Zelda D'Aprano is renowned for her activism on behalf of the Women's Liberation Movement in Australia. She was a founding member of the Women's Action Committee in 1970 and took direct action, campaigning against salary inequaliity by chaining herself to the Commonwealth Building in Melbourne and with other members of WAC paying only 75 per cent of tram fares.

Zelda D'Aprano has written for many publications, is a well-respected speaker and has represented women's liberation on numerous committees. In April 2000, Zelda D'Aprano was awarded an Honorary Doctorate from Macquarie University, Sydney.

T0164446

Other books by Zelda D'Aprano
Zelda (1995)

KATH WILLIAMS:
THE UNIONS AND
THE FIGHT FOR EQUAL PAY

Zelda D'Aprano

Spinifex Press Pty Ltd
504 Queensberry Street
North Melbourne, Vic. 3051
Australia
women@spinifexpress.com.au
http://www.spinifexpress.com.au

First published 2001 by Spinifex Press

Cover design by Deb Snibson
Typeset in Garamond by Palmer Higgs Pty Ltd
Printed and bound by Australian Print Group

National Library of Australia
Cataloguing-in-publication data:
D'Aprano, Zelda, 1928– .
    Kath Williams: The Unions and the Fight for Equal Pay.
    Bibliography.
    ISBN 1 86756 02 0.

1. Williams, Kath. 2. Women labor union members –
Australia – Biography. 3. Women labor union members –
Australia – History. 4. Equal pay for equal work –
Australia – History. 5. Labor unions – Australia – History.
I. Title

331.478092

This publication is assisted by the Australia Council,
the Australian Government's arts funding and advisory
body.

For my mother Rachel Leah Orloff who always
dreamt of a more caring and sharing world

The dead need history for the voice it gives them; the living need history disturbing enough to change the present.

Greg Dening, *Australian Book Review*,
June 1998, p. 17.

People who have been real movers and exciters got left out of histories … Often, reading histories, there are events which stick out, do not make enough sense, and one may deduce the existence of some lunatic, male or female, who was equipped with the fiery stuff of inspiration—but was quickly forgotten, since always and at all times the past gets tidied up and made safer …

Women often get dropped from memory and then history.

Doris Lessing, *Under My Skin*, 1994, p. 12.

Contents

Acknowledgements

I wish to give a special thanks to the late Kath Williams' son and granddaughter, Ray and Lynda Clarey, for their co-operation and use of interview tapes and transcripts.

Special thanks are also due to the following people for their help in giving interviews, supplying documents and answering miscellaneous questions: Pauline Armstrong, the late John Arrowsmith, the late Fred Benbow, the late Iris Benbow, the late Harry Bocquet, Marge Broadbent, Peg Cregan, the late Ruth Crow, Joan Crump, Kath Dimitrin, the late Agnes and Wattie Doig, Jenny Doran, George Edson, Bradon Ellem, Jane Farrell, Joe Godard, Kath Golding, Jack Hutson, Grace Jane, Emma Jolley, Geysler Kaplan, Marilyn Lake, Vic and Vida Little, Frances Eodelyn Loeber, Mrs E MacSween, Marion Miller, the late George Mitchell, Maggie O'Sullivan, Vera Perry, the late Eric Pipgrass, Bill Richardson, Flo Russell, Linda Rubenstein, Lyndall Ryan, Jocelynne Scutt, Sylvie Shaw, John Shields, Hilda Smith, Naomi Steer, Anne Summers, Bernie Taft, Lois Williams.

I also wish to express my appreciation of the assistance given by staff and/or officers of the Alexander Library, West Australia; Australian National Archives: Australian Security Intelligence Organisation; Australian Council of Trade Unions; Sarah Brown, Archivist, Victorian Trades Hall Council; Camden Haven Adult and Community Education; Federated Liquor and Allied Industries Employees Union, Victorian Branch; Geelong Historical Records Centre; Katherine Herrick, Education History Unit, Department of Education, Victoria; Jessie Street National Women's Library; Labor Council of New South Wales; Laurieton Branch of Hastings Library, New South Wales; Mitchell Library,

ACKNOWLEDGEMENTS

State Library of New South Wales; National Library of Australia; Noel Butlin Archives, Australian National University; Queensland Teachers' Union Library; School of Industrial Relations and Organisational Behaviour, University of New South Wales; Union of Australian Women; University of Melbourne Archives; Western Australian Museum; Brendan Wood, Textile, Clothing and Footwear Union.

Many thanks to the following for permission to use material: New South Wales University Press; Harper Collins; Penguin Books; University of Queensland Press; Australian Liquor, Hospitality & Miscellaneous Workers Union; Margo Oliver; Jeni Thornley and Megan McMurchy (*For Love or Money*); Stella Lees and June Senyard (*The 1950s*); Belinda Probert and Ray Juriendini for permission to cite Bradon Ellem. 1996. 'Hell for Leather'. *Labour and Industry*, 7 (1)); Heather Radi (*200 Australian Women*).

I also wish to acknowledge just a small sample of women whose involvement in the campaign for equal pay during the 1940s to 1960s to the best of my knowledge remains unrecorded:

Clothing Trades Union: Dot Castles, Stella Cooper,
    Grace Taylor (Gale)
Metal Trades Union: Thelma Pryor, Aileen Beaver
Iron Workers Union: Evelyn Taylor, Sally Bowen
Postal Workers Union: Janne Ellen (Reed), Doreen Burrows
Clerks Union: Irene Arrowsmith, Monica Chalmers,
    Dela Nicholas
Hospital Employees Union: Jessie Davies
also, Olive Howe, Peggy Erry, Jillian Hopkins,
    Ruth McDougal

Thanks go to the writers of many books and articles whose research I have used.

Many thanks go to Mavis Barnes and Elaine van Kempen

for your assistance, corrections and positive criticism. You were both a constant source of encouragement.

And to Susan Hawthorne of Spinifex Press who, in publishing this book, validates the grassroots campaigns of women in history.

Finally, I would like to thank Ron, whose support, patience and assistance over the years helped to make this book possible.

Zelda D'Aprano
Laurieton, New South Wales
April 2001

Foreword

I have long been skeptical about the conventional image of women in 1950s Australia, which sees them passively adhering to their prescribed roles as mothers and wives, acquiescent in their subordination. Now Zelda D'Aprano, in this exciting study of left-wing activist Kath Williams and the fight for equal pay in the 1950s and 1960s, sets the record straight. Australian women, she notes, have shown great spirit in their activism and the 1950s was no exception. Based on extensive original research, Zelda's account documents the significance of the political campaigns led by women in the trade unions, notably Kath Williams, a member of the Communist Party and paid official of the Liquor Trades Union, who was elected secretary of the newly-formed Trades Hall Council Equal Pay Committee in Melbourne in 1955. Angered by 'the rank injustice of paying women less for their labour than men', Williams organised demonstrations and seminars, rallies and deputations, for some twelve years. In 1957 she presented the Equal Pay Petition, with 62 000 signatures, to the Commonwealth government. In 1960 she organised an Equal Pay Rally outside the Victorian Parliament. In 1967, the year in which she retired, aged seventy-two, the ACTU finally decided to pursue an equal pay claim with the Arbitration Commission. Zelda was, of course, involved in the struggle herself and she writes about it with passion and commitment. History, she believes, should engage the heart as well as the head—this is such a history.

Marilyn Lake
Melbourne, 2001

Abbreviations

ABS	Australian Bureau of Statistics
ACSPA	Australian Council of Salaried & Professional Associations
ACTU	Australian Council of Trade Unions
AEU	Amalgamated Engineering Union
ALP	Australian Labor Party
AMIEU	Australian Meat Industry Employees Union
AMWU	Amalgamated Metal Workers Union
ANU	Australian National University
ASE	Australian Society of Engineers
ASIO	Australian Security Intelligence Organisation
BTU	Boot Trades Union
CAEP	Council of Action for Equal Pay
CAR	Commonwealth Arbitration Report
CIG	Commonwealth Industrial Gases
CPA	Communist Party of Australia
CPML	Communist Party Marxist Leninist
CPSU	Community & Public Sector Union
CTU	Clothing Trades Union, now the Textile, Clothing & Footwear Union
EP	Equal Pay

EP Committee	Equal Pay Committee
ETU	Electrical Trades Union
FEDFA	Federated Engine Drivers and Firemen's Association
GPO	General Post Office
HCCPSO	High Council of Commonwealth Public Service Organisations
HEF	Hospital Employees' Federation, now the Health Services Union of Australia
ILO	International Labour Organisation
LTU	Liquor Trades Union
LVA	Licensed Victuallers Association
MHR	Member of the House of Representatives
MTHC*	Melbourne Trades Hall Council
NPEC	National Pay Equity Coalition
NSW	New South Wales
NSWNA	New South Wales Nurses Association
OECD	Organisation for Economic Co-operation and Development
SLV	State Library of Victoria
THC*	Trades Hall Council
TLC	Trades and Labor Council
UAW	Union of Australian Women
UMA	University of Melbourne Archives
UN	United Nations
VBU	Vehicle Builders Union
VEWOC	Victorian Employed Women's Organisation Council
VTHC*	Victorian Trades Hall Council
VTHC EPC	Victorian Trades Hall Council Equal Pay Committee

WEB	Women's Employment Board
WEL	Women's Electoral Lobby
WLM	Women's Liberation Movement

* MTHC, THC and VTHC are the same organisation with name changes occurring over the years. It is now known as the Victorian Trades Hall Council (VTHC). Equal Pay Committees operated during the period which covers these name changes. The documents drawn on therefore variously refer to these committees as the Melbourne Trades Hall Equal Pay Committee (MTHC EP Committee), the Victorian Trades Council Equal Pay Committee (VTHC EP Committee), the Trades Hall Council Equal Pay Committee (THC EP Committee)). To prevent confusion, all references in the text are to the Victorian Equal Pay Committee (VTHC EP) or to the Equal Pay Committee (EP Committee).

Preface

For some years there has been serious concern for the rapid decline in interest young people have in History. Could it be that the usual historical depiction of static one-dimensional beings whose heads have been separated from their hearts is an underlying reason for this lost interest? All people have strengths and weaknesses and, depending on circumstances, are capable of performing heroic or cowardly deeds, but men wished to preserve an untarnished image and remain immortal for posterity, so they created history: a record of their deeds only.

Because there is more to life and living than is recorded in history books, the novel provided the place in literature where human experiences could be portrayed. In the anonymity of the novel men were safe, and all emotions, human frailties, weaknesses, illnesses and hang-ups could be recorded. History's splitting of the human so as to preserve egos may be partly responsible for the present dilemma.

The recording of history, apart from being a collection of known facts, should, where possible, embrace a combined record of the hearts and heads of those involved. However, when adhering to this theory, difficulties arise in attempting to write a record of motivations, thoughts, feelings and pain experienced by people—important factors which may have given rise to decisions influencing the course of history.

There is always the inherent danger, when writing history, of the writer being sympathetic or unsympathetic to an individual and presenting them with a halo or demonising them or, failing that, portraying them as flat, disembodied cardboard cutouts. In the main, this has been the method of portraying history and in recent years when referring to the history of the Equal Pay Campaign, there has been a tendency to concentrate on the decisions made by wage tribunals and the Arbitration Court. Although recognition has been given to a small number of women involved in the campaign over the many years, one could be forgiven for thinking that all it required was several learned people placing well-researched arguments before male judges or wage tribunals to obtain wage justice. Little has been recorded about the efforts made by the trade union movement and the women who carried out the struggle within their workplaces and the unions.

Without diminishing the vital efforts made by women from all sections of society, it would be denying reality to assume equal pay could have been achieved without involvement by the trade union movement. Kath Williams made an outstanding contribution to the trade union movement and to the achievement of equal pay.

When writing the history of working-class experience in or around any period of time, authenticity requires language to adequately reflect industry, the institutions, the organisations and the culture of that era. Having a working-class identity meant being part of a society which developed a jargon widely used to depict the current situation in industry, and the trade unions often adopted many of these expressions. *Sweated labour* refers to employees being overworked and underpaid, the *sweat shop* was commonly used to describe a workplace

where conditions were often substandard and where employees were overworked and underpaid, the *speed up* described a situation where pressure was applied for employees to
produce more.

Part of the disciplining of the workforce commences at
school and continues to inculcate its reverence for authority
throughout almost all of our institutions and organisations. The
trade unions are no different, and while members attending
meetings may be addressed as brother, comrade, member or
formally, as Mr, Mrs and Miss, all the research of written union
records for this book revealed almost all members were
addressed formally. This usage has been retained in this book.

It is not now politically correct to use the infantilising word
girls when applied to women, but this was the common term
widely used in the workplace and culture until the late 1900s,
and it appears once in the book.

Women who played an outstanding role in the equal pay
campaign over the years were almost always known by their
given name as well as surname and are recorded as such in this
book.

Writing this book on the late Kath Williams has given me
insight into the problems confronted in trying to record all
aspects of her life, her family, her children—and all that
entails—plus her commitment to the equal pay campaign,
politics and the trade union movement.

In times prior to electronic communication, letters often
gave a lasting record of people's lives. Telephone conversations
leave no such record to assist a writer in accessing the feelings
and thoughts of individuals long dead. Kath, being a very busy
woman, did most of her communication by phone.

The ontological combination of heart and head, intuitive
understanding and broad, honest intellectual analysis is
essential for history to come to life. I was faced with many

frustrations when attempting to record the life of Kath Williams, a very private person. Interviews with family, comrades, friends and work associates provided testament to her involvement with politics and trade unions but showed very little of Kath the woman.

When conducting research for this book, it became patently clear that, like almost all history, women's history too has minimised the involvement of grass roots activism. It was not until 1991 that an adequate record of Emma Miller and Leontine Cooper's major contribution to women and the trade union movement during the late nineteenth and early twentieth century, was finally recorded.

The need to write this book arose from the necessity to recognise Kath's contribution in the struggle for equal pay and place her among other great campaigners.

While there is more material available, such as leaflets, posters and general campaign documents resulting from Kath's work over the years on the VTHC Equal Pay Committee, the key aspects of all the material have been included in this book.

I have listed a great deal of detail and my analysis of it in the hope that in reading this book, people will be inspired to be more thinking, studious and active about wage structures and how the entire system works, and about the confusion that can be created to impede justice. The fight for equal pay has been a lengthy political campaign, involving the political structures of government, employers and the trade union movement, all embroiled in what at times resulted in incomprehensible outcomes. It was in this environment that Kath Williams operated.

To deny recognition of a radical woman's contribution to the cause of equal pay is to distort history.

Editorial note

The sources for this book are varied and variations in spelling between sources—as they appear in legislation, newspaper reports, union material and academic research—have been retained: for example: Fruit Pickers, fruit-pickers and fruitpickers; woolen, as have the changing titles for unions.

MEDICAL GAZETTE

SATURDAY, MARCH 15TH, 1918.

WOMEN'S WORK AND WOMEN'S DUTY

During the travail of child-birth, the medical man comes to the aid of suffering women, at the time when they are fulfilling their highest physiological function. ...
Biologically speaking, a woman's whole life is centred round that one function—childbearing. She is anatomically differentiated to accomplish this act and to protect the young life during its first nine months of existence. Thereafter she is specially mentally endowed to tend it during infancy and childhood, to supply its many little wants, to educate it for the battle of life ... Unfortunately, in our civilised communities many of both sexes remain unmarried. It is a regrettable circumstance, ... but can never be eliminated. What is the duty of this army of marriageable but unmarried women to the community at large? What walks of life most nearly meet their physiological requirements?

We have already indicated that a woman's sphere is in her home—the nursery of her children. If these are several, as they should be in a healthy community she must have assistance in the house and must seek for this amongst the unmarried. In many instances, later on these will be mothers themselves, and they thus have a chance of learning much in domestic economy (in its broad and original sense of the 'science of the home') as well as in the proper bringing up of children. Other assistants may never have the chance of being selected as a wife, but these, though not themselves to be mothers, may still vicariously meet that other need of their organization, the desire to love and cherish children. They will be fulfilling,

to some extent at least, their original physiological intention.

But what do we see in our great cities of the South? No sadder sight can meet the eye of him who 'loves his fellowmen' than to stand at one of the railway stations in our capital cities between 8 and 9 in the morning. An immense number of persons are hurrying to their daily occupations, a large proportion being young girls in their teens and just out of them. These are going to work in factories, stand behind shop counters, and type in large offices. Eventually many will marry, but what will have been their training and what will be their tastes? From leaving school, life has been a whirl, wages have been spent on dress, evenings have been devoted to picture-shows and theatres, and the dignity of the relations between the sexes has been tampered with by flippant flirtations. Instead of learning to keep house, to cook simple dishes, to make the most of limited means, to nurse the baby and mend the children's clothes—instead of doing services which the community needs and demands—we have this butterfly and parasitic existence ...

... The only solution to the problem seems to lie in the passing of legislation which will prohibit the employment of girls and women in any walk of life which is not unquestionably women's work, until they shall have passed through an apprenticeship in household work. Such apprenticeship should be for six months, preferably longer, the housewife being responsible for the conduct of the girl and for giving her opportunities of obtaining knowledge. At the end of her time, a certificate would be granted, and thereafter, if she still so desired, she might seek other avenues of employment. The apprenticeship need not be confined to the homes of the well-to-do; in the humblest cottage, provided the mother was accepted as capable enough to teach, a thorough grounding could be acquired ...

Source: The Australasian Medical Gazette, March 15 1913, pp. 234–5

1

Cath the housewife/mother becomes Kath the activist

Catherine Mary Isabel Chambers (Cath) commenced her teacher training for the Domestic Arts in 1913.[1] We do not know what dreams or ambitions she may have had during adolescence but, with the pervading culture inculcating domesticity for girls and opposing participation of women in the workforce, the demand for teachers qualified in Domestic Arts created opportunities for young women to obtain a profession. Choices for women were few, and perhaps Cath recognised the potential this training would give her for a career, the means of a livelihood as well as providing skills and knowledge befitting her for marriage.

Cath was born on April 23 1895 at Lara, a tiny settlement south-west of Melbourne, in StoneLea Cottage, the home of her maternal grandparents, built by her stonemason grandfather William Harding. By the 1890s Lara, with its population of 250, had developed the charming air of an English village. Even its railway station, according to the *Werribee Express*, had the rural cottage home cosiness which might be seen on country branch lines in England.

Cath was the second-born of five children, four daughters and the youngest being a son. While little is known of Cath's parents or about her childhood, her father, Edward, was the foundation Secretary of the Victorian Clerks Union.[2] Her parents were able to live a comfortable existence and had the financial means to provide their children with advanced education. Lois Williams, an early pupil of Melbourne University High School, recalls seeing Cath's name heading the list on the old school's Honour Roll.[3]

Early in the twentieth century tertiary education was a luxury few could afford, and, of the five Chambers' children, Cath attended The College of Domestic Economy situated in Lonsdale Street, the precursor to Emily McPherson College, and obtained her Diploma to teach Domestic Arts in December 1915.[4]

Eileen, the eldest daughter, was said to have been a Magistrate in the Children's Court; Bobbie was a librarian; and Connie came down with tuberculosis, a disease rampant at the time, especially among young women. Ted, unlike his sisters, found schooling difficult, worked in numerous unskilled and semi-skilled jobs and spent several years humping his swag during the depression years.

Having obtained her qualifications to teach, Cath being classified as a temporary assistant, was placed by the Education Department in various schools from Collingwood to Daylesford.[5] World War 1 was in progress and what money was available went for the war effort, not education. Cath's teaching report after completing her first year of teaching, described her as 'A teacher, bright in appearance, prepares and presents a good lesson, demonstrates and questions well, but needs experience in methods. Is an energetic and willing worker and should with experience become a very good teacher. *Good 84.*'[6]

It was through her father's involvement with the trade union movement that Cath first met her husband-to-be, Percy James Clarey. When visiting the Chambers' home to see Edward on union business, Percy met Cath, and expressed words of

'This morning, girls, we are going to make spotted dick.'

So wrote Kathy Skelton in her account of her experiences as a student in Form two at a domestic school during the 1950s. She describes how the girls were allowed to clean the flat at the end of the Domestic arts wing, make pasties, lemon sago, Irish stew, baked custard, rice pudding and jam roly-poly. They never made spotted dick and nor were they ever asked to open their Education Department Recipe Book at page forty-two, although longing for the teacher to direct them there and pronounce the forbidden words.

Cath Chambers during her teaching career was responsible for adhering to the curriculum established by the Education Department and, as a domestic arts teacher, was responsible for preparing girls for their housewife/mother role.

The curriculum Kathy Skelton describes was the sort Cath was required to teach.

Drawn from Michele Lonsdale, *Liberating Women:
The Changing Lives of Australian Women since the 1950s*, p. 19

interest to Edward about his attractive daughter. At a later visit to the Chambers' home, Percy and Cath spent some time conversing and Cath accepted his invitation to visit him at his union office at Unity Hall at the Spencer Street end of Bourke Street. This was the beginning of their relationship.

Percy was born in 1890 at Bairnsdale, Victoria. When he was a child, the family moved to Melbourne where he was educated at South Yarra State School and later at the Working Men's College. Crippled in his youth by rheumatoid arthritis, he was dependent on crutches all his life. Percy spent some years in hospital because of his affliction and, with plenty of time on his hands, he was able to use this period of incapacitation to continue his education and indulge himself in reading, a

Private collection

Cath in her early twenties

pastime he loved. On leaving hospital, he attended the Royal Melbourne Institute of Technology where he studied gold and assaying.

Percy was employed as a clerk at George Pizzey and Son, leather merchants, Percy became involved in trade unionism and politics. He was an ambitious young man and at the early age of twenty-four became the Victorian President of the Federated Clerks' Union of Australia and Federal President three years later. He was to become an organiser of the Amalgamated Food Preservers' Union of Australia and of the

Federated Storemen and Packers' Union of Australia. He served as Federal President of both organisations and maintained a close relationship with them throughout his long industrial career.[7]

At a time when most young men were away at the war, it is easy to understand the impression Percy, a successful young man who had already attained a position of power and respect, made upon Cath. Shortly after their relationship began, Cath spoke to her mother of her love for Percy and of his proposal of marriage.

In 1990, when interviewed by Cath's granddaughter Lynda, Agnes Doig, long-time friend and comrade of Cath's, said '[Cath's] mother disapproved of the relationship on the grounds that "she would be foolish to marry a cripple"'. In time, Cath wondered if her mother's strong reaction to the prospect of her marriage made her more determined at the age of twenty-two to make her own decisions and assert her right to live her own life. Many years later and in hindsight, 'she wondered whether she would have married so soon, having known Percy for two months only, or at all, if her mother had not made her feel sorry for him and his disability'.[8]

With the forthcoming marriage in sight, Cath was forced to resign from her teaching position due to Education Department regulations at the time which stipulated that 'No married woman shall be eligible for appointment to any office in the public service. Every woman employed in the public service who marries after the passing of this Act shall immediately upon her marriage retire from the public service.'[9]

Cath would have been fully aware of Departmental policy regarding married women teachers and although she may have resented it, like most women of her time, she accepted the housewife/mother role and was prepared to sacrifice her career. The Education Department waived the penalty when she broke her bond: the bond being an undertaking that she would teach at government schools for a specific number of years after qualifying.

Cath and Percy were married on 31 March 1917. The marriage was conducted at the Chambers' family home at Box Hill and Mr. J. L. Mudford, minister of the evangelist Church of Christ officiated. The newspaper advertisement of her nuptials is attached to Cath's Education Department Record.[10]

Taking a great interest in helping her husband in his political ambitions, Cath made great efforts in the home, socially and politically, in support of his aspirations. Her training in the domestic arts equipped her with the necessary skills for being a competent housewife and she was noted for her splendid cooking. She was always well groomed and was considered to be a good wife and mother, qualities which were deemed to be of the utmost importance. Cath was pleased when their first child, Bruce, was born in 1918, just prior to the end of World War 1. She didn't want her child born while the war was in progress.[11]

Cath and Percy lived in Inkerman Road, Caulfield, a well-established 'middle-class'[12] suburb, and Cath was more than satisfied in assisting Percy along the road to political success. Whilst doing this, Cath herself was becoming more learned and aware of politics and of the hardship and suffering the working class endured. Cath had been brought up in a family in which the labour movement and politics were broadly discussed, and was a keen reader and incisive thinker. Although being 'gentle', she was not shy about discussing her ideas or opinions and could be quite forthright in doing so. She believed strongly in trade unionism and the Labor Party, believing it to be a true party, dedicated to bettering the lot of working-class Australians.

Cath's committment to the Australian Labor Party (ALP) was

profound. She was to become prominent in the labour movement, attaining a position on the Victorian Executive of the ALP.[13] Being an extremely competent woman, she was able to manage her home and devote much of her time to Labor Party activities. It was twelve years before Cath gave birth to her second son. This delay was caused by problems associated with her first confinement and, wanting another child, she underwent surgery to enable her to be a mother for the second time. Raymond was her last child.[14]

One can only speculate as to why, after all these years, Cath decided to have another child. To have undergone surgery as

Cath and Percy's wedding

Private collection

she did indicated her genuine desire to have another child. However, in view of what was to transpire, perhaps she thought another child would hold the marriage together.

The economic crash in 1929 ushered in a lengthy period of deprivation, poverty and hardship which, for many people, endured until the beginning of World War 2 in 1939. During these years when the economic depression was at its worst, Cath was often distressed when meeting people who came knocking on their front door asking for handouts, mainly food, money or clothing. It was during these bad years that 'Percy would on occasions bring home a box of fruit, a bottle of expensive alcohol or some other luxury item. When first asking Percy how he came by the "gift", she was told it came from a mate in return for a 'favour'.[15]

Cath, after giving several years of devoted service to the ALP, eventually became President of the ALP Women's Organising Committee. Her observations and experiences of the poverty all about her, and seeing no end in sight or improvement in the economic situation, caused her to develop doubts about the policies and practices of the ALP and its ability to deliver the promises made to working-class Australians. She believed the Liberal and Labor parties had different platforms and represented different people: the Liberals looking after the interests of the moneyed class while the Labor Party looked after the working-class, and they both had different visions for Australia. She initially believed in the parliamentary system, a democratic political system—representing all Australians—and that it would in time create a fair and equal Australia; but with one-third of the workforce unemployed during the worst years of the depression, Cath gradually came to believe that the parliamentary process was far removed from the reality of ordinary workers' lives. She questioned the adequacy of the Labor and Liberal party structures to meet the needs of the desperate people who were turning up on her doorstep and began a serious analysis of her own political beliefs and those of her husband.

By 1933 when Hitler came to power in Germany, people who understood capitalism and how it functioned were rapidly becoming alarmed by the threats of Hitler's policies, and Cath developed an interest and involvement in causes and activities more radical than Percy preferred. The Movement against War and Fascism was one of these causes and, knowing the threat fascism posed to the world, Cath became one of the Movement's foremost speakers, proving to be quite capable of holding her own among the male speakers.[16] It was on one of these occasions, when addressing an overflow audience of over 1000 people at Unity Hall in 1934, that Flo Russell, who was to join and become an organiser for the Communist Party of Australia (CPA), first heard Cath speak. She was most impressed by Cath's 'clear, thoughtful and powerful address'.

With the passage of time, Cath and Percy's marriage developed problems, political differences being a major issue. Agnes Doig felt that Cath had eventually become 'more interested in assisting Percy to overcome prejudice towards his disability and achieve his goals than feeling any love for him'.[17] Percy was determined to enter Parliament and having a wife like Cath, who was averse to hiding her growing radicalism, became a constant embarrassment to him.

During 1934 when Cath was Secretary of the Caulfield Branch of the ALP, she met a man with whom she had an affair, a common experience among people but which in those years was strictly frowned upon. Percy saw his opportunity and took it. He would no longer be embarrassed by Cath's revolutionary behaviour.[18]

Is it unreasonable to wonder if Percy had ever associated with another woman?

It is interesting to note that, during these years, a 'quick' divorce was possible only on the grounds of adultery. A woman had to be caught only once, while hearsay reports a man had to be caught on two occasions with the same woman.

In 1935 Cath was removed from the position of President in the Australian Labor Party's Women's Organising Committee for taking sides with Abyssinia when Italy invaded that country. Cath supported the imposition of economic sanctions on Italy, as Britain and other European powers had already done, but this was rejected by the ALP in Victoria.[19]

This caused a great deal of dissension in the Victorian Branch of the ALP. Mrs Cath Clarey from the Women's Group was one of the speakers at a mass meeting arranged to take place at Wirth's Olympia near Prince's Bridge. The members were warned not to take part in this meeting, and all who did were automatically excluded from the ALP and not readmitted until the following Easter Conference of the Party.[20]

It was in this same year of 1935 that Cath was the Labor candidate for the Legislative Assembly seat of Caulfield but withdrew before the poll.[21] Why did she withdraw from the election? Was pressure applied to make her do so?

Apart from the strength of her own political commitment and her desire to further participate in causes of her choosing, Cath, being an intelligent woman, would have known there was little hope of Percy maintaining a parliamentary career while married to her. Her activities jeopardised his career and although the ending of their marriage, like most marriage endings, had problems, it was inevitable that it would end.

Cath and Percy finally agreed that she take young Raymond, while Bruce, the older son, remained with his father and went on to university to become a doctor.

Cath was determined to keep Raymond, and friends recall how she doted on this young son, his father paying one pound a week for his upkeep. Raymond remembers his mother taking him to the bedroom and packing a small suitcase. She went on to explain how they were leaving home and going to stay with Cath's brother, Ray's Uncle Ted and Auntie Betty who lived in Prahran, a working-class inner suburb.

Jobs were extremely scarce in the thirties, and for women forty years of age it was almost an impossibility to get work. Women fortunate enough to obtain employment received half the male wage for doing the same work. Cath's siblings were divided in their attitude towards her over the marriage breakup, and she appreciated the assistance given by Ted and Betty. She knew she would have difficulties in supporting herself and Ray.

Almost every woman has a story to tell and only Cath would have known what pain and anguish she felt when going through this period of disillusionment with the ALP, her marriage breakup after eighteen years, an affair that came to nothing, the fear of being alone with a young child, the need to find work at a time when the economic depression was severe and the uncertainty of it all.

At this stage, Cath was still legally married to Percy which prevented her from seeking re-employment as a teacher. To make ends meet, she undertook a variety of jobs, 'spruiking in stores like Coles etc., selling jewelry or other goods' as Wattie Doig's letter describes. One venture saw 'Cath and her brother Ted, going from door to door endeavouring to buy gold. They carried a small test kit to perform the acid test which determined whether a metal was in fact gold.' They pursued this venture day after day, and Raymond heard many stories of how his 'mother and uncle carried sticks to fend off aggressive dogs'.[22] A sign commonly displayed on gates at the time read 'No Hawkers or Canvassers'. Ray visited his father regularly.

Cath told Marjorie Broadbent, a friend and comrade, of 'one occasion when Percy failed to return Ray after weekend access.

Cath was frantic with worry. She didn't know what she could do to get her son back. She carefully considered her situation and the consequences of a custody battle for Ray.'[23] Percy was a successful and well-respected trade union leader who had the standing and resources to provide for his children. Cath was a very warm and loving mother and did any job she could get to provide for herself and Ray, but she didn't have the power, the money or equal standing with Percy in putting a case forward in court for the custody of her son.

> The arrangement with access had been informal until this incident took place and Cath felt that Percy was now attempting to challenge her right to custody. Cath walked the city streets for some time trying to reach a decision on what she could do and how best she could assure her custody of Ray.
>
> She finally used the only strategy available to her. She was in Flinders Street near the *Herald* office when she remembered all the 'kick backs', a practice of Percy's she strongly disapproved of. She went into a telephone booth and rang him. She told him of her proximity to the *Herald* office and threatened to inform the *Herald* of the rorts, and 'gifts' he received from 'grateful people' if he didn't return Ray within one hour. Shortly after, Ray arrived in a taxi with his small case and she had no further trouble from Percy.[24]

Many friends remember the love Cath bestowed on Ray and her determination in wanting to keep him with her. Being a single mother and a divorcee in the thirties was a situation of vulnerability and extreme difficulty, but not knowing what experiences Cath may have had, one can only assume that she was fortunate in being involved in left-wing politics where people were, perhaps, more likely to be sympathetic and supportive.

Despite these upheavals, Ray recalls a time when Percy came into his uncle's house when returning him from access and Ray came upon his parents embracing; he hoped they would come back together but it wasn't to be. While Cath's politics were heading more to the left, Percy's were heading more to the right. The divorce was finalised in 1936. That was when Cath joined the CPA.

Cath was dedicated to the class struggle and socialism, and there is no evidence of any participation or connection by her with the feminists who were particularly active during the mid-1930s.

By the late 1920s Percy had emerged as a national trade union and political leader through his affiliations with increasingly powerful federal unions and his work for the newly-formed Australian Council of Trade Unions (ACTU). He presided over the ALP Victorian Branch in 1934 and next year was elected President of the Melbourne Trades Hall Council. By 1937 he was strongly identified with the right wing and was elected to the Victorian Legislative Council as member for the province of Doutta Galla. He held this seat until 1949 when he remarried and went into Federal politics, holding the seat of Bendigo.[25]

As a divorcee, Cath was able to seek employment again with the Education Department but it wasn't until July 1938 that she obtained a teaching position in Portland on the south-west coast of Victoria.

Unknown to anyone living in the vicinity, Cath and Ray moved into the 'Claremont' Guest House run by Mrs. Kosh. Cath soon began to enjoy her work and develop friends among her teacher colleagues. Apart from teaching domestic arts, she was also teaching geography and history, subjects she wasn't qualified to teach, and even though initially this caused some problems with some members of the staff, these difficulties were soon overcome and she was frequently invited to their homes.[26] Ray recalls becoming very bored on one occasion when the teacher friends were playing 'Monopoly' and he 'played up' to force his mother into taking him home. Ray usually accompanied Cath to her many activities including political meetings.

The only political contact Cath had when she arrived in Portland was Dougie Cross, a man whom the CPA knew of as having similar political beliefs. He turned out to be the town drunk. Being the only person Cath had political contact with, she rapidly got to work on him and within a short time he became involved in activities which gave him a sense of purpose. He was grateful to Cath for helping him overcome his drinking problem.

Cath met up with the Benbow family, a pioneering family who had been early Wonthaggi miners and had moved to the Heywood area, eleven miles out of Portland, where they established Heathmere, their farm. The entire family held radical political views and Cath spent most of her weekends at Heathmere. She loved the farm, the old weatherboard farmhouse, the large open fireplace with the huge burning logs and the Benbow family who made her and Ray more than welcome.

Cath left 'Claremont' and moved into a house in town. Being the 'vivacious, outgoing and likeable' woman that she was, she often welcomed many associates and friends to her home, the more regulars being Fred Benbow, Fred junior, his sister Iris and George Mitchell, a young cadet journalist.

World War 2 had commenced, and, when Stalin signed the non-aggression pact with Hitler, Communists were regarded as Nazi sympathisers, and Menzies took this opportunity to make the CPA illegal. Known and suspected Communists were followed and watched with suspicion. It was illegal to possess books or other items of literature considered to be radical or revolutionary. Apart from the possibility of having this material confiscated, one could be charged with possession of illegal material.

On one occasion, when seeking assistance from the Party, Cath was obviously unimpressed when informed that Flo Russell would call to see her and told the Party she didn't think a woman was capable of doing the job of Organiser. Flo related how Cath changed her mind after meeting her.[27]

Cath was remembered as the brains behind a small group of left-thinking people who met together and produced a newsletter which, although being illegal, was distributed in the town and to local farms. She wrote and typed most of the articles which appeared, cut the stencils and then they all took turns in running the old Gestetner duplicating machine to print the final product. When it was not in use, the group hid the typewriter down a nearby farmer's well, suspended on a long rope. When the typewriter accidentally fell into the well, another was found to replace it. The Gestetner was wrapped in oil cloth to keep the moisture out and was planted on a high, dry, sandy bank amid bushland marshes for safekeeping. The normal print run was 200 copies, which took several hours to deliver at night by people on foot or on the 'Little Beesa' motor bike, the BSA.[28] Ray has many fond memories as a child of the great excitement he felt when, as a pillion passenger, he helped distribute this secret material.

Because of the risk involved in hiding the press near Heathmere, it was moved from one place to another when necessary. Sometimes it was placed in a firebreak at the local tip. It was generally well known that this group of people were responsible for the leaflets because their political views were well known; however, the group felt their newsletter spoke truthfully of what was going on locally, as well as elsewhere, and, as people, they were accepted within the community and were never troubled.[29]

Freddie Steen, the local policeman, was suspicious of Cath and the group. George Mitchell recalls Freddie Steen being observed on an island in the swamp, perched with his telescope, looking for evidence of the activity he suspected them of undertaking, but with obvious frustration for he was never able to prove their complicity.[30]

On one occasion, when Cath and Ray were at Heathmere, the Federal Police called in and interrogated Iris Benbow and Cath for some time. They looked through each book and pamphlet in the house. It was claimed that, on one occasion, Percy, who was now a Member of Parliament, called to warn them of an impending raid.[31]

Cath decided to reduce her visits to Heathmere after the police interrogation; she didn't want her friends feeling continually threatened by further intimidation.

Fred Benbow junior remembers Cath as a 'bright, bubbly woman, looking younger than her years and the driving force behind the local ALP meetings which were held at the old bluestone building, the Foresters' Hall'.[32] Young Ray accompanied his mother to ALP meetings where he slept on a wooden bench as the meeting proceeded. Fred thought Cath would have made a 'first-class politician' and recalls Cath telling his mother that, 'before their political differences became paramount, she worked her guts out to assist Percy in his rise in politics'. That Cath came to be attending meetings of the ALP while being a member of the CPA indicates that at this stage of her life she was a member of both Parties.

Cath was never known to complain. Perhaps she was a stoic, or fortunate to possess a happy disposition, for whatever hardship she endured she always appeared to be in control, smiling, laughing and in good cheer. She was noted for having a great sense of humour as well as being a heavy smoker. It didn't matter where she was, and though always elegantly dressed, she would take the 'makings' from her old battered tobacco tin and roll herself a cigarette.

CATH THE HOUSEWIFE/MOTHER BECOMES KATH THE ACTIVIST

Aside from Cath's political activities, her teaching career in Portland was going well. Reports state that:

> [She] has taken up her duties with enthusiasm and is attacking her problems in a hardworking fashion. Class control is pleasant and effective … Has organised her special subjects on sound lines. She is very interested in her work and has a sound practical attitude to it. Gives thorough attention to all matters which come under her care …
>
> A hardworking and reliable teacher, makes good preparation, is capable in centre management, teaches along good lines and is willing and helpful in all school activities.[33]

Cath taught at Portland for five years before deciding to move to Wonthaggi where she commenced teaching in 1943. What prompted her to make this change is unknown, perhaps she was being pestered with attention by an unwanted suitor, a common occurrence experienced by women living alone. Cath was never afraid of living life to the full and this means taking chances.

Wonthaggi was a coal mining town on the south-east coast of Gippsland in Victoria. This mine was famous for the many technical difficulties in the getting of coal, the great number of lives lost through accidents, the horrific working conditions and the staunch militancy of the men who worked there. The town had a history of fierce union battles over the many years of the mine's existence and it wasn't long before Cath became involved in local activities.

Cath became known as Kath with a K and formed a close-knit group with Wattie and Agnes Doig, local communists who had migrated to Australia from Scotland. It wasn't long before Kath became Secretary while Wattie, a miner, was President of the local branch of the CPA. 'At its peak, the local CPA branch had 130 members and regularly sold over 300 copies of the communist weekly paper in the Wonthaggi area'.[34]

And again Kath found herself being kept very busy. 'Kath was in her element, a good speaker, good appearance and plenty of courage. It took guts to campaign in those days when the 'groupers' (anti-communists) were active ... Agnes and she worked close together working among the women and women's organisations and the work was of a very high standard.'[35]

Kath had been a single mother for ten years when she met and developed a relationship with a miner and CPA member named Andy Williams, whom Agnes described as 'a good looking bear'. Being attractive, intelligent and highly respected in the area, Kath would have been seen as a 'good catch' and, although thirteen years older than Andy, she agreed to marry him.

There is no evidence to indicate whether or not this is what she really would have preferred given that the moral values of the time were so restrictive. There was a public and private code of behaviour in the CPA, and as long as you were discreet and male you could do almost anything. Kath, however, was female, very active in the CPA and living in a country town where her private life was open to view, circumstances where any sort of liaison other than marriage would have been seriously frowned upon by the CPA leadership. Being the sort of woman Kath was, it's not difficult to envisage Andy's need for marriage to give him a feeling of security. Kath resigned from teaching and married Andy in August 1945.

At this stage of his career, Percy, Kath's ex-husband, had managed to hold the position of both President of the ACTU and Minister for Labour and Employment in the Victorian State Parliament.[36] 'Clarey was criticised in Parliament and the press after he accepted the ostensibly incompatible post of Minister for Labour in 1945. He shrugged off the protests and conducted his portfolio without any evident conflict of interest.'[37]

With the Soviet Union involved in World War 2 and allied with the democracies, both the ALP and CPA played a major role in the Wonthaggi area. Kath took up the challenge and accepted the position of running the CPA bookshop as well as being an Organiser for the CPA in and around the countryside. To be an Organiser or a member of the State or Central Committee of the CPA meant having power, prestige and status.

This new responsibility meant Kath was often out and about in her dealings with people and organisations, and she rapidly developed a close relationship with the people of the area, leaving Ray, now fifteen years old, at home with Andy. This wasn't what Andy wanted. He resented her absence from home when attending meetings, her intelligence, her association and involvement with numerous organisations and people. The characteristics which first attracted him to Kath became the very same characteristics which then annoyed him. Agnes Doig spoke of his extreme jealousy of Kath's working relationship with Agnes's husband Wattie, the President of the local CPA branch. Andy's drinking increased, and with this indulgence he became more difficult. Kath realised the mistake she'd made and returned to Melbourne with Ray.

Kath did weaken and succumb to Andy's pleas for forgiveness and his request for a reconciliation; however, it didn't last and Kath remained in Melbourne.

In 1948, Kath was offered a position in the Liquor Trades Union (LTU) by Jim Coull, the Acting Secretary. The LTU had a history of activist women, and Kath wasn't the first woman communist to become involved in it (see chapter 2). The union was a well established left-wing union, and the Secretary was well aware that, when seeking this type of work, communist women, because of their ideals and commitment to the working class, would see the job not only in terms of a career but as an opportunity to make every effort to improve the conditions of the workers they represented.

Kath's good teaching record would have allowed her to return to teaching since the Education Department had been forced to relax its rules on the employment of married teachers due to the desperate shortage of teachers during and after World War 2. But all the experiences she had gained from her involvement in political organisations and political parties made Kath aware and confident of her own ability, and she undertook a career change: a change which would, because of her political commitment, fulfil her desire to have a more potent influence on improving the wages and conditions of the working class while moving towards a change in the system.

However, Kath needed to comply with the rules of the union which required her to work in the trade before being eligible to hold office. She commenced work in the cafeteria at Manton's Store and stayed there long enough to entitle her to be employed by the union. In 1948 both Kath and Jim Munro were employed as organisers in the LTU. It was in this same year that she was elected to the State Committee of the CPA. Kath was now fifty-two years of age, a late starter in some respects, 'but her past achievements and her organising skills were already widely acknowledged'.[38]

2

An early history of
women and unionism

Kath's teenage years were in an era when there was much emphasis on women's role as housewife/mother. When she began her activities as a union organiser, she joined a long line of outstanding women from the early history of women in unions.

It is interesting to note that not all Australian women of the past were the passive ladies often depicted in women's magazines or novels. On the contrary, women in industry and the public service have a reputable past of courage and tenacity in working to improve the conditions under which they toiled.

In the nineteenth century women in every State were campaigning for a livable wage and better working conditions. In 1882, in Melbourne, 500 tailoresses at Beath Schiess and Co. went out on strike against threatened reductions to their 'already paltry wages', and presented their own log of claims to the employer. This was the first strike organised by a women's trade union in Australia. Their solidarity 'gained them considerable public support ... (and) Trades Hall Council backing led to the enrolment of several thousand women in the union, extension of the strike to other factories, and recognition by the employers of the log of claims'.[1]

As early as 1890, the women of Queensland, working in various enterprises, formed a women's union and May Jordan,

Source: unkinown

THE EIGHT HOURS MOVEMENT.
Oh, if you please, Mum, I'm an eight 'ours wonner, I am, and as you insistes on my
working after four p.m., I must soot myself with another missus.

when outlining the policy of the union, said it aimed to raise a
woman's wage to a level which would allow her 'to keep
herself honestly if she had no home to fall back on'. She also
pointed out that if a woman didn't feel fit enough and strong
enough to do her daily work, it was either because she hadn't
enough to live on, was worn out by long hours, or worked in
an unhealthy atmosphere. She argued that work should be paid

for by value whether performed by men or women and the best work should get the best pay.[2]

By the end of September, membership of the women's unions in Queensland included nine occupations: waitresses, nurses, milliners, machinists, photographers, domestics, shop assistants and, the best organised, the tailoresses.

'The Women's Union first set out to abolish the no-sitting rule for shop assistants [an issue still unattained] and school teachers, and to gain shorter shop hours, equal pay, payment for apprentices, payment for overtime, and improved working conditions in other areas'.[3]

The Working Women's Political Organisation, which was established in Queensland in 1903, 'raised feminist issues' and had 'equal pay high on the agenda'.[4] When Labor gained office

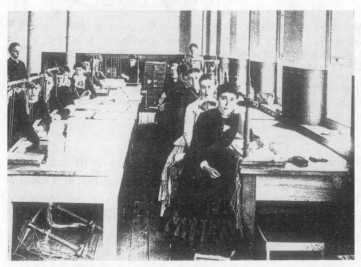

New South Wales Government Printery Collection. Mitchell Library Archives, State Library of New South Wales

In the late nineteenth century jobs were scarce for young women. Women depicted in this photo were employed in the sewing room at the New South Wales government printing works in 1892. Their work hours were long and their wages low.

Foy & Gibson Collection, University of Melbourne Archives
(Inset) Myer Emporium Collection, University of Melbourne Archives

The Whitework and underclothing section of Gibsonia Woollen Mills in Victoria, 1922. The factory was well lit and the women sitting either side of the bench were able to converse with each other but their chairs had no backs.

(Inset) Workers at Myer on Lonsdale Street, Melbourne, in the late 1920s had chairs with backs. Note the obvious sexual division of labour.

in 1910 it was pledged to equal pay, thanks to the efforts of party activists such as public servants Annie and Belle Golding and their sister Kate Dwyer, the first President of the Women's Organising Committee of the Political Labor League'.[5]

In 1910, the clothing trades were paying men twenty-four shillings for making a Norfolk jacket and a woman fourteen shillings. The right to belong to a union, union access to a workplace or the right of a union to exist had become extremely difficult. The Tramways Union was bearing the brunt

AUSTRALIA TO-DAY

December 1, 1909

The sample of weekly wages paid to employees as published below are those in force in one State, but may be taken as applying to practically the whole Commonwealth.*

Shilling(s) &Pence (d)	Males	Females
Bookbinding	59s 9d	18s 4d
Boot	50s 2d	22s 4d
Cardboard Boxes	56s 4d	23s 8d
Cigar	45s 5d	33s 4d
Clothing	55s 7d	22s 10d
Confectionery	51s 4d	20s 5d
Dresses, Mantles, Etc.	52s 1d	21s 3d
Furniture	57s 8d	25s 6d
Jams, Pickles & Sauces	39s 9d	17s 7d
Jewelry	62s 4d	38s 9d
Leather Goods	48s 7d	20s 0d
Paper Bags	59s 0d	17s 4d
Shirt	55s 2d	20s 0d
Under clothing	37s 6d	19s 5d
Waterproof Clothing	47s 3d	20s 10d
Biscuits	39s 4d	18s 11d
Carpets, Curtains, Cushions	54s 8d	21s 7d
Dye Works	41s 11d	16s 4d
Flock Mills	35s 2d	15s 6d
Furriers	54s 10d	20s 3d
Grocers' Sundries, Spices etc	49s 9d	17s 1d
Hats	61s 5d	21s 10d
Hosiery	50s 7d	20s 10d
Paper Patterns	50s 0d	26s 7d
Photography	47s 9d	20s 5d
Tea Packing	36s 8d	19s 6d
Tinsmiths (food tins)	37s 10d	15s 4d
Tobacco & Cigarettes	54s 0d	23s 5d
Toys	41s 7d	14s 11d
Umbrellas	49s 7d	19s 10d
Woolen Trade	44s 10d	19s 6d

* A selection from the original list.

Workers' weekly wages in 1909, compiled from *AUSTRALIA TO-DAY*, an annual plublication of The Commercial Travellers' Association of the anti-union onslaught, and women from the Clothing Trades Union came out in support of the Tramways' employees.

This campaign led to the first Brisbane General Strike on 30 January 1912, when most of the working population downed tools for the basic right to form a trade union. Thousands of people took part in the march through the city streets, including a contingent of six hundred women from the Clothing Trades Union led by seventy-three year-old Emma Miller. 'The women lined up to march to Parliament House to interview Premier Denham. The day was hot and humid and the women were dressed in the unsuitable clothes of the day with ankle-length skirts and long sleeves. They also wore large hats anchored with long hatpins.'[6]

At Parliament House, when informed that Premier Denham was not there, Emma Miller and Helen Huxham addressed the tightly packed crowd. Police began to disperse the crowd and as the women headed along George Street the mêlée in the city was becoming ugly. Finding their way barred by police at Queen Street, 'The women showed a bold front and defied the police, and walked through their ranks. The crowd was hilarious with derisive laughter, and gave hoots and cheers.' The police drove the women back with a violent baton charge. The procession 'advanced again and the main thoroughfare was soon thronged with a formation of ladies' and the procession was again attacked by mounted police. 'The women, bruised and outraged at this unwarranted attack, brandished their umbrellas and drew their hatpins. As the mounted force rode roughshod over people … Emma Miller thrust her hatpin into Police Commissioner Cahill's horse.' Major Cahill was thrown from his horse and injured.[7] This day became known as Black Friday.

Elsewhere, in the late 1800s, Jean Beadle, another working-

Pam Young, Proud to be a Rebel—The life and times of Emma Miller

Female members of the Clothing Trades Union marching to Parliament House on Black Friday (*Queenslander* 10 February 1912)

class activist, had 'gained first-hand knowledge of "sweated labour" in the clothing trade in Melbourne', and so learned to become an activist on the job and in the union. She moved to Perth, where she fought for unionisation of women in industry, 'equal pay, maternity allowances and child endowment to be paid directly to mothers'.[8]

Age was never a deterrent to activism and in Victoria, in 1907, Sara Lewis, a twenty-year-old, was the main organiser in forming the Waitresses Union. By 1911 she had managed to have this group formally accepted into the Hotel and Caterers Association, creating the 'Female Branch' which already numbered 700 members. She played a leading role in initiating the hotel union's federation in 1912 and remained active in various unions throughout her life.[9]

Margaret Hogg, a typist in the Stores Supply Department in New South Wales, began her long campaign to improve the pay and opportunities of women in the public service. When

Photo: D. Elford. Collection of History Department, Western Australian Museum

Black and white photo of a colourful historic banner depicting both women and men at work in the clothing trade. The man, in traditional practice, is sitting cross-legged on the table while the woman uses the sewing machine. A branch of the Amalgamated Tailors and Tailoresses Society was formed on the eastern goldfields of Western Australia in 1897.

writing for the *Public Service Journal* in 1914, she said that the twentieth century was:

> the period which has brought [women] into the industrial world to face the serious fact that they are capable, industrious and conscientious as men. Having come into this self-knowledge in spite of the obstacles which have been strewn in their path for the

last fifty years, they ask for equal opportunities and equal remuneration.

The days when the single man supported his women-folk are past, and women of spirit are glad of it. The single man of the present day, paid on a higher scale than the single woman, more often than not uses his surplus for amusements, not for the support of kith and kin … I would suggest that single men and single women be remunerated on the same scale, and married men and married women on the same basis, positions being equally open to both sexes.[10]

In Western Australia, after commencing work as a kitchen maid in a miners' boarding house in Kalgoorlie, Cecilia Shelley worked in a number of different jobs in the hotel and catering industry. 'Her experience of the appalling working conditions of women in this industry prompted her to take an active role in the Hotel, Club, Caterers, Tearooms and Restaurant Employees Union'.[11] In 1920 she was elected Secretary of this union in Perth, becoming one of the first and youngest women to be a paid trade union secretary in Australia.

Under Shelley's stewardship, that union became one of the largest predominantly female unions in Western Australia. She led the union in a 22-week strike in 1921, which began over the dismissal of a waitress who was collecting union dues and escalated into a major confrontation on the issue of 'preference for unionists'. 'She led a second strike in 1925 to gain a five shilling wage increase and a working week of forty-four hours'.[12]

As union Secretary Shelley often appeared in the Arbitration Court. Small in stature, with a quick wit and a strong person-ality, she was not easily overawed by the court atmosphere and not impressed by officialdom or titles. From the 1920s she campaigned for equal pay and equal opportunities for working women and, like Kath, she experienced a period of expulsion

Private collection

Ivy Oliver and Flo Davis marching with the Hotel, Club and Restaurant Employees Union, 1937

from the ALP. Cecilia Shelley remained as Secretary of the union until reaching the age of seventy-four in 1967 when she retired.

In Victoria, women employed in the confectionery industry organised on their own behalf and established the Female Confectioners' Union which functioned as a separate union until 1944. Miss Margaret Wearne and Miss Daisy Diwell, the

In *For Love or Money*, Flo Davis was quoted as having written of the conditions under which she had worked in 'Forty Years Organising', *Sixty Years of Struggle*, Vol. 1, Red Pen Publications, 1980. Pp 3738.

'I worked in a cafe in Pitt Street and hours didn't mean anything. You served breakfast, dinner and lunch, and we had a late-shopping night as well – on a Friday. Then you worked from half past seven in the morning till about half past nine at night, to serve the dinner at night for the late shoppers and picture crowds and so on... But in the afternoon when you were supposed to have a break, you went into the dressing room and did the beans and peas and that sort of thing. We never got anything extra for working on a public holiday... and that's what brought me into the union...'

Flo went on to write of meeting up with Topsy Small who had a big influence on her and of how both women became organisers in their union.

'We used to go around the shops, Sargents mainly, and the hotels, to try and get the girls to do something about their conditions. We started to build the union up, by policing the hours and the pay and whether they got annual leave pay. At the same time we would take our awards to the courts, to the Conciliation committees, to get better awards. That was a long struggle too, but eventually we got somewhere, with a good membership behind us'.

Cited in Megan McMurchy, Margo Oliver and Jeni Thornley, *For Love or Money*, p. 104

pioneers of the Female Confectioners' Union, were in the main responsible for the success of this union. As shop steward, Miss Wearne was able to enroll 95 per cent of the women and girls employed in MacRobertson's huge factory where some departments boasted one hundred per cent membership.[13]

Earlier than this, the Victorian Lady Teachers' Association, the Women's Post and Telegraph Association and the Women's

Public Service Association were very active in taking up women's demands. Most instrumental in the formation of the last two associations was Louisa Dunkley, who worked as a telegraphist in Melbourne. 'She had a far-sighted understanding of the need for public service unionism, and of the need for equal pay.'[14]

Australian women have shown great spirit in their activism. When lengthy negotiations failed to deliver satisfactory results for clothing workers, and strikes were held in Adelaide in 1922, and Melbourne in 1932 and again in 1935, one 'girl' was quoted as being typical of the strikers: 'We just went out, the boss nearly had a fit. By gee it was good.'[15]

Over the many years, numerous women, most of whom are unknown, contributed to the fight for pay justice. In 1935, Muriel Heagney, an active campaigner in her long working life, gave a report to the President and Executive Committee of the Amalgamated Clothing Trades Union. This six-page report was on the special organising campaign Muriel and the Union had conducted in the factories in Brunswick, after allegations of sweatshop conditions had been made public. It describes the methods adopted and the reactions of women in the factories to being organised for union membership. It made recommendations to improve the system of collecting dues and suggested that a social club be set up, or informal union meetings held, so that women would not be intimidated by formal meeting structures. It also emphasised the need for a full-time women's organiser.[16]

Despite her sterling work and comprehensive report, 'No structural change took place to follow up Heagney's powerful arguments in favour of appointing a female organiser'. 'The role of women activists did not notably change. Over the decade 1935 to 1945 the representation of women on branch committees barely altered. Leadership remained male.'[17] It was

La Trobe Collection, State Library of Victoria

Muriel Heagney

almost another twenty years before a women attained a leadership position, when Muriel Dosa succeeded, in June 1954, in becoming Secretary of the Adelaide Branch, the first woman in the history of the Clothing Trades Union to attain that position.[18]

In the LTU, three women were early militant activists: Jean Young, Susan McComb and Loretta Shore. Jean Young and Susan McComb both migrated to Australia from Scotland during the twenties, a period of economic hardship. They soon became militant activists in the unemployed movement, and

The cover of Muriel Heagney's booklet, published by Hilton & Veitch, 1935

together with Grace de Lande organised the first International Women's Day (IWD) March in Melbourne in 1931. (Sydney also saw its first IWD March in 1931).[19] Their story is recounted

Victorian Female Operatives Hall built alongside the Victorian Trades Hall Council Building where the 'Female Branch' of the Hotel and Caterers Union met

In 1883 the Victorian government of the day was approached by the Trades Hall for a grant of land, adjacent to the land on which the Melbourne Trades Hall was built, for the purpose of building a Female Operatives Hall. The grant was given and a small hall was built within the same year, alongside the Trades Hall, accommodating three unions which had a proportion of female members; the hall contained a clubroom which was used by the female staff of unions with offices in the Trades Hall.

The Female Operatives Hall was demolished in 1936. By 1975 an exclusive female operatives area no longer existed and there was no provision anywhere in the Trades Hall for women operatives or women staff.

During 1975, International Women's Year, the Trades Hall council unveiled a plaque in honour of the contribution of women to the labour movement.

Where is Our Female Operatives Hall?
(Title of Kathie Gleeson's article in *Vashti*, Winter 1975)

in Alleyn Best's *The History of the Liquor Trades Union in Victoria*:

> Loretta (Lorrie) Shore was part of the Union's 'Rank and File' team in the 1930s which finally won leadership in the 1937 elections. She worked closely with Jean Young and Susan McComb in their attempts to bring more women into the union and gain a better deal for women workers in the industry … [and] these three women activists formed a good team in unionising women workers in hotels and restaurants.[20]

Jean Young was the first woman to be elected to the position of full-time Organiser of the Victorian LTU. Her organising talents were put to the test when the first hotel strike in Victoria's history took place.

Susan McComb migrated from Scotland in the 1920s. She joined the Communist Party in the early 1930s. After being defeated in 1936 for a position in the LTU, in 1937 she became the first elected female member of the management committee.

Jean Young was born in Dumfries, Scotland, migrated to Australia in 1927 and for nearly two years was forced to work as a domestic under the migration scheme of the time. She then obtained a job as the linen keeper at the Esplanade Hotel in St. Kilda. While in Sydney, Jean joined the Communist Party and on her return to Melbourne in 1931 became very involved in the unemployed struggle. She ultimately obtained a job at the Victoria Palace Hotel and with her friends, Susan McComb and Lorrie Shore, began attending meetings of the LTU. In 1938 Jean became the first elected female organiser of the LTU in Victoria.

An earlier restriction the executive placed on her not to organise hotels 'because they were not suitable places for a woman to enter' was changed at her insistence and also because male organisers were not too successful in organising 'back-of-the-house' hotel workers who were mostly female. Nevertheless the executive allocated only some city hotels to her—the 'better type'—as well as a few country hotels. In exchange she requested lowering the entrance fee for females from two shillings and sixpence to one shilling and sixpence since all female workers were on unequal pay (approximately 60% of the male rate) and that the unions should adopt a militant and progressive policy for equal pay for the sexes.[21]

Union of Australian Women, Melbourne

The first Melbourne International Women's Day March, 1931. The march went along Russell Street, down Bourke Street to Swanston Street, then on to the Yarra Bank where Grace de Lande spoke from the platform on the need for women to organise politically. (Photo by Grace de Lande, using a small box camera)

By adopting these policies, Jean Young argued, women workers would see that the union was trying to help them out of their wage exploitation. 'Union members agreed and her success in hotels began to equal her success in restaurants, even in the refreshment room at Parliament House in November 1940'.[22]

One of the best-remembered events of Jean Young's organising years is the waitresses' strike at the Alexandra Hotel, the first hotel strike in Victoria, which occurred in April and May 1941. After joining up the hotel's female staff, she took their complaints about not having a changing room to the management. The waitresses in particular who were required to wear uniforms were forced to change in a passageway leading to the men's toilet. The publican refused Jean Young's request for a separate changing room. When she conveyed this news to the waitresses they decided to strike. After two weeks the stoppage developed into a lengthy stalemate, with Jean supporting the waitresses in requesting patrons to boycott the hotel. 'Then there was a sensation', recalled former secretary Jim Munro:

> A whole number of 'stink bombs' exploded in the bars and dining room at the busiest time of the day. Customers left in a hurry. The next day the management sought a conference with the union. As a result a change room and rest-room were provided, with a guarantee that these facilities would be kept in an up-to-date condition.[23]

Twelve months later, in 1942, and after five years of daily organising 'combats', Jean Young resigned as union organiser due to ill health. At Jean's last union meeting on 6 May 1942, Jim Coull gave warm praise for the work she had done and on behalf of the union, he placed on record the union's appreciation of her efforts. Within a few months of Jean's departure an agreement was reached that gave equal pay to barmaids in Victoria.[24]

In 1942 the ACTU called three conferences to discuss equal pay. The 1941 ACTU Congress heard a report from a Conference of Unions with women members and adopted two of its recommendations. It recommended that:

1. this Congress requests the Federal Labor Party to take the necessary action to provide for equal pay for the sexes.

2. The Congress affirms the right of women to earn their living in industry; the professions and the public services; and demands for all workers 'the legal right to equal occupational rates based on the nature of the job and not on the sex of the worker.'[25]

Following the Congress, Percy Clarey (Kath's ex-husband),

8,000 TO LEAVE JOBS
General Strike in Textile trades

A general strike in the woollen, worsted and cotton sections of the textile industry has been declared, and by tomorrow morning every mill in the metropolitan area will be idle.

As a result, about 8,000 employees, the overwhelming proportion being girls ...

Sydney Morning Herald, 22 February 1943

when addressing a conference on industrial matters in Canberra, made clear the reasons for the Congress's decision:

> Women must be permitted to come into industry only upon such principles and under such conditions that when the men who have gone overseas return to Australia and are available for absorption in civilian industry, they will not find their positions and their standard prejudiced because it is found cheaper to keep women in certain jobs rather than have men engaged in them.[26]

The LTU was already in action and 'The most significant gain achieved by the Victorian Branch (of the LTU) was equal pay for barmaids in 1942, followed by equal pay for women in distilleries when distilleries first began employing women in 1943'.[27]

With the various laws enacted to prevent women from being employed as barmaids, the shortage of bar attendants during the war (in 1942) was acute. The Licensed Victuallers Association (LVA) were deeply concerned about hotel-keepers being unable to 'take full advantage of free spending soldiers, including the well-heeled American soldiers who had recently arrived to set up camps in Melbourne … Now in court, hotel-keepers were "promising the world" in order to be allowed to employ more women.'[28]

The shortage of bar attendants was not solved by the Women's Employment Board (WEB) who were placing women in employment during the war and who saw their responsibility as providing female staff for munitions and other vital services but not barmaids. It was pointed out that the Board did not have jurisdiction over women aged forty-five and over, most barmaids being of this age.

The Labor Federal Government made appointments to the WEB and Muriel Heagney, who had been continuing her activism in the Allied Clothing Trades Union and more widely in the union movement, was known to be angry when, after all her efforts, the Government excluded her from being on the Board, reputedly because she was known for supporting the ACTU policy of full equality for the sexes while 'a number of unions was anxious to change this policy'.[29] The Common-wealth's representative on the Board was Mel Cashman from the Printing Industry Employees' Union. Cashman did not press for equal pay: 'she voted usually with the majority, usually for between 60% and 95% of the male rate'.[30]

Nevertheless, after a lot of toing-and-froing between war regulations and State and Federal government laws, on 8 September 1942 Judge Foster 'brought down his equal pay order, including a "face-saving" clause: "In deference to the ex-pressed wish of the Government of Victoria the Board decides that no female under the age of 30 shall be employed in terms of this order"'.[31]

The Victorian Government, who had presumed the responsibility for the morals and safety of Victorian women, had at first demanded that no barmaids be employed under the age of thirty, a requirement which met with the approval of the WEB. However, when Justice Foster complied with their wish, the Government then changed its demand to thirty-five years. The parties, including the Federal Government, finally agreed on thirty-five being the minimum age. Equal pay was another condition of employment. It must have been assumed by the politicians and moral guardians that, by thirty-five years of age, women were well able to deal with violent inebriates and look after themselves, or that their morals were intact or way beyond concern.

During the 1940s great emphasis was placed on obtaining the 40-hour week and, after twenty-five years of vigorous campaigning by the unions, and an intensive drive of rallies, stoppages and strikes throughout 1946–1947, a claim for the 40-hour week was co-ordinated by the ACTU. The Arbitration

---

IDLE TEXTILE FACTORIES
Strikers Defy Union

About 6,000 striking textile workers, mostly girls, defied the instructions of their union yesterday and refused to return to work.

The factories had been working at full pressure to cope with defence orders. They had just about met this demand and were concentrating on arrears of civilian orders when the strike started.

Sydney Morning Herald, 4 March 1943

THE SYDNEY MORNING HERALD,

TRAM WOMEN PROTEST

Stopwork Plan To-day

Bus and tram traffic may be dislocated in Sydney to-day because a number of tram and bus conductresses have decided to hold a stop-work meeting this morning, to protest against the dismissal of women from the service.

13 March 1946

Court then reduced the working hours from forty-four per week to forty hours and this was implemented through industry from 1 January 1948.

In the immediate post-war period 'Female wages became a casualty ... Most women workers suffered wage decreases as employers moved to drop female rates of pay back from their war-time averages of 80% or more to the pre-war rate of 60–75% of the male rates.'[32] All the old laws pertaining to the employment of barmaids in hotels resurfaced and the law prohibiting the employment of barmaids was once again in force. However, the LVA did not want to lose the services of women. Male labour was hard to get and women were renowned for their courtesy and efficiency. The opinion of those who said that bars employing women would become 'cesspools of vice' was proved wrong.

The 1950s pub was a man's world, the place where men went to relax, 'not the home, but the pub. There were pubs for every occasion and every occupation.' Some catered for wharfies and workers, some for lawyers, some for shearers, some for journalists, some for farmers, but 'good' women did not go to hotels. 'The barmaid was not there on terms of equality: her role was to serve, and perhaps provide an expansive bosom for a weary head'.[33] Women were not admitted into Public Bars: the Lounge was where a women, when accompanied by a male, could purchase drinks at a higher price.

In her autobiography, Caddie describes the deplorable conditions then existing in Sydney hotels and how, when working in the saloon bar of a large and well-known city hotel, Caddie found 'The Missus' a cold, hard woman with diamonds smothering her fingers, who had rigid control. The staff were not permitted to have a drink of water while serving in the bar, and if, at any time, a drink of water was requested, the manager took over that section of the bar while the barmaid raced upstairs to the staff washroom and drank from the dribbling tap, over the basin.[34] She recounts the many experiences endured by the staff when coping with the six o'clock rush. It was some time before Caddie managed to handle the evening stampede with any degree of skill. By four o'clock in the afternoon during the week, the bar would be lined six deep with the first arrivals crowded against the counter while those who arrived later jostled, shouted and swore in an attempt to be served before closing time.[35] Some men were known to urinate where they stood rather than lose their position at the bar.

Working conditions for staff in Melbourne hotels were no better: back-of-the- house staff, the cleaners and domestics were, in the main, confined to working in airless, dingy, smelly rooms and in corridors where the carpets, floor coverings and furniture had not been replaced due to World War 2, while most beds for guests resembled hammocks.

Several years were to pass before building materials and commodities were available to enable great alterations to be made to improve conditions prevailing in hotels.

The LVA was attempting to reduce barmaids' wages and Commissioner Morrison's decision came as a surprise in June 1949 when he reduced barmaids' wages to 75 per cent of the male wage in every State except in Victoria. In justification he said:

> I agree with the union that a barmaid must be a capable businesswoman who attracts custom by her personality and ability. Above all she must be honest. Her honesty is really the true measuring rod in determining the value of her services.
>
> Then in laying out the wages, state by state, he continued the equal pay rate in Victoria without stating why.[36]

Did the above criteria for good barmaids also apply to barmen?

The Local Option Alliance (an organisation set up to protect the morals of Victorians) immediately petitioned the Victorian Government to return the bars to prewar conditions. That meant no women barmaids. A fierce struggle followed. While many hotel-keepers wanted to retain barmaids at 75 per cent of the male rate, the union was adamant: equal pay or no barmaids.

It was in this climate of action that Kath Williams, as organiser, first undertook her responsibilities in the LTU and commenced work on a very low salary. She was expected to 'bring in her

PAY RATIO REDUCED
Women Strike

About 270 women process workers employed at three factories struck yesterday after the companies had refused to continue paying them 90% of the male wage.

Sydney Morning Herald, 12 January 1951

own wages', which meant walking from one hotel to another, going from restaurant to restaurant and also being responsible for canteens. Her job entailed recruiting staff into the union, collecting dues, listening to the members and taking up the issues which concerned them. She was on her feet all day and

Women's Strike At Ironworks

NEWCASTLE, Sunday.
Women ironworkers in heavy industries in Newcastle will strike tomorrow for increased wages.

They claimed at a meeting today that an award which became operative in December reduced a margin which they had received since they entered the steel industry as a war effort.

Three hundred women ironworkers are employed at five plants – B.H.P. steelworks, Stewarts and Lloyds, Rylands, Australian Wire Rope Works, and Henry Lane's.

Sydney Morning Herald, 19 February 1951

constantly dealing with difficult employers reluctant to negotiate or agree to a settlement of disputes.

Kath had responsibility for back-of-the-house staff in hotels while the men attended to the front of the-house, the bar. She proved herself a 'magnificent organiser: tenacious, hardworking day and night'.[37] Her hard work was rewarded. 'From 1948, new membership applications leapt from the previous monthly 50 or so to more than 200. Soon after Kath Williams started, it was noted she "enrolled over 40 new cafe members in six weeks and corrected many evasions of the award".'[38] By April 1949 around 500 new members a month came onto the union's records.[39]

Kath Williams also organised the first general meeting of cafe and restaurant members since Jean Young's retirement in 1942. At this meeting:

> Discussion followed on the many evils affecting working conditions of the employees in many cafes and restaurants ... lifting of weights, a greater number of chairs per waitress and filthy conditions under which employees change ...
>
> A new log of claims was drawn up to incorporate increased wages for all classifications on the basis of equal pay for the sexes—straight shifts of 5 days, rostered over 7 days, and better overtime, sick pay and casual rates.[40]

Kath had become part of a left-wing militant union, one of the few unions committed to its members and prepared to do battle for equal pay for women, a commitment which demanded constant struggle, and at no time was it ever easy.

In 1948 when Kath took up activities not a great deal was happening in the trade unions on equal pay. The Victorian Trades Hall Council recommended the ACTU approach the Commonwealth Government to ascertain the reasons behind the announced intention to intervene in the Female Minimum

WOMEN STOP WORK

◆

With knitting bags, thermos flasks, and sandwiches, more than 800 women attended a stopwork meeting in the Town Hall basement yesterday.

Members of the Electrical Trades Union, they are demanding wages equal to at least 90 per cent. of the male rate.

They decided unanimously to hold another stopwork meeting if their claims were not fully heard by the Conciliation Commissioner before September 16.

Union officials said it was the largest E.T.U. meeting they had ever attended.

Sydney Morning Herald, 6 August 1948

Rates matters and the class and nature of material proposed to be placed before the Court which was being conducted at the time.[41]

On September 22, 1948 an application for Equal Pay for Women in the Metal Trades came before Conciliation Commissioner Mooney. 'Between thirty and forty women attended the Court (evidently not usual, judging from the surprised look on court officials' faces). They were mostly women employed in the Metal Trades, to whom success of the Application was

48

extremely important.'[42] It was pointed out that, while equal pay was the policy of the Status of Women Commission at the United Nations Organisation, a resolution of the International Labour Organisation, a plank of the ALP and the aim of many women's organisations in Australia, 'it will not become a reality for Australian women until they themselves demand it, and demand it in terms which the Conciliation Commission understands, i.e., by showing, on the job, that they are serious, and they mean to get it'.[43]

Kath continued walking the streets of Melbourne while doing her job and, in the meantime, she became familiar with how the trade union structures worked. She observed the techniques and methods used when embarking on large campaigns and had time to analyse the equal pay campaigns that preceded her involvement. Kath was aware of how the capitalist economic system operated and believed that, because of the economic system and the lack of support from the larger trade union bodies, the achievement of permanent equal pay by individual unions was most unlikely. Hence her initiation of the drive towards a larger and all-embracing campaign.

Most women entering the workforce after World War 2 had other preoccupations. They saw their involvement in paid employment as a temporary undertaking, an effort solely for the purpose of buying a vacuum cleaner, refrigerator or other newly available goods for their home. They may also have wanted the necessary finance to educate their children and perhaps buy a car or have a holiday. Despite numerous women remaining in the workforce for many years, in the main they saw their home and children as their first priority and their husbands as the breadwinners. Their own personal income was for 'extras', and because their own paid employment was not seen as permanent or as a future career their interest in unions was of secondary importance.

It was not unusual then for women who went into paid work to take their housewife-mother-role with them, not seeing their labour and presence as a commodity to be sold to their employer in return for money. They had been conditioned to serve freely and be passive in the home, and men were then reluctant to have these passive women in their industries where they would be used as cheap labour and become a threat to men's jobs and salaries.

For most women, learning about paid labour, industry, trade unionism and the vital need for involvement is dependent on their union's role together with their experience in the labour force, particularly when working in large, predominantly male industries. But for Kath, the situation was different. Apart from several large canteens, she was involved in individual hotels and restaurants where small groups of women were employed and more easily intimidated. It was Kath's experience, knowledge and the support of a strong union behind her that brought the realities of paid work and unionism to women workers under her care.

3

Women's postwar moves on equal pay and the ACTU

With the men returning from the war, great emphasis was placed on women leaving industry and returning to the home. It was this period that became known as the 'baby boom'. The austerity of the war years had passed, girls were getting married younger and people were striving to obtain housing and commodities.

Of the ex-service women who returned home there were those who had no wish to live as their mothers had done. Among them, Claire McNamara who, in *Labor Digest*, asked, 'Must women return to the kitchen?', while Margaret Harland demanded equal pay and equal opportunities of employment in her article in *Women's Place in Society*, published in 1947. Margaret, then a housewife, had been a member of the Army Education Service in wartime and felt that women—whether in the services, on the land, or in the home—had proved their worth during the war, had earned a stronger place in society and it was time for their voices to be heard.[1]

Women schoolteachers had also developed increased awareness and resentment towards discrimination by working side by side with men in a profession where the difference in male and female rates of pay was blatantly observed. In the outback areas of Queensland, women teachers incurred the same expenses for board and lodging as men teachers, yet they received a lower allowance than men teachers. At a union meeting in 1949 when a motion was put in favour of equal allowances, Miss Flannery pointed out that 'if we are going to be intimidated by the Arbitration Court or any other tribunal in this State because we are afraid of getting less, then we will never get anywhere'. Miss Davies, in supporting the motion, said 'a man is given £25 because he has to support a wife and children but more than half of the male teachers on our staff are unmarried men.'[2] It would seem that most of the men attending the meeting were opposed to women receiving equal pay or benefits and defeated the motion by using the possibility of the department reducing their benefits to the level of women.

The 1950s presented a new dynamic where acquisition and 'femininity' became the economic, political and cultural scene. Despite the promotion in the press and women's magazines of 'women's place being in the home' the demand for goods and the growth in industry created a rapid increase in the need for workers, resulting in great numbers of women entering the workforce. In June 1954 'There were 845 402 women in the workforce—128 240 or 18% greater than at June 1947. Of the total female population, 19% were in the workforce, the same percentage as at the 1947 Census.'[3] Also in June 1954 proportionately more women were in the workforce in Victoria (21 per cent of the female population) than in the other States; New South Wales had 19 per cent, the lowest being Tasmania with 16 per cent. Of the total workforce in each State, the female component was highest in Victoria with 25 per cent followed by New South Wales with 23 per cent.[4]

> 57% of the female work force were girls or women who had never married, 30% were married women and living with their husbands, and the balance of 13% were either permanently separated, widowed or divorced. The proportion of married women in the work force was lowest in Queensland (23%) and

highest in Victoria and South Australia, both with 33%. Virtually the entire increase in the female work force between 1947 and 1954 was made up of married women. The proportion of married women who were in the working population increased from 8% in 1947 to 14% in 1954.[5]

While more married women were moving into the work-force, most novels and women's magazines written during this period ignored this trend and built a world where there was a natural order and where males and females, obeying 'immut-able' laws, fulfilled their destinies. In this world the rewards for women, as wives and mothers, were idealised, yet as Australian factories swung into mass production advertisers claimed that happiness was to be found through the purchase of consumer items, necessitating a change of attitude towards frugality,

How the 1952 catalogue of the department store, Farmers, suggested we should dress

finance and credit.[6] With the availability of colourful dress materials, rapid changes occurred in women's fashions. No longer were women confined to the austere, rationed, wartime clothing and the change brought in 'heavy pyramid coats with jutting collars and pencil-slim hobble skirts or flared skirts that stood out like tents, supported by layers of underskirts in the new 'crackle' nylon. Beneath seamless stockings of sheer nylon were shoes with stiletto heels which ruined floors in the name of style'.[7] With the advent of washable, drip-dry fabrics, the working girl's wardrobe was transformed, making it possible for her to wear a different outfit every day. The 'Bra' assumed great importance and, for the first time, the young had a fashion identity of their own; the word 'teenager' became known and the 'teenage' market established.

'In many ways, the fifties were a unique historical epoch for women. A period of tremendous repression after the "freedom" of the war years, particularly in relation to sexuality; a period when passivity was conflated with femininity, while simultaneously femininity became women's sole legitimate employment'.[8] The film stars who stood out from it:

> in papier-mache relief—Jerry Lewis, Elvis Presley, Marilyn Monroe and Doris Day—had an unreal quality, images at once bland and tortured. They were all about sex, but without sex. The fabulous fifties were a box of Cracker Jacks without a prize; or with the prize distorted into a forty-inch bust, a forty year-old virgin.[9]

Movies were beginning to suffer a credibility gap, a gap between the screen and their mass audiences, between what the movie stars were and what we were:[10]

> It was as if the whole period of the fifties was a front, the topsoil that protected the seed of rebellion that was germinating below. The cultural disorientation had begun, but it had yet to be acknowledged ... The word 'alienation' was adopted to express the new alignment of 'us' against 'them'.[11]

It was during 1951 that the press publicised the case of Mrs. Irene Dempsey receiving the sack for wearing slacks to work at a Brunswick factory. Wearing slacks was not readily acceptable and was considered to be unfeminine.[12]

It was in this economic, social and cultural environment of the late 1940s and early 1950s that Kath organised the women members of her union and began her work on equal pay.

Three decades earlier, in 1920, a claim for equal pay by the Cardboard Box Makers had been 'dismissed by Justice Brown on the grounds that if women got equal pay or a minimum wage it would make work more attractive and women would not fulfil their family duties'.[13] The Melbourne Trades Hall Council (MTHC) was also calling for equal pay rates at this stage. Over a decade later, during the depression, the ACTU presented its first equal pay case in May 1937, requesting that, as a first step, female wages be fixed at 60 per cent of the male rate in place of the existing 50–54 per cent. The Arbitration Court refused the claim.[14] In 1949–1950 when the Supreme Commonwealth Arbitration Tribunal considered a claim for an equal male and female basic wage, the Tribunal rejected the claim. Mr Justice Foster then gave his reasons for doing so, reasons which reveal the power a judge had to reinforce women's place as being in the home, the place where women's labour received no remuneration. His points were:

(a) the male basic wage was a social wage for a man, his wife and family;

(b) no claim was made for a unit wage upon which equality of wages could be based;

Justice Foster noted that it was easily understood why the union did not make a claim for a unit wage on which equality of rates could be based since it might have resulted in a lower male basic wage.

(c) 'equal pay' based on the male basic wage would put an intolerable strain on the economy;

(d) it was socially preferable to provide a higher wage for the male because of his social obligations to fiancée, wife and family;

(e) while single females were said to be anxious to receive the higher wage, their interest changed on their marriage ... As married women they became concerned that their husbands should bring home the largest possible pay envelope;

(f) the needs and the responsibilities, etc., of females were substantially less than that of males in this community; and lastly,

(g) the redistribution of the wage fund so that young unmarried females would receive very substantially increased spending power would disturb the economy in a manner certainly to the disadvantage of the married basic wage worker and his wife and family, and, probably, of the whole community.[15]

This Commonwealth Arbitration Court Case made the first determination of a female basic wage set at 75 per cent of the male basic wage, thus making it institutionalised.[16]

When analysing Judge Foster's seven reasons for rejecting the claim for an equal male and female basic wage, one can see how the need to 'provide a higher wage for the male because of his obligations to fiancée, wife and family' placed women's responsibilities in the home as being 'substantially less [important though necessary] than that of males in this community';

in other words, women's work, whether it be in or outside the home, was of less value; thus women were unworthy of receiving a wage in their own right for work performed. This placed women into the position of near total dependence on a husband.

It was taken for granted that pay justice for women was a burden on the economy; thus women were condemned to go on being financially dependent on men and to subsidising the economy both by their cheap labour in the workforce and by running their homes for their men in the workforce.

In the early fifties, the female professional officers in the Commonwealth Service Association had their request for equal pay rejected; in two further determinations, the Arbitrator refused claims by the Hospital Employees' Federation (HEF) and the Repatriation Department Medical Technologists Association for equal pay for certain categories of females in quasi-professional positions.[17]

When examining the tactics and actions employed by Kath over the years, one can detect her concern about the overall perspective of equal pay and the role of the trade union movement. Within a short period of becoming an organiser in the LTU, and observing how the Arbitration Courts and Wage Tribunals dealt with equal pay claims lodged by individual unions, it would appear that she worked with a long-term goal in view.

Kath noted the rejections the various unions' equal pay claims and began applying pressure for combined action to be taken. Although the ALP had adopted equal pay as national policy in 1936, followed by the ACTU in 1941, it was difficult 'to convince Labor and trade union officials that the male 'breadwinner' concept of the basic wage and the award wage should apply equally to women'.[18]

Efforts made by individual unions campaigning for equal

pay were rarely successful and, even when they were, they proved to be of short-term duration or were of benefit only to women covered by militant unions or professional associations. Most employed women were in industries where, although women predominated, men controlled the union and, while giving official support to the cause of equal pay, were not prepared to take substantial action.

It was in this context Kath undertook a campaign intending to obtain equal pay for all women: one rate of pay for the job performed, a campaign which would require massive support from the ACTU, professional associations, all Trade Union Labor Councils, the trade unions and the support of women all over Australia.

As a member of the State Committee of the CPA, Kath began her campaign among communist trade union officials and members who attended meetings of trade union cadres. Her prime task was to convince these trade union officials; and she is remembered for spending a great deal of time talking to and addressing meetings in an effort to convince and coerce her comrades and others into taking up active struggle for equal pay. The great majority of those present at these meetings were men who, in the main, worked in predominantly male industries and it was important to get their support if the entire union movement was to be activated.

The year 1950–1951 was a very trying time for communists and trade unionists. With the Senate's approval, the Menzies Government passed a Bill for the dissolution of the Communist Party, a Bill which had far-reaching threats for the trade union movement and democracy. When the decision was made to hold a referendum on the issue all of Australia was geared up for the campaign with both sides applying all they had. The Menzies' Bill was defeated.[19]

It wasn't difficult for Kath to convince her comrades in the

CPA of the need for equal pay as they were well aware of the threat women's cheap labour would be if the owners of industry were to decide to employ more women to displace men. But trying to convince them to take action took more persuasion. The reality was that most male trade union officials didn't know how to go about organising women and preferred to avoid the situation.

In 1951 a CPA factory bulletin claimed the Menzies Government, through an approach to the Public Service Board, was trying to revoke the award, made during the war, to women working in the munitions factories of 90 per cent of the male rate.[20] The article went on to say that the Ironworkers Union 'would fight like hell' to preserve the women's rate of pay. Apart from calling on all men workers to support women in the fight against wage cuts, they claimed that, if women's wages were reduced, women would be employed to replace men so it was important to stand behind the women and safeguard their wages.

In the same year, the Victorian Trades Hall Council (VTHC) requested the ACTU call a conference of unions with women members for the purpose of preparing plans to meet the attack of employers on the standard wage of women workers.[21]

In August, the employers lodged a claim to come before the Arbitration Court demanding that the rate of women's wages be reduced from 75 per cent of the male rate to 60 per cent.

Obtaining wage justice for women has always been a constant battle. The daily press was almost silent on this issue.

The right of women to earn their living in industry, the professions and the public service had been affirmed at the 1941 ACTU Congress.[22] The need to affirm the right for women to be employed in the paid workforce may seem strange to women today but the threat of pushing women out of the workforce is ever present.

In 1942, the first women to become mail officers entered the Melbourne General Post Office (GPO) as a wartime measure. They understood and agreed to the men resuming their positions when returning from the war but, after the cessation of hostilities, and in spite of several advertising campaigns, men did not enter the Mailroom in sufficient numbers to allow the dispensing of women's services. Women employed by the GPO received the same salary as the men and did 90 to 95 per cent the same work, making up the leeway by being more dexterous at some parts of the job and more amenable to the monotony.[23]

By the end of 1950 the Government had decided that women employed as mail officer would receive 75 per cent of the male rate, a decision threatening men's jobs. The women had remained employed for seven years after the war and had come to hold different views in regard to it being a man's job. 'And this position continued until early 1951 when a slump began to appear and the men decided to avail themselves of the shelter of the Mailroom!'[24]

At this time, there were approximately 300 women employed in the Melbourne Mail Branch, about 100 of these were married when the retrenchment of women started in May 1951 and continued to the December. On New Year's Eve 119 single women were given approximately three weeks' notice. 'The women sought and received an interview in Melbourne with the Superintendent of Mails, but he informed them that the matter was out of his hands'.[25] (The following year, in 1953, 125 Sydney women were also dismissed from the GPO. By the time these dismissals occurred, some women had been employed in the service for eleven years. These dismissals were part of the Menzies Federal Government plan to retrench 10 000 Commonwealth public servants.)

Despite the massive amount of overtime worked by the

remaining staff, the retrenchment of women resulted in chaos in the service and delivery of mail and although the union made no attempt to save the jobs for women at the Melbourne GPO it claimed it would seek jobs in other government departments for the women. The reasons given for this stand by Mr J. E. Hickey, Acting Secretary of the Postal Employees Union, was that 'the union regarded the industry as basically a male industry and also considered that the appointment of women during the war years was purely a temporary measure'.[26] This was typical of the prevailing male attitude towards the right of women to work and the fear of women undermining their wage standards.

In 1953 the Melbourne GPO, after an advertising campaign

Photo: Viv Méhes

Pia Patrizia, married with three children, worked in a factory making corrugated metal sheets for ten years, then spent many years working as a spot-welder.

Photo: Viv Méhes

Rada Usak from Yugoslavia, employed in meat works

in the press, were unsuccessful in recruiting sufficient male mail officers for the job. Further attempts to recruit men were still being made in 1954. An advertisement appeared in October 1954 seeking male and female staff to handle the Christmas mail, but stipulated the 'Employment of women will not extend beyond 31st December, 1954'.[27] It wasn't until the mid-1960s that women became part of the regular workforce at the GPO.

From the 1950s onward, Australian policy-makers acknowledged that migrant men and women were needed to expand the Australian workforce and accept the jobs nobody else wanted and the influx of migrant workers into the workforce became very visible. Many migrant women were employed in sweatshops on the process line—cleaning, sewing and processing food for the whole of society, while they were taken for granted and denied any economic or social recognition. As late as 1978 the Royal Commission on Human Relationships found that some unions had not responded to the entry of migrants and women into the workplace. It was claimed that this neglect amounted to discrimination in that they accepted subscriptions for services they failed to give.[28]

Mrs Jean Daly, the Australian representative on the UN Commission on the Status of Women, had asked the Federal Government in 1952 to state where it stood on the question of equal pay for women. Such a declaration was urgent in view of the application from employers to the Arbitration Court for an extra 15 per cent reduction in women's wages. In her letter to the Minister for Labour, Harold Holt, she pointed out that the International Labour Organisation Convention in June 1951 recommended equal pay, but the Australian Government abstained from voting, the emploiyers voted against it and employee representatives voted for it.[29]

In 1953, among all the States of the Commonwealth, Victoria alone approved the concept of Equal Pay for Equal

Equal pay float in the May Day March, c. 1950

Communist Party of Australia Collection, University of Melbourne Archives

Work of Equal Value and agreed to the ratification of the ILO Convention 100 by the Federal Government.[30]

Moves made by the Menzies Government to reduce women's wages stirred the campaign for equal pay among trade union circles in Victoria—notably in the Liquor Trades Union which had large numbers of female members employed in circumstances which left them open to exploitation by employers. Pressures of this sort, together with the climate produced by the ILO recommendation, persuaded the ACTU Congress meeting held in Sydney in September 1953 to carry the following resolutions:

> That this Congress calls on the Federal and State Governments to legislate for the provision of equal pay for the sexes in all occupations and, in the first instance, to grant equal pay to their own employees.
>
> We call upon the ACTU to establish Equal Pay Committees to undertake the task of campaigning for legislation and to arouse the interest of male and female workers in the demand for equal pay; such committees to be co-ordinated on a national basis by the Executive of the ACTU.[31]

With the lower wages paid to women, Kath found it necessary to enlighten men in the trade unions who found it easier to oppose women entering their industry than to support equal pay even though such a move would prevent women being used against them.

Kath set her mind on becoming a delegate of her union to the Trades Hall Council, the structure with the power to make important decisions. The THC met every Thursday evening, a commitment she willingly undertook, knowing that if she was going to succeed in mobilising all the unions, getting onto the THC was the first step. Achieving this goal depended entirely on Jim Coull, then Secretary of her union.

Jim Coull was an old Scottish socialist who did not belong

to the CPA. Kath had a constant 'battle with Jim'. He was a 'supreme bureaucrat and chauvinist' while at the same time being a 'terrific orator'. He often spoke at the Yarra Bank, an open-air forum held regularly on a Sunday afternoon in Melbourne situated by the Yarra River, where speakers from various political parties, religious groups and faith-healers were able to expound their theories and philosophies. Jim was known to be capable of 'mesmerising and/or entertaining' his audience for two hours 'talking a lot of bull'. With his broad Scottish accent he often had the listeners 'roaring with laughter', but 'his depth of understanding of trade unionism was sadly lacking'. His obvious study of adjectives, and his great ability with invective, gave him the skills 'to tear any opposition to ribbons' if they dared oppose or heckle him.[32]

Kath had to work under this man's authority 'and he could be ruthless, he was a smart operator'; nevertheless, he supported her in her determination to be on the THC and she was duly elected to this body in 1954. Kath was now able to have a direct influence on the entire representation of the Victorian trade union movement which assembled weekly at the THC meetings.

Kath was to have many heated disagreements with Jim over the years but, when speaking of these incidents with friends, without minimising the seriousness of her arguments, she always managed to present a tolerant and sometimes humorous side to the narration.

Average attendance at THC meetings was 150 males and about ten females. Most of the women delegates in attendance were selected by their unions to be supportive when votes were taken but they added little to the discussion. Most women found the atmosphere of union meetings alienating. Kath wasn't overawed or intimidated by the heavy male presence or atmosphere. Her experience over the many years of involvement in political parties, and dealings with hotel managers on the job, had given her the strength to address meetings with confidence.

The type of workplaces Kath was responsible for in her job had a high turnover of staff making any attempt at unionising difficult'. She would no sooner enrol a woman into the union when, within months, the employee had left the job. 'By establishing good shop stewards, Kath was successful in winning absolute support from the women working in the cafeterias at Coles and Myers, both having been difficult places to organise.'[33] 'Women members of the LTU remembered the dedicated service Kath gave over the years and indicated their gratitude for her support in time of need'.[34]

There can be no doubt that being a 'first-class' organiser, successful in recruiting members and able to deal with the problems confronted on the job, made Kath's job reasonably secure. Despite the fact that she stood up to Jim Coull and argued over what she considered to be important issues he did not dismiss her; he had a deep respect for Kath even though at times he thought she was on about a lot of 'froth and bubble'.[35] Ultimately, Kath went on to become a delegate from her union to the ACTU Congress. Only those attending the ACTU Congress or Conferences would know of Kath's contribution when present. Knowing what men were like in politics and the unions, I suspect that while the men were supposedly listening, they were not really hearing what she said.

From here on, Kath continued with a consistent campaign of talking, lobbying, cajoling and coercion for the proposed Equal Pay Committee to be established. Much of this lobbying took place at a personal level, at the faction meetings prior to the THC meetings, and in the meetings.

In November of 1954 a special meeting of women union members held at the Trades Hall in Melbourne resolved to approach the THC requesting the THC establish an Equal Pay Committee (EP Committee) in keeping with the decision made by the ACTU Congress of 1953. In March 1955 the Executive of the THC called a meeting of unions with women members which resolved to set up the desired committee.[36]

In all, it took two years of discussions, consultations and meetings after the initial ACTU Congress decision in 1953 before the THC EP Committee sent a circular to all affiliated unions in 1955 notifying them that the EP Committee had been established.

The years of effort Kath expended in getting the THC EP Committee up and running were acknowledged by the unanimous decision of the THC when electing her to the honorary position of Secretary/organiser of the THC EP Committee.[37] Yes, it was another unpaid job for a woman, but a very important strategic position, and one which Kath with her experience was able to utilise to the utmost degree.

Those elected to the committee were: Messrs. G. Hayes, Boot Trades; D. MacSween, Clothing Trades; A. Williams, Electrical Trades; G. Collaretti, Hospital Employees' Federation; W. Steel, Federated Clerks'; and Mrs K. Williams, Liquor Trades Union. Kath was the only woman on the committee and the only communist.

The THC EP Committee aimed to carry out ACTU policy by all possible means: using leaflets, meetings, press, radio and election campaigns appealing for moral and financial assistance to help carry on the campaign for equal pay.[38] The Committee did not waste any time before getting into action. At the impending ACTU Congress, it was decided to consult with state governments to enact equal pay legislation and for State and Labor Councils to establish EP Committees. It was also decided to convene a conference of unions with women members to be held in March 1956.[39] The circular went on to stress the importance of the work in view of the attacks being made on women's wages, and the use being made of women as cheap labor which depressed general wage levels. As well, it stated: 'We would be pleased to send a speaker to your next Committee of Management or General Meeting to put the case to your membership'. The circular was signed by Mrs K. Williams, Hon. Secretary.

A circular from the THC EP Committee was sent to all affiliated unions with a bundle of free copies of a leaflet for distribution among union members. Thirty thousand leaflets were printed and a request was made for financial assistance as well as promotion of the availability of speakers.[40] Again, Kath alone signed the letter.

The VTHC EP Committee sent a circular to numerous women's organisations notifying them of the formation of the Equal Pay Committee and the steps being taken by the trade union movement to secure social and economic justice for women workers. It further explained that the Committee was to give effect to the policy of the ACTU on equal pay for the sexes and went on to indicate how efforts were being made by employers to have women's wages reduced. Leaflets explaining the issues were also included with an order form for same. Support was invited for the campaign and a call was made for resolutions to be sent to parliamentarians.[41] Once again Kath was the only signatory to the circular.

The significance of Kath being the only signatory is because the time came when the signature of Gil Hayes, the President, also appeared on the letters. It would seem that the President's signature started appearing on the correspondence to allay fears that Kath may have been making unilateral decisions. Perhaps the signature of a male was required to give the document and Committee more credibility and authority.

It is interesting to note that Gil Hayes of the Boot Trades

Union (BTU) played a major role in the fight against communism during the 1940s and 1950s. Bradon Ellem in his paper on
the BTU, drawing on Robert Murray's *The Split*,[42] tells of
meetings of anti-communists in the BTU union's office in the
THC before World War 2 had ended. From these gatherings
emerged an informal group, the 'Boot Trades Group' which
operated against communists in the Trades Hall. Although
communists and their allies never 'controlled' the union, the
industrial groups would be active in both branches, generally
bolstering the positions of officials. With the ending of World
War 2, young men like Gil Hayes and Frank Carmody had
already prepared for the fight at home against communism
even though their union was controlled by the 'right'.

Gender relations were part of the struggle in the BTU and
heated arguments occurred over how the union should res-
pond to speed-up and incentives, how the union should be
structured, at what level women's wages should be set and
what role women should play in the union. 'The Industry was
marked by a rigid sexual division of labour which remained
intact: in 1947, 42 per cent of the workforce was women: in
1955 it was 45 per cent'.[43]

With the right wing firmly entrenched in the union in the
1940s and 1950s, the union 'became more introspective than it
had ever been',[44] letters from equal pay committees were
ignored and any discussion of equal pay at meetings resulted in
the decisions being left to Federal Council to decide. Women
were all but excluded from an active role in the union. There
was no attention given to equal pay. Ellem notes that:

> The majority of men had long ignored any calls for action with
> women's groups be it for International Women's Day, a Women's
> Conference, the United Associations of Women's Charter or a
> Labor women's organising fund ... It is not unfair to say that the
> groupers and their allies were even less interested in the question

of women's pay conditions and participation than were others ... Earlier, the militants had briefly overcome the officials' inertia on women's post-war wages, successfully arguing for 90 per cent of the male rate as against 75 per cent. The formal commitment to equal pay irrespective of the work performed was not backed up with much action despite calls for special meetings.[45]

It must be said that when the union did mention women's wages at the National Wage Case hearing in 1947, 'the judge simply said 'Skip them' ... and 'after much delay, increases were handed down to the men in 1947 but the women received nothing'.[46] While there is no record of women attending meetings in NSW until 1952, in Victoria Ivy Thompson, the only woman to speak at meetings, was leading the left's call for equal pay, for a thorough assessment of wage-fixing of the sexual division of labour. Gil Hayes became Secretary of the BTU in 1947. And 'When the Victorians finally did send delegates to an equal pay conference in 1955, half those who attended were male officials. None of those who had been in the decade-long push for equal pay were elected'.[47]

Gil Hayes was elected to be the President of the Victorian Trades Hall Council Equal Pay Committee. Why?

Mr Gus Collaretti, also a member of the VTHC EP Committee, had between 1954 and 1967 held various positions in the HEF as President of the Victorian No. 2 Division, as staff representative on the Victorian Public Service Board, was appointed Secretary of No. 1 Division and, ultimately, Federal President of the HEF.

The records of the HEF between the years 1950 to 1967 seem to have disappeared and, as the writer of this book, I had to depend firstly on my experiences as a member of the HEF which were recorded in the book *Zelda*.[48] In 1954 after serving my trial period of employment as a dental nurse at Larundel

Psychiatric Hospital, Victoria, I pursued the shop steward in order to join the union. Four months after joining the HEF, Division 2, I attended the first general meeting held since becoming a member and discovered it was the only meeting the union had called for a period of twenty months.[49] This occurred even though the union rules stipulated that quarterly general meetings were to be held. The numbers attending this meeting were insufficient for a quorum but the meeting still went ahead. Gus Collaretti was acting Secretary of No. 2 Division at the time. Like Gil Hayes, Gus Collaretti's main concern was controlling the union and playing a prominent role in combating communism.

When doing the research for the present book, I discovered that, while being active in the HEF, Gus Collaretti, who was a full-time official of the Federation and a member of the VTHC EP Committee, was also involved in the ALP split.[50] During all the years of his association with the EP Committee, the members of No. 2 Branch of the HEF were not informed of his association with the EP Committee. One can only surmise that the reason the Executive kept this information from the members was so as to save themselves the bother of having pressure applied for action on equal pay.

At the HEF Branch No. 2 General Meeting in September 1960, a woman member asked the newly elected full-time Secretary for the HEF policy on equal pay. He said all these points would be discussed by the Executive. In reality, this meant that the issue would rest in the archives: the usual method used to discourage the members from asking for action and which proved to be successful, for the members never heard any more about it.[51]

Without any prior notice being given at a General Meeting or notification of any sort, in 1961 the Federal Executive of the

MAKE UP OF TRADE UNION
STRUCTURE BETWEEN THE
1950s AND 1960s

Delegates to the Trades Hall Council in
the capital city of each State could be
elected by the membership, or appointed
for an agreed length of time determined
by their union, to represent the interests of
their membership.

ACTU Congress or Conference delegates
were appointed by the Federal Council, or
federal body of the union to represent the
interests of the membership.

Federation decided to take the serious step of disaffiliating the
HEF from the ACTU. This was done without the members'
knowledge or approval.[52] Disaffiliation prevented the union
from any further contact with the VTHC EP Committee.

What then was this HEF Federal Trade Union Leader doing
on the VTHC EP Committee? Was he still attending the meetings
or did he resign? Many strange games are played out in
hierarchical structures!

At the General Meeting of February 1963, it was decided to
donate twenty pounds to the Equal Pay Committee and for the
union to contact them and invite a speaker to visit every hospital during lunch hours to address the members on the equal
pay question. These meetings never took place.[53] Research also
revealed that, of the steady flow of leaflets issued from the EP
Committee over the years, the members of No. 2 Division
received leaflets only on one occasion Perhaps the one bundle
of leaflets received by the union was in response to the twenty
pounds donation? When I asked the Executive for the identity

of people on the VTHC EP Committee, the reply was they didn't know.

After attending the 1963 Federal Conference, where we were informed that the ACTU was making 1964 Equal Pay Year, I reported this information to our next General Meeting but nothing occurred. In hindsight, it would seem that the 1964 Equal Pay Week was mistakenly reported as Equal Pay Year.

In October of 1967 No. 2 Division of the HEF appeared as a sponsor of the 'Equality for Women Talk Out'. This was as far as the union was prepared to go. Gus Collaretti, while on the ACTU EP Committee, never attended any of HEF No. 2 Division General Meetings to report on the EP Committee's activities.

4

Decisions on equal pay, 1891 to 1955

Reams of paper have been written stating the various reasons why the Arbitration Commission and wage tribunals should grant equal pay and why these Tribunals rejected the claims brought before them.

As early as 1891 the Brisbane Royal Commission heard testimony from workers in manufacturing and service industries such as hotels and restaurants. Among the many issues raised was equal pay. The two women commissioners, Elizabeth Edwards and Leontine Cooper, asked the most questions. Elizabeth Edwards was particularly persistent in her questioning of the government printer, Mr J. Beal. While the private employers were inclined to hedge on equal pay questions, Beal, in opposing equal pay, flatly stated, 'You cannot put a woman to do a man's work'. When pressed by Elizabeth Edwards on whether the girls would get the same pay if they did the same quality and quantity of work, he said 'They could not do the work … it is a physical impossibility'.[1]

As well as asking questions on women's right to equal pay, the two commissioners also asked questions about the right of women to equal work itself. Leontine Cooper pursued the questioning: 'Can you give any good reason why a woman should not be allowed to earn her living at anything she is capable of doing?'[2]

In Victoria a decade later:

The issue of equality of pay and opportunity in the public service gained especial prominence between 1900 and 1902 when the Victorian Women's Post and Telegraph Association, led by Louisa Dunkley, drew on the New South Wales example to campaign for equal pay and opportunity for women in the newly constituted Commonwealth Public Service.[3]

Though at first equal pay was sought as an act of justice to those women in the Public Service who had 'year in year out' been doing the same work as men, the Victorian Women's Post and Telegraph Association then decided to advocate it as the only method of keeping up the value of the work and providing fair opportunities for employment for both men and women in the future.[4]

In his 1907 Harvester Judgement, Justice Higgins created the Basic Wage, a wage sufficient for an unskilled labourer to maintain himself and his family in frugal comfort. Higgins' definition of frugal comfort did not allow for such elements of living in a civilised community as light, clothing, furniture, utensils, loss of employment, books and other reading matter, sickness and death, religion or charity in the wage. His explanation of how he arrived at this figure was to prove disastrous for equal pay claims for the next sixty years.[5]

Justice Higgins' judgement was responsible for drastic reductions in the wages earned by women and girls, leaving girls to 'dream of eventual rescue through marriage'. Emma Miller, Helen Huxham, members of the Women's Union, and others claimed working women found it difficult to grasp that, as individuals, they should be economically independent on a livable wage; an equal wage that was their right. They mounted an educational campaign explaining the true position, and continued to call for equal pay.[6]

During the Basic Wage Royal Commission of 1920, its chairman, A. B. Piddington, said, 'The doctrine of the living wage has … never yet been consistently carried into actual practice in Australia',[7] yet its acceptance by the trade union movement made its maintenance and continuous containment of women's pay at less than men's possible. Piddington went on to say that the living wage theory could not 'be eliminated from the beliefs and convictions of the Australian people',[8] adding further strength to the exploitation of women. The unions accepted this situation believing they would gain more support when seeking wage claims for a man and his family, thus leaving women wage-earners without support.

In the 1912 Rural Workers Union Case, Justice Higgins established an Arbitration Court precedent when contrary to his previous judgement, he gave fruit-pickers equal pay. Higgins said the claim had 'an attractive sound, and seems to carry justice on its face; where a woman produces as good results as a man in the same kind of work, she ought not to get less remuneration'.[9] Despite this substantive comment, his decision confirmed some differentials in pay between women and men in this industry. Equal pay was given to women whose work was directly in competition with men, whereas other women in the industry, the wrappers and packers, were performing tasks men did not do, so they were kept on women's rates.[10] Justice Higgins was not prepared to give women pay justice.

Responding to the decision brought down in the Rural Workers Union Case, at the Women's Industrial Convention held in September 1913, women delegates agreed 'the time had arrived in the Commonwealth of Australia when women must organise industrially and politically'. 'Sara Lewis from the Hotel and Caterers' Union, and one of the organisers of an equal pay rally in Melbourne in July of that year, insisted that women workers did the same quality and quantity of work as men'.[11]

Women and men grape pickers at 'Yalumba' in the Barossa Valley, South Australia, c. 1900
From *Australia and New Zealand Complete Book of Wine*, p. 31, compiled by Len Evans, published by Paul Hamlyn, 1973

In the 1919 Clothing Trades Case: 707, Justice Higgins said, 'It is not for me to find a scientific basis for the distinctions in the wages paid to the various skilled employees as between themselves and the unskilled, and one another'. Due to the fact that distinctions existed, he went on to say 'they exist and are recognised in the practice of society for me, in a practical inquiry with the view of settling disputes'.[12] Justice Higgins adhered to the social norm. However, there was always discontent and agitation among the clothing trades employees because of the exploitative methods used by the industry employers and, in 1926, 'The Clothing Trades Union again claimed for an equal minimum basic wage for men and women in the industry at 21 years of age. This represented a departure from the policy of differential rates hitherto adopted, and reflects the modern viewpoint on the value of women's labour and social rights.' Every worker should enjoy the highest possible standard of living in her own right and not merely share in the pleasures and comforts of life through the beneficience of her menfolk.[13]

It was not until 1935 that the first substantial and widespread organisation for equal pay occurred, the year which also saw the founding of the Equal Status Committee in Victoria. Muriel Heagney was responsible for both, and in that same year published her important book, *Are Women Taking Men's Jobs?* Born in 1880 and raised in a Labor Party home, Muriel Heagney spent most of her working life campaigning for the Labor Party, the unions and women.

Muriel was passionately committed to feminism. This was to bring her into conflict with Labor men because of her stand on the need for women at home to receive an income, an endowment, a claim seen by the men as class collaboration and a threat to the male basic wage. They may have also seen the advent of women receiving an income as undermining their role as the provider, a threat to their security and the security of the family. Distressed by the attacks on women's employment during the depression, Muriel 'had decided that women must win their independence as wage earners in the labour market, working with men, not against them'.[14]

When moving to Sydney, Muriel played a leading role in the setting up of the Council of Action for Equal Pay (CAEP) in May 1937 which drew together representatives from twenty-eight unions and several feminist groups. This was achieved by resolution of a conference of fifty-three organisations convened by the left-wing NSW Branch of the Federated Clerks' Union to consider equal pay and female labour problems. At its first Interstate Conference, the CAEP decided to 'lobby for a change in the Australian Constitution to give women a constitutional right to equal pay and equal opportunity of appointment'.[15] John Hughes, the assistant secretary of the Clerk's Union, when addressing the conference, affirmed their feminist goal: 'Equal pay means the establishment of economic independence for women and provides a basis upon which they can struggle to secure the consummation of full equality'.[16]

It was during the depression year of May 1937 when the Basic Wage case was being heard that, 'For the first time the ACTU presented its case for EP, asking that as the first step, female wages be fixed at 60% of the male rate in place of the existing 50–54%'. When evidence and arguments were presented for the need and provision of more food and medical care to be factored into the basic wage, Judge Brockman, the former president of the Central Council of Employers of Australia, commented that 'while such evidence was ... useful for ... propaganda purposes' it was 'wasting the time of the Court'.[17] The Claim was finally rejected on the grounds 'that the Basic Wage had to be determined in terms of industry's capacity to pay', and the *Labour Daily* of 26 March 1937 reported, 'If that wage is the highest that industry can pay, nothing the Court will do will remedy the position of the basic wage earner'. The Court refused to set the female basic wage at 60 per cent of the male rate.

During the 1930s and 1940s, Muriel and Jean Arnot undertook speaking engagements and wrote well researched papers. Muriel's 'Equal Pay for The Sexes, a survey on Women's Wages', was prepared for the 1948 ACTU Congress. 'Feminists' and 'laborites' worked together in the CAEP, campaigned actively among women and forced statements on equal pay from political party leaders.[18]

It is interesting to note the approaches women made in the early years when presenting arguments in favor of equal pay: almost half the claims were based on ethical grounds while the other half were on economic grounds on the basis of women's lower wages and/or the threat to men's jobs. For instance, Jean Arnot, in her presentation to the Annual Conference of the Public Service Association said:

> The case for equal pay is based on the strong foundations of justice and the claim of every individual to impartial treatment as number 1 priority ... [and secondly], Women are the community, just as well as men, and there is no reason to suppose that an injustice put upon one part for the benefit of the other, is of any advantage to the whole.[19]

In a further attempt to gain pay justice for women, the United Nations Association of Women, during the late 1930s, briefed a Sydney Barrister, Nerida Cohen, to appear in the Clerks Union Case in the NSW Commission, in support of phased-in equal pay. In 1940, she was again briefed, this time to apply for leave to intervene in the Federal *Basic Wage Case* by a coalition of twenty-five women's organisations. Intervention was disallowed by the Court on the basis that the question of equal pay was not before the Commission. The episode shows how women banded together and worked through the unions to achieve a common goal, for, out of this apparent failure, came a solidarity with unions. Nerida Cohen and Jessie Street held talks with Trades Hall. Thirty-one unions were represented at the meeting, which resolved to recommend a combined application to the Court for equal pay. The experience drew women's attention to the realisation that unless *women themselves*, whether Trades Unionists or members of social organisations, *are prepared to take an active part in pressing the claim for equal pay* and the improvement of the rates of pay for women workers in proper quarters, that *such claims would not be pressed.*[20]

In 1941 the ACTU Congress adopted the right of women to earn their living and the legal right to equal occupational rates based on the nature of the job and not on sex of the worker.'[21]

In October 1941, Murdoch's Melbourne *Herald* published what was billed as 'Australia's first Gallup poll', a survey on whether women deserved to get the same pay as men for

MEN

18 to 40 years

required as

MAIL OFFICERS

The Postmaster-General's Department requires men aged between 18 and 40 years for employment as Mail Officers, General Post Office, Melbourne.

Duties include letter sorting and associate work in the Mail Branch.

Congenial Conditions Planned Shifts

SALARY at:

	per week
18 years	£7/12/2
19 years	£9/7/5
20 years	£11/2/9

Adult:
£12/13/9, rising to
£15/4/5 per week
Penalty Rates for Shift Work

APPLY NOW TO

The Staff Employment Officer,
Postmaster-General's Department,
3rd Floor, G.P.O.,
Spencer Street,
MELBOURNE, C.1,

or telephone MY 4491

Commonwealth of Australia
SEPT, '54 'H'
P.M.G.'s DEPARTMENT

MEN REQUIRED

for employment as

MAIL OFFICERS

from October 4

PROSPECTS OF PERMANENT EMPLOYMENT

●

DUTIES: Letter sorting and handling Christmas Mail.

No previous experience required.

SALARY: Commencing adult salary is £13/5/3, rising to £15/6/8, a week. (10% penalty rate is paid for shift work.)

FOR FULL INFORMATION

Call on the

**Staff Employment Officer,
3rd Floor, G.P.O., Spencer St.,
Melbourne—or 'phone MY 4491**

POSTMASTER-GENERAL'S DEPARTMENT.

MEN
(over 18 years)

and

WOMEN
(over 21 years)

are offered
IMMEDIATE EMPLOYMENT AS

MAIL OFFICER

to handle the Christmas mail

Commencing Adult Salary for MEN — £13/5/3 rising to £15/6/8 a week. Women previously trained in sorting — £12/16/- a week.
Untrained — £12/6/- to commence, £12/16/- on completion of training. An additional 10% penalty rate is payable for shift work.
Good prospects for continued employment and permanent appointment for MEN.
Employment of Women will not extend beyond 31st December, 1954.

Eleanor Masters Collection, University of Melbourne Archives

Advertisements for jobs in the Melbourne press, offering permanent work for men. Far right advertisement states, 'Employment of women will not extend beyond 31st December, 1954'.

doing equal work: 59 per cent favoured equal pay while 33 per cent were opposed.[22] It would appear that while the Murdoch claim is disputed because of the earlier work carried out in 1940 by Sylvia Ashby, head of one of the country's first market research companies, it is possible that Morgan's was the first Gallup poll to be published.[23]

Jean Arnot gave early recognition of the need for a minimum wage for both sexes, based on the cost of living for a single person, with allowances for dependents. She claimed that the assumption that all men have dependents and all women have none was false. She did a great deal of research into the position of women in other countries in the hope of furthering efforts in Australia, and presented an extensive document to the Institute of Public Administration in 1945. In her ABC broadcast on 'Should Both Sexes Receive EP for Equal Work?', Jean detailed all the reasons why claiming equal pay was fair and just. She said,

> What are the main factors which have resulted in the universal ideal that the remuneration for women's work must be lower than that for men? First of all, the laws and customs associated with marriage, in that the expectation of marriage tends to discourage extensive training of girls at special skills, thus keeping women in the ranks of the less skilled workers at lower rates of pay; and the possibility of marriage makes girls content with lesser wages and more routine work and whatever the actual facts of an individual woman's life may be, the potential fact of motherhood constitutes a disability from the working point of view. Secondly the standard of money earning for women is always in danger of being kept down because of the unpaid work in the home, by women, mothers and wives. This fact which is the lot of a large body of women, lowers the money value of domestic work which has a large influence on other types of women's work.[24]

Jean went on to speak of the need for women to organise and campaign for equal pay. On 18 November 1946, CAEP met in Sydney and Muriel Heagney, as Honorary Secretary, gave the report. The delegate from the Teachers' Union followed, pressing for recognition of the situation regarding women's wages, and urged that action be taken immediately to secure implementation of equal rates for all workers without any sex differential. Two nights later, Jessie Street held a Conference on equal pay at Federation House.

Very little action by the top trade union bodies occurred on equal pay during 1947. The emphasis in that year was on the 40-hour week; however, the Australian Railways Union and the Sheet Metal Workers Union (two predominantly male left-wing unions) moved at the ACTU Congress for the ACTU to take up the issue of equal pay.[25]

Women continued to press for an equal pay hearing at Federal level, and in 1949 the court reviewed the principles upon which the basic wages of adult males and females were fixed. When women's organisations were represented at basic wage, national wage or minimum wage hearings, these were the occasions on which more attention was given to women's pay claims.

In the Basic Wage Inquiry during 1949 and 1950, the ACTU claimed an increase in the male basic wage sufficient to support a family of five, and the same basic wage for women as a matter of equity.[26] The ACTU submitted that workers, 'irrespective of sex, should be paid at the same rate and the elimination of differing rates is necessary to prevent unfair discrimination by employers as between male and female workers'.[27]

The claim was rejected, but the Court boosted women's pay from 54 per cent to 75 per cent of the male rate. The Court reached this decision not on the basis of need but because it claimed that employers had already been paying women employees at that rate.

In 1951 the Queensland Branch of the Clerks' Union placed a Claim for Equal Pay before the Industrial Court of Queensland. This was an unusual case which came about after continual pressure on the Executive by the membership proved fruitless; they were too busy to prepare a case was the excuse used, and so Daisy Marchisotti, a member of the union, under-took the research with the support of Berenice Collins, another member, and Val Howard, a clerk in the Sheet Metal Workers' Union Office. When Ken Sanders, the Union Secretary, inter-viewed the women, he pointed out the 'difficulties' they would face when being cross-examined in the court and urged them to drop the idea of being advocates.[28]

Left with the final preparation of the case Daisy went ahead and sought help from experienced people. Muriel Heagney sent her all the information she had plus a great mass of figures and Daisy obtained other information from the State Statistics Bureau. Berenice and Val turned up at the State Industrial Court where the case was being heard and Joan Riordan, an extreme right-winger, the only woman branch councillor in the union, put in an appearance. The court was crowded with journalists, members from the Union of Australian Women (UAW), and Mrs. Byth, President of the National Council of Women. Mrs Byth sought permission of the court to intervene because of the vital interest of the case to women.[29]

Daisy had prepared a thorough case, with most of her material based on statistical and economic data. 'I was hellishly nervous, but my voice is pretty strong and I was always good at reading. I read the whole ten pages of the submission, bar the tables, which I had typed and carefully double-checked.' When the case was over, the newspapermen crowded around, they seemed to be amazed that a woman could put up such a case.[30]

Daisy finalised her submission by demanding a 'rate for the job' regardless of sex, and stated the reasons for the demand.

Mr. Sanders, the Union Secretary, notwithstanding his earlier attitude, was shamed into addressing the Commission in favor of the case and in support of the women.

Following the conclusion of the case, Justice Matthews tried to get the witnesses to agree that they were not just ordinary clerical workers, but quite above average in intelligence and thus might be getting over the award. But none of the girls were getting male rates.

Despite the evidence presented, the judges decided this had not proved that all females in the industry were 'performing the same work as males or producing the same return of profit to their employer'. The judges in their judgement so confused the issues and contradicted themselves that it was obvious they had difficulty in refusing the claim. They were determined, come what may however, to refuse the claim.[31] The judgement agreed with the submission that it was 'most difficult to prove that women produced the same profit as men', and, given that they had reached this conclusion, the judges decided there was no reason to grant the claim.[32]

With all the publicity this Equal Pay Case received, Daisy had difficulty in obtaining employment following the Case.

Where was the union? What were they doing to help her obtain work?

Constant vigilance is always necessary to guard against attempts to downgrade women's wages. 'In 1953 the Women's Christian Temperance Union joined with other women's groups in protesting against the employers' application to the Arbitration Court to reduce the basic wage of women to sixty per cent of the male rate'.[33] The Application was refused and the wage remained at 75 per cent of that of men. This case took place when a shortage of labor existed. This occurred only eight years after World War 2 during a stage of economic growth.

With the newly established VTHC EP Committee now in action, more circulars were sent to affiliated unions drawing attention to women receiving 75 per cent of the male rate of pay and noting even this was under attack. Clothing Trade

Eleanor Masters Collection, University of Melbourne Archives

Employers were seeking a reduction of wages for women from 75 per cent to 54 per cent of male rates. 'Needless to say, should they be successful, a general onslaught can be expected on women's wages in other industries, and in fact on wage levels generally'.[34] A request was made for orders of the enclosed leaflet explaining the issues and again, the offer was made of speakers available for meetings. Support was invited for the campaign and a call was made for resolutions to be sent to parliamentarians.

As Honorary Secretary, of the EP Committee, Kath did almost all of the preparation for the circulars and leaflets and researched articles for the trade union journals in her own time at home. She now had very little time for herself being engrossed in trade union work, involvement in the CPA and the EP Committee. When visiting Kath of an evening, friends remember her constantly being preoccupied with writing. 'There she would be sitting at the table, pen in hand writing and smoking'.[35]

Towards the end of 1955, leaflets co-signed by both Gil Hayes and Kath Williams advertising an EP Rally at the MTHC Chambers were circulated. Delegates from factories and workplaces were requested to attend.[36] This Rally was important to

Private collection

Kath Williams in her early fifties

Myer Collection, University of Melbourne Archives

Myer's Cafeteria in the early 1950s was one of the workplaces Kath organised on behalf of the union.

inspire and encourage participation, not only in the equal pay campaign but to encourage the unions to participate in the approaching Federal Union Equal Pay Conference early in 1956.

At the very first history-making ACTU Federal Union Conference on Equal Pay, held on 13 March 1956 in Melbourne, Gil Hayes presented a report on behalf of the VTHC EP Committee and said they had adopted a comprehensive program in furtherance of the campaign of stimulating interest in the equal pay question.[37]

He went on to add that a series of leaflets had been issued, radio talks conducted, and a deputation had waited on the State Government. Articles had also been directed to the daily press and union journals, whilst unions had been circularised offering speakers' notes and speakers when required. Research had also been undertaken on what had been attempted or achieved in other countries and Unions were advised to claim male rates for all classifications when submitting claims in the courts for equal pay.

SUNDAY, NOVEMBER 27, 1955

at 2 p.m.

•

Trades Hall Council Chamber

Cr. Lygon and Victoria Streets

•

EQUAL PAY RALLY

Speakers include:

The Hon. JOHN CAIN

Leader State Parliamentary Labor Party

Trade Union Leaders

followed by open discussion

ITEM: Short Comedy Sketch on Equal Pay

Factories and Work Places are entitled to representation on the basis of
two for the first 100, one for the second 100, up to 500, and one for each
additional 1,100 workers.

Unionists!

Appoint YOUR representatives to attend the RALLY and report back to you

HELP PUT MORE MONEY INTO THE POCKETS OF WORKING-CLASS
FAMILIES BY ACTIVELY SUPPORTING A.C.T.U. POLICY OF EQUAL PAY
FOR THE SEXES

Called by Equal Pay Committee (sponsored by T.H.C.)

Industrial Print, Carlton

G. HAYES, President.
K. WILLIAMS, Hon. Secretary.

Equal Pay Collection, University of Melbourne Archives

WHY

You Should Support

EQUAL PAY!

Working women number two out of every
three in the whole of Australia.

There are over 800,000 of them.

They represent 27 per cent. of the total
wage and salary workers.

The majority receive only three-quarters
of a man's wage for doing the same
job.

These women are not working for fun—
but because they have to.

Six out of 10 are wholly supporting a
dependant.

About half of these are helping to
support two or more.

Equal Pay Will Give Wage Justice
to These Women

Equal Pay Collection, University of Melbourne Archives

Leaflet issued by the VTHC Equal Pay
Committee

Hayes went on to say that much confusion existed as to what was meant by the term equal pay. The Victorian Committee had formed a panel of experts from prominent people in the trade union movement, which decided that *equal pay* meant *the rate for the job* based on the full male basic wage and margins for skill. When concerning a female industry with no comparable male wage, then the wage was to be equal to that of a male when engaged in that particular industry.

Delegate Davis, from the Hotel, Club & Restaurant Employees Union NSW, said she regretted to report that there had been little activity by Trades and Labor Council of NSW in the creation of an equal pay committee. However, arrangements had been made recently for the distribution of 40 000 leaflets, and it was hoped to do something in the way of radio propa-

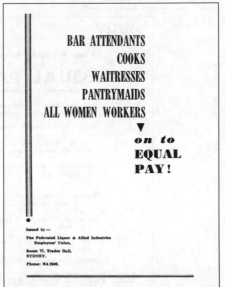

Cover of pamphlet prepared by Flo Davis,
Acting Secretary of the Labor Council of
New South Wales Equal Pay Committee

ganda through 2KY. She and her co-delegates from NSW had learned much from the report submitted by delegate Hayes, the result of which was that a deputation would wait on the State Government of NSW after the conference was over.

One wonders how Kath felt when Gil Hayes received much of the kudos for work she had done when, in his own union, he was one of the male leaders who quashed any moves for equal pay. Despite what Kath may have thought, she accepted the situation knowing, as others did, that the 'rightists' in the EP Committee were there to '*keep the balance*'.[38] They were there to see she didn't push her 'communist line' and, in the meantime, there was always the hope these men would perhaps be convinced and inspired to make an effort to support equal pay within their own unions.

The conference resolutions passed aimed to apply pressure on both Federal and State Governments for the implementation of the 1951 decision of the ILO and to grant equal pay to their employees. This also included equal pay in all State Awards.

The ACTU was also asked to organise a national petition in support of equal pay and that all possible support be given to the unions when claiming equal pay before the Commonwealth Arbitration Court.

State Labor Councils were to intensify their campaign for equal pay by strengthening the EP Committees; organising meetings and representative conferences; assisting unions engaged in struggles for equal pay; and participating in the distribution of literature, radio talks and all other avenues of publicity and propaganda; and individual unions were urged to press demands for equal pay by direct negotiations with employers, and to include this claim in award applications.[39]

This was the very first conference the ACTU had organised for unions with women members to campaign for equal pay. The daily press gave scant publicity to this historic Equal Pay Conference with the evening's Melbourne *Herald* featuring the conference under the heading, 'Equal Pay New Union Moves'. The Melbourne *Sun* of the following morning featured a tiny article on page 11.

The Roy Morgan Gallup Poll of June 6 1956 stated that public opinion was in favour of equal pay. Sixty-seven per cent said 'Pay her as the man', 31 per cent said 'pay her less', and 2 per cent said 'not sure'. The report went on to add 'It is rarely that 98% have opinions on a subject. Equally rarely this majority (67%) hardly varies State by State.'[40]

The MTHC distributed a well designed, compact Equal Pay leaflet to all the unions for distribution.

Don MacSween, member of the EP Committee and editor of the left-wing union journal *Scope*, began 'changing values and conditions on its "women's page"'. Cooking and beauty tips made way, although not totally, for articles on equal pay, politics and prominent women activists and officials.[41]

Kath enjoyed sharing some of her experiences as a union organiser on the job and one could appreciate her humour when relating the incident that occurred when arriving at a certain hotel. On this particular morning she was feeling on top of the world when she entered the hotel and proceeded towards the kitchen, at which moment, two burly men approached. With one on either side of her, they lifted her under the arms, carried her out of the hotel and deposited her on the footpath. She finished her anecdote with a healthy laugh. Encountering this type of behavior didn't deter her; she was able to deal with many of the toughened characters in the hotel industry of the times.

Kath had been a member of the UAW for some years and it was suggested she go overseas to attend a working women's conference taking place in Budapest, Hungary. Included in this trip was an invitation to spend two weeks in the Soviet Union and one month in China.

The UAW formed a committee with interested women from trade unions to raise funds for Kath's fare and she left Australia on the 26 May 1956.[42] Prior to her leaving, Kath and Cecilia Shelley, the delegate from West Australia, and Esther Taylor from New South Wales addressed a round of meetings of women workers in factories to discuss the issues which needed to be raised at the conference and also to raise money to cover the cost of fares.[43]

In her personal contribution, Kath set out to give delegates a picture of her country. She told them of the democratic and militant traditions of Australia going back to the days of Eureka, when the miners of Ballarat fought the redcoats and how, out

Photo Courtesy of the Union of Australian Women, Melbourne

Australian women attending the first World Conference of Women Workers held in Budapest 1956. (left to right) Cecilia Shelley of Western Australia, Esther Taylor and Flo Davis, both of New South Wales, and Kath Williams of Victoria

Cover photo of Pauline Armstrong and child, for Kath Williams's report on the World Conference held in Budapest 1956

of these early battles, a strong, virile trade union movement had emerged. She went on to speak of the minimum basic wage for the family and how it gave rise to the deep-rooted tradition of women's place being in the home and how women employed during World War 2 joined their unions and were able to gain equal pay in many industries. She explained that after the war, it was expected that women would retire once again to their homes, but the needs of industry and inflation determined otherwise. In 1950 a struggle took place to increase the basic wage and the unions claimed equal pay for women workers. Many stoppages and overtime bans were carried out in support of these claims before the Arbitration Court, with the result that the 40-hour week was won, cost-of-living adjustments reintroduced, and a female basic wage of 75 per cent adopted.

Kath spoke of the recession in 1952, the attempts made to reduce wages, increase working hours, put women back on the old 54 per cent pay rate and of the peak reached in women's employment in 1955 when over three quarters of a million women were in paid work. 100 000 more than in 1943. With the large percentage of women in industry and the attempt to cut their wages, the trade unions brought about the most determined bid in the history of the Australian working class for equal pay. The move began in Victoria with strong support from the MTHC and spread throughout the Commonwealth. Equal Pay Committees were set up in all states and a wide campaign got underway. Support for this campaign came from teachers, the public service and women's organisations. In 1956 the ACTU launched a national petition which was presented to the Commonwealth Government by deputation, demanding that it legislate for equal pay, in accordance with the 1951 ILO Convention 100, on Equal Pay for Equal Work to which it had been a party.

Kath described the men trade union leaders who were taking part in the campaign and the effect this was having on breaking down male prejudice. She looked forward with confidence to an end to discrimination against women workers and the adverse effect this had on the life and well-being of working people.

The General Conference Resolution endorsed the need for the delegates to denounce the discriminations against women practised in many countries and that:

1. the ratification of I.L.O. Convention No 100 on equality of remuneration for equal work be accompanied by its practical implementation.

2. energetic and persevering action be carried out in the broadest possible unity necessary to win the most important demands, application of the principal 'Equal Pay for Equal Work' for all categories of women workers, including young girls, establishment of a guaranteed minimum wage equal for both men and women, equal opportunity, the right to work, reduction of working hours, abolition of speed-up, laws for the protection of the health of women workers and safety at work, unemployment allowances, old age pensions for women, free medical and hospital care, protection for working mothers, paid maternity leave, payment of nursing time, more schools, crèches, after-school centres, etc., improvement of housing programs and lowering of rents; and

3. the conference asks women workers, together with their trade unions, to draw up programs of their demands on the basis of this resolution as applicable to the conditions in each country, to take a more active part in the struggles of the working class for increased wages, trade union rights and democratic liberties.

The conference also decided to send the adopted documents to the executive bodies of all international trade union organisations and their trade departments, and expressed the hope that they would examine these with the aim of reaching agreement, and would co-ordinate their efforts in defence of the rights and demands of women workers.

Kath wrote an extensive report of her experiences at the Budapest Conference:

Early in March last year I was asked by the Victorian Branch of the Union of Australian Women to attend as an observer, the World Conference of Women Workers, which was being organised by the World Federation of Trade Unions, assisted by the Women's International Democratic Federation, to which the U.A.W. is affiliated.

The invitation came at a time when the Australian Trade Union Movement had launched its campaign for Equal Pay for Women Workers, in which I was vitally interested, and I realised the value such an experience could be in the struggle for economic justice for Australian Women workers.

I put the proposition to my Union, the Liquor Trades, and they readily granted me leave of absence to attend for they were great supporters of equal pay and realised the value of the Conference. They did more; they gave me a wonderful send-off at the Melbourne Trades Hall, at which leading officials of the Trade Union, THC and ACTU, together with many rank and file unionists, friends and supporters, wished me well and charged me with the responsibility of reporting to the Conference the steps taken by the Australian Trade Union Movement to secure equal pay for women workers and to bring them back a report of my experiences.[44]

Kath detailed the contributions made at this Conference by women from around the world—their work situations, conditions, salaries, the changes they wanted to see and their fervent desire for economic justice and world peace. Women from Mexico raised sufficient money to send ten women to the conference by selling postcards depicting a Mexican woman breaking the chains binding her wrists. She outlined how women from the developing countries spoke of the harrowing conditions prevailing in their countries, and described how Germaine Guille, Secretary of the French General Confederation of Labor said the 'principal problems of the world's 300 million women workers were low wages, unequal pay, lack of opportunity, speed up, bad working conditions, insufficient social services and homes, unemployment and insecurity'. She pronounced the effective application of the principle of equal pay for equal work as the basis of the work of Conference.[45] All the delegates supported the need for women to play a greater role in their unions and to seek office where they could make their demands more effective.

After Kath had completed her report on the overseas Conference, she went on to write of the progress made on the home front since her departure and of the 40 000 signatures collected from outside as well as inside the trade union movement on the ongoing Equal Pay Petition. She wrote of the many women's organisation who were actively supporting the campaign and of the President of the Federation of Business and Professional Women's Clubs who when addressing their annual Conference in 1956 said, 'The greatest single hurdle facing Australian working women is Equal Work Pay for Equal Work'. This demand was endorsed by the Victorian Branch of the Australian Physiotherapy Association, Association of White Collar Workers, Bank Officials' Association, the Association of Architects and Draftsmen and the Australian branch of the British Medical Association.[46]

Kath wrote to the President of the Australian branch of the British Medical Association endorsing on a Federal and State basis, the demand of women doctors in the State Public Service for equal pay and instructing their official journal not to accept any advertisement from any government body offering different or lower rates for women doctors. Women teachers too had a very important win, when they forced the Victorian State Government to pass the *Teaching Service (Married Women) Act*, 1956 which gave married women the same rights as single women and widows, except in the matter of superannuation.[47]

Kath also drew on the UN General Assembly recommendation of December 1955, which urged that member nations should promote human and women's rights by various means, one being by the organisation of seminars. She went on to detail the British Seminar on the Status of Women organised by British women's organisations, and of the British trade union movement which took part in it for the first time, Lady Street, Australian social activist and fighter for women's equality, being one of the seminar's organisers. Kath went on to quote her words:

> While women remain unorganised, and while society is prepared to accept discrimination against women workers – such discrimination will continue. The answer to this is to organise and unite women workers by all available means, to fight for their democratic and human rights to the point where society will no longer tolerate the injustices and indignities to which they are subjected.[48]

Kath coming to the end of her booklet described how the Australian trade union movement, 'which by its sustained activity has by its strength, united around all sections of the Australian people with like objectives, and with growing determination of the World Movement of Women Workers is an inspiration and a guarantee for the future – a future of EQUALITY – SECURITY AND PEACE'.[49]

Kath concluded her booklet with the 'Composition of the Conference'. Here, she made note of all the countries represented and noted the eighteen different trades from whence the delegates came.

Kath, while being a very forthright woman, was also a modest person, and never mentioned the role she had played or was still playing in the equal pay struggle. When reading this material, one can detect her great feeling of optimism and the satisfaction in playing a part in overcoming injustice.

5

The fight for equal pay, 1956 to 1959

In accordance with the resolutions of the 1956 ACTU March Conference on Equal Pay, the Labor Council of NSW was asked to sponsor a States-wide conference on equal pay. The Labor Council organised this National Equal Pay Conference, but at its Council Meeting following the conference, it refused to hear or accept the Conference Report because of its right-wing bias and opposition to the ACTU. The Council adopted the conference minutes at their August meeting. It would seem that the members of the Labor Council of NSW were insufficiently interested to hear the outcome of the National Conference on equal pay.

At the Federal Unions' Conference 21 March 1956, Delegate Flo Davis, of the Hotel, Club & Restaurant Employees Union, said she regretted to report that there had been little activity by the Trades and Labor Council of NSW in the creation of an Equal Pay Committee, but it was hoped to do something in the way of radio broadcasts. Flo's union initiated regular broadcasts on Station 2KY. Arrangements were made for the distribution of 40 000 leaflets, 1100 of which were sent to Brisbane.[1] A request was made to the Labor Council for an urgent deputation to the Premier of NSW and unions were to be asked to participate in the radio broadcasts. The Teachers' Federation was to contact Melbourne direct for 10 000 copies of the Equal

Pay Petition and it was agreed that copies of the petition be sent to all ALP branches.[2]

The Conference inspired the NSW Delegates and 'during 1956 the Labor Council of New South Wales began to revive its EP campaign'. 'Moreover, the NSW Trades and Labor Council endorsed its recently established Equal Pay Committee's objectives of pressuring the ACTU to hold a conference to discuss EP and to pressure the Federal Government to ratify the ILO Convention of 1951'.[3]

From here on, the NSW Equal Pay Committee became active and was distributing leaflets, speakers notes, conducted a questionnaire and organised the occasional seminar.

Ruth Don, the first woman President of the Queensland Teachers' Federation and a committed activist for equal pay,[4] initiated the distribution of equal pay leaflets and the petition throughout the membership.

The VTHC EP Committee, with support from the THC, called a meeting of unions and organised a rally to which all unions and a number of other organisations were invited to send representatives. *SUNDAY, MARCH 24, 1957 AT 2.30 PM* appeared in large lettering on the Equal Pay leaflet for the rally at the THC Chamber in Melbourne. The main speakers were Albert Monk, President of the ACTU, and J. Stout, Secretary of the Victorian Trades Hall Council, who were to be followed by an open forum.[5]

Circulars were sent out from the Equal Pay Committee encouraging participation in the collection of signatures on the petitions as well as attendance at the rally. The circular also detailed how British women, through their efforts, were successful in obtaining equal pay which was to become effective for British public servants by 1961. It was expected that the rally would enable representatives from all the organisations present to report on their activities. Massive numbers of leaflets advertising the March 24 Rally were distributed.[6]

SUNDAY, MARCH 24, 1957
at 2.30 p.m.

★

Trades Hall Council Chamber
Cr. Lygon and Victoria Streets

★

EQUAL PAY RALLY

Speakers:

Mr. A. MONK   Mr. J. V. STOUT
President Australian Council Trade Unions   Secretary Melbourne Trades Hall Council

Open Forum for Discussion

YOUR ORGANISATION IS ENTITLED TO ATTEND

Basis of Representation: A.L.P. Branches and Factories: Two delegates for the first 100, one for each additional 100 up to 500, and one for each additional 500. Trade Unions, Public Service and Women's Organisations: One delegate for first 500, one for second 500 and one for each additional 1,000.

All Visitors Welcome

Equal Pay Benefits all Working Men and Women

RALLY to the RALLY

Issued by Melbourne T.H.C. Equal Pay Committee; G. Hayes, President, Mrs K. Williams, Honorary Secretary.

The Industrial Printing and Publicity Co. Ltd., 24 Victoria St., Carlton, N.3

Equal Pay Collection, University of Melbourne Archives

When addressing the rally, Stout suggested strike action should be taken in support of equal pay. Gil Hayes submitted a report on behalf of the MTHC EP Committee and spoke of the many ACTU leaflets and radio broadcasts, and of the deputation to the Victorian State Government. Articles he said had been sent to the daily press and union journals and he encouraged unions when lodging claims for equal pay with wage tribunals to ensure they were claiming male rates for all classifications. He went on to say that the EP Committee had decided that equal pay meant the rate for the job based on the full male basic wage and margins for skill and called for more union meetings to be held on the job where signatures could be collected for the petition.[7]

Whenever the daily press featured an article or news item on equal pay, it was almost always presented from a negative point of view.

BOLTE SAYS NO TO EQUAL PAY FOR WOMEN[8]

Why couldn't they have written 'Bolte Refuses Wage Justice for Women'?

On the same page and just below the above article, a smaller heading stated: *We'd aid strike says Woman:*

> If women went on strike for equal pay, the Women's Christian Temperance Union would probably support them', the State Secretary, Mrs F. J. Nicholls, said today. 'We were behind the suffragettes once and we have sent petitions to the Government. I imagine we would support women in a strike.

Bolte's response to the Rally was made quite clear. He said the State Government would not legislate to give women public servants the same salary as men. The *Herald* reported him as saying that equal pay for the sexes would have a tremendous effect on Victoria's economy:

> Other Ministers said equal pay now would force up the cost of living to a dangerous level … It was also remarkable that when the Tramways Board last year tried to employ women tram drivers at equal pay rates with men, the union threatened to strike to stop

the move. In view of this, how much of the present equal pay campaign is genuine and how much is political bally-hoo?[9]

The same issue of the *Herald* quoted the Principal of the Melbourne University Women's College, Miss Myra Roper, as saying that, 'Today's women doing the same work as men should get men's pay'; she then went on to speak of the tendency for commercial interests to use women as cheap labor.[10] This tiny press article was one of the very few to appear in the daily press lending support to the equal pay campaign.

Kath came out fighting after Bolte's comments:

> How long does Mr Bolte think his or any government is going to buck the demands of over three quarters of a million women wage and salary earners, backed by the trade union movement, and becoming more aware every day of the rank injustice of paying them less for their labor than men?[11]

She wrote of the difference in salaries of women and men in the postal service, female and male clerical assistants in the public service and female and male doctors in hospitals, and suggested that women should march on Parliament as they had done in England.

On occasions, Kath spoke at the Yarra Bank open-air forum. The forum attracted regular Sunday visitors and was for many a learning experience, while for others it was purely entertainment, a source of amusement. 'Kath's personality, good health and commitment made it possible for her to feel comfortable in that environment and her material was always well prepared. She was very patient with hecklers until able gain their attention or they left.'[12] Kath attended all types of functions, addressing people on the injustice of women's wages and the need for them to become involved in the equal pay campaign.

When Kath sought my assistance to provide the music for the equal pay float she was organising for the forthcoming May Day Rally, this was my first association with her. The entire exercise was arranged with several women singing while I accompanied on the piano accordion. Kath had written the lyric to a popular tune, the intention being to get the equal pay message across as the float drove slowly along the route. Kath was no lyricist and cramming a great number of words into the melody made it come across as a lot of gabble, particularly when the float was moving by. When trying to point this out to Kath, she wouldn't budge. Kath could be tough, she had learned to survive in a man's domain. The truck on which the group performed was adorned with colourful streamers and banners proclaiming the justice of equal pay. Television had arrived in Melbourne and the May Day Committee assured her that the equal pay float would be towards the front of the march where it would be visible to the TV cameras.

Kath wanted people to be aware of the equal pay campaign and was excited in anticipation of the publicity this first TV appearance offered. The march started off and the male marshalls directed all the men to head the procession, while the equal pay float was way behind. There was no TV publicity for the cause of equal pay. Kath was visibly distressed and angry. How often did she have to endure this treatment?

Prior to May Day, I arrived to attend a rehearsal at Kath's home in Clifton Hill. I was early and was admiring the various knickknacks displayed in her lounge room. She walked over when I drew attention to a particular ornament, and taking it in her hand she gazed at it in silence for several seconds, then said it was a gift from her first husband. It was her body language and the way she made this comment that struck me. There was a combination of nostalgia, and perhaps a blend of the memories of her first lover, the father of her children and their happy early years together.

Kath, in her determination to set the record straight, wrote to the *Guardian* (the Communist Party Weekly) when the Melbourne *Herald* refused to publish her press release in response to a statement made by Mrs D. McLarty of South Yarra who, when addressing the annual conference of the Housewives Association, said women should not get the same pay as men. Shortly afterwards, two separate articles appeared side by side in the *Guardian* on 6 June 1957. Kath's article began: 'Everyone agrees that the home is the main thing, but I would say that it is the job of both parents to keep the home together. The overwhelming majority of parents accept this responsibility, but they can only do this job to the extent that the money coming into the home will provide for the family.' She also highlighted the plight of women who were sole breadwinners, and went on to say, 'Money may not be everything as Mrs McLarty stated, [but] lack of it is a serious matter for the family'.

The other article noted the criticism by P. J. Clarey, MHR, from the Bendigo Trades and Labor Council, for drawing the ballot to select youths for national service training. Kath and Percy were certainly at opposite ends of the political spectrum.

During the 1950s and 60s, it was customary for the daily press to assign an industrial reporter to cover all matters pertaining to the trade union movement. These reporters were always on hand and were provided with the latest information from the trade unions on disputes or difficulties within the workforce. Their assistance was always sought when publicity was needed for functions, meetings or rallies but if there was any doubt over its publication, a press statement was released.

Gil Hayes did not make any headlines as President of the EP Committee in the daily press; on the contrary, research revealed that the entire issue of equal pay was a non-issue and only made headlines when, on rare occasions, the liberal politicians or business leaders made heated attacks against equal pay for women. Gil, with his religious and right-wing background, would have been loath to be featured in the *Guardian*, however, regular snippets on him appeared in the *Guardian*'s reporting of conferences, meetings and demonstrations.

All the Victorian daily newspapers received regular correspondence and press releases from the VTHC EP Committee pertaining to their activities but almost nothing appeared.

Accusations were made at the interstate meeting of the Executive that the ACTU Executive was not giving equal pay its full support and that governments were fobbing off legislation on equal pay by claiming the Industrial Commission was responsible for this matter.[13] The NSW delegate reported that their Trades and Labor Council (TLC) had set up an equal pay committee but refused them the right to co-opt women from outside organisations. It would seem that, initially, the TLC was reluctant to establish an equal pay committee and women from several unions, together with women from outside organisations, formed an equal pay committee. The TLC eventually established its own EP Committee, and subsequently the two committees eventually combined.

Kath was selected to represent the Liquor Trades Union on the delegation to present the Equal Pay Petition to the Commonwealth Government. The deputation to Harold Holt occurred in August 1957 and was led by Albert Monk, President of the ACTU. The two women on the seven-person delegation were Miss Osborne, the Teachers' Federation representative and Vice President of the NSW TLC Equal Pay Committee, and Kath. They pressed the government to implement the articles of ILO Convention 100, and presented the petitions with over 62 000 signatures, a tremendous effort.[14] Holt's public response to the issue of equal pay was ten months in coming.

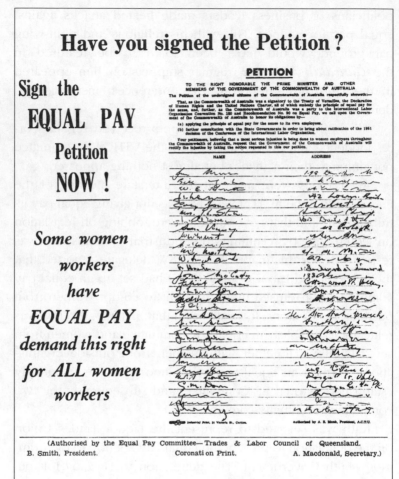

Labor Council of New South Wales Collection, Mitchell Library Archives, State Library of New South Wales

The *Sun* reported Dr Lorna Lloyd Green, President of the Australian Federation of University Women, as saying that 'Women should boycott low-paid jobs. Women are still rated at about 75% of male rates of pay and the rate should be for the job done irrespective of sex.'[15] She went on to tell the story of a Victorian woman graduate who, when applying for the position as a personnel officer and when stating the salary she expected, was told, 'We can get a man for that wage'.[16]

The *Guardian* published Kath's letter, obviously sent because the *Sun* had rejected it, in which she wrote, 'Reg Leonard, the *Sun's* columnist, recently launched an attack on the campaign for Equal Pay which he called "... the hardy annual"'. She described how his attack was prompted by the discussions which took place at the biennial conference of the Federation of University Women in Canberra, and how Leonard used Dr Green's comments and interviews of a number of prominent women, to highlight some differences of opinion while overlooking the fact that 'all the women he quoted were strongly united on the main point, they all agreed that women should fight for Equal Pay'.[17]

At the September ACTU Congress held in Sydney in 1957, Albert Monk moved that the ACTU call a National Conference of Unions with women members to discuss equal pay, wages and conditions and to pursue every method to ensure Federal and State Governments introduce legislation to grant equal pay to employees. Kath as a delegate to the ACTU Congress supported the motion.[18] Agreement was reached to hold this special conference and the NSW Labor Council requested this Conference on Working Women to be held in March 1958 in Sydney with the widest possible representation; however, it was decided that women from women's organisations, if invited to attend, could do so only as observers.

The Equal Pay Rally held at the Melbourne Trades Hall in March 1958 was a great success. The rally was attended by 130 delegates from sixteen unions with women members. Among those represented were the VTHC, nine women's organisations, the Victorian Teachers' Union, the Bank Officers' Association, the Medical Officers' Association, the Victorian Public Service Association, seven Labor Party Branches and eight factories.

A. E. Shepherd, Leader of the Victorian State Parliamentary Labor Party, addressed the rally indicating that the ACTU National Conference on Equal Pay to be held in Sydney towards the end of the month would help to frame Labor Policy. He went on to say that if the previous policy was again adopted, and Labor was returned, it would be incumbent on them to bring in equal pay. 'If we did not do this' he said, 'we would deserve to lose the confidence of the people in the Labor Party'.[19] The Assistant Secretary of the VTHC also pointed out that delegates from other countries at the ILO Conference criticised Australia's failure to give effect to the ILO Conventions.

When giving her report to the Rally on behalf of the EP Committee, Kath summarised the work carried out by the trade union movement over the previous twelve months. She spoke of the many letters submitted to the Minister and how the deputation also pressed the Government to implement ILO Convention 100. She went on to say that the ILO was aware of the number of countries still practising discrimination based on sex, that the United Nations and the ILO repeatedly called upon governments of all countries to take appropriate measures to put the principle of equal pay for equal work into effect, and taking into consideration the demands of millions of women workers from around the world for equal pay, the time had come for member nations to consider implementing equal pay either by legislation, by collective bargaining, a combination of these, or by other means if such measures have not yet been adopted.[20]

Bold headlines in the *Sun*, in May, featured Harold Holt, the Federal Minister for Labour in the Menzies' Liberal Government, making a policy statement to the House of Representatives following the announcement by NSW Labor Premier Cahill that he would legislate for equal pay. Holt was adamantly opposed to any legislation for equal pay, claiming that this should be left to the Commonwealth Arbitration Court. He made use of Justice Foster's 1949/1950 basic wage hearing decision which was that equal pay would put an intolerable strain on the economy based on the male basic wage.[21]

The daily press began to trivialise the importance of equal pay with articles such as 'Should she pay for him?'. This demeaning and distorting of the facts and arguments pertaining to equal pay were methods used to divert attention away from the vital issues.

Bolte adopted an arrogant, dictatorial role, refused to have meaningful dialogue with the unions and, with total support from the media, was able to elicit the support of the electorate. In representing those who sought greater profits he was adamant that women would not receive equal pay.

Meanwhile, the ACTU was making arrangements to send a deputation to Harold Holt in Canberra. The trade union movement believed it was essential at all times to bring pressure to bear on politicians and the government.[22]

The VTHC EP Committee invited Officers of the ACTU to hear Miss M. Woodford, Honorary Secretary of the NSW TLC EP Committee, speak at the Melbourne Rally. Another woman doing an unpaid job.

Kath wrote an article on the campaign, 'Equal Pay Reaches New Heights in Australia', for the *World Federation of Trade Unions Journal*, a magazine available in many countries.[23]

Following the Melbourne Rally in March 1958, the VTHC EP Committee sent a letter to organisations with women members drawing attention to the resolution passed at the conference dealing with the need to circularise state parliamentary candidates seeking their views and support. Kath urged immediate action be taken for widespread publicity when receiving the replies. Publicity was also given to the Committee's

'Best Letter Competition', the topic being 'Should women receive Equal Pay with men?'.[24]

The Equal Pay campaign had gained momentum and the National Working Women's Conference held in Sydney on 20 and 21 March 1958 inspired those in attendance. There were 200 delegates and observers from ninety-four organisations, representing thirty-six affiliates of the ACTU and fifty-eight non-affiliates.[25] Miss M. Woodford notified Mr J. D. Kenny of her disappointment prior to the conference when sixteen organisations with women members were not invited to attend as observers.

Among the many resolutions passed at the Sydney National Working Women's Conference held in March 1958 supporting the introduction of equal pay was one applauding the action of NSW Labor Premier Cahill and his government in deciding to introduce legislation giving effect to the principle of equal pay for women. A NSW delegate reported that since their EP Committee had got underway they had 'given wonderful support to the Trades and Labor Council in its campaign for Equal Pay'. Disappointment was noted regarding the fact that the Commonwealth Government had not legislated for equal pay in the Commonwealth Service. The NSW TLC EP Committee now had high hopes of the NSW Government legislating to implement equal pay for State employees, to be followed with a strong campaign for the ultimate objective of equal pay for all working women in Australia.

Of the many delegates in attendance, Stella Nord from the Queensland EP Committee indicates that the conference was significant and one of historic importance to all women of Australia. She went on to say that women were the Cinderellas of industry and were a cheap labour force, and that in Queensland, in 1954, employers sought to widen the scope of work for women at lower rates of pay. She added that, in her view, factory laws should be enacted over conditions such as seating facilities for women in industry.[26]

Delegate Miss Osborne from NSW Teachers' Federation pointed out that Australia was only one of seven countries which did not give equal pay to teachers. 'She reminded the conference that Minister Holt said that Australia did not wish to find itself out of step with other industrial salary structures throughout the world, yet he must be aware that Australia is well out of step in regard to equal pay with leading industrial countries'.[27] The delegates, both men and women, who attended these inter-union equal pay conferences, represented a wide variety of employees—from factories to the Public Service—and participated in the discussion, all making contributions on how best equal pay could be implemented.

Conference resolutions called upon Federal Government to honour its obligations as a Member-State of the ILO, to grant equal pay to its own employees, to bring the matter before the next Premiers' Conference, and provide extra finance to the States for payment of equal pay to State Government employees. Attention was drawn to Mr Holt's presidency of the Annual Conference of the ILO during the 1950s, and to

---

STOPPAGE IN

SMOKES PLANT

More than 800 Tobacco and Cigarette Workers' Union members employed by W.D. and H.O. Wills (Aust.) Ltd. will hold a stop-work meeting tomorrow to discuss the firm's new work system for women piece workers.

Herald, 12 January, 1959

---

failure to give a satisfactory reply to the deputation which presented petitions. All the other demands were listed plus 'Labor Councils to intensify campaign so that decisions of this conference be made more effective'.[28]

As mentioned, it was the policy of all Liberal or Coalition Governments, both State and Federal, to strongly oppose legislation and press those wanting equal pay to go to the Industrial Tribunals. The vast majority of appointees to the Tribunals, Wages Boards and Arbitration Commission were (and are still) conservative and rarely made (or make) a decision which would establish a precedent contrary to a government's wishes. These structures were established to preserve the status quo and, in the main, will not diverge from it unless approval is indicated by government, whether State or Federal. It is for this very reason that the trade union movement continued to urge all the governments to legislate for equal pay while governments insisted that the unions take their case to the Wage Tribunals.

As Justice Gleeson was to say in 1994, 'It is wrong to assume that, running throughout the law, there is some general principle of fairness. Much of the policy behind laws, statutory or judge-made, is based upon other considerations'.[29] Justice Gleeson, as Chief Justice of the High Court of Australia, is now the most powerful judge in the land.

At a daily level, Kath was always active about injustice. Marjorie Broadbent relates how, on one occasion, when Kath was attending an equal pay conference in Sydney and sat down to breakfast with other delegates at their hotel, she was duly served with a small portion of bacon and eggs. When noting her helping was less than those served to the male delegates, she asked the waitress for an explanation and was informed that breakfast helpings to women and children were smaller than men's servings. Upon asking if there was a difference in price she was told that all the prices were the same. Kath demanded to see the manager and no one at the table commenced eating. The manager eventually appeared in pyjamas and dressing gown. Kath told him who she was and who they all were, and tackled him over the discrimination and unjust pricing of meals in his hotel. Agreement was hastily reached and all at the table received fresh and equal helpings, a policy which the hotel adhered to from then on.[30]

Kath also spoke at one of the Sunday Night Series of lectures, held at the Unity Hall, Melbourne, and for her session Kath chose the topic of equal pay. She was also one of the very few women who gave up their Sunday afternoons to speak at the Yarra Bank.[31] Like Muriel Heagney, Kath was able to address all interested people and mix in all company. She could take her place on the State Committee of the CPA and at the same time feel at ease and enjoy the company of workers. She was no snob.

Kath's respite was in her garden where she enjoyed her many plants and flowers and their perfumes and colour. She took great care in their cultivation and paid extra attention to the many hanging baskets with their need for constant watering. She was tidy and house-proud and obtained great satisfaction from seeing her small cottage surrounded by nature's bounty. Another of Kath's pleasures was attending CPA social events or going to the local cinema with Ray. When Ray graduated as a chemist, married and had a family, she obtained great pleasure when baby-sitting her grandchildren whom she loved dearly.[32]

One can understand why, to a large degree, researchers avoided the 1950s period of the equal pay struggle and concentrated on the previous or following years. Cognisant of the amount of detail recorded in this book, it is disturbing to think that people interested in learning of the involvement of individuals and the trade union movement in the campaign for equal pay over the many years, have to plough through pages and pages of dry data. Unfortunately, this is unavoidable and yet the amount of effort required to organise all the recorded activity during these years—the conferences, meetings, or even getting the information together to issue circulars or letters—cannot be detailed. Nevertheless, it was this ongoing concerted campaign which created the foundation for what was to follow.

When observing the commitment and all the work Kath did, one can understand why her position on the VTHC EP Committee was designated as Honorary Secretary/organiser in 1955. Male-controlled unions were reluctant to provide the finance to make this responsibility a paid position and Kath did all this work for the VTHC EP Committee while also attending to her job which provided her livelihood.

All told, Kath held three responsible positions during the 1950s and 1960s: Honorary Secretary/organiser of the VTHC EP Committee, State Committee member of the CPA and—her only paid position—organiser of the Liquor Trades Union. With all the voluntary work Kath undertook on behalf of the EP Committee, one may ask why the union movement did not contribute the funds to employ her specifically to carry out these vital tasks. One can only assume that lack of interest and commitment by male-controlled unions together with the overall reluctance by women to take action enabled this situation to prevail.

Kath's commitment to the CPA, together with her organisational abilities and tremendous personal appeal, made it possible for her to call on the services of left-wing union leaders and staff, including her own, when assistance was required. Colin Wilman of the Painters' Union was often called upon to help. The VTHC on occasion would also give assistance through their office staff and facilities to accommodate the many letters, circulars and other material Kath produced. All expenses incurred by the organisation of equal pay committees, conferences and leaflets distributed were met by the trade union movement. It was the union fees paid by members that enabled the entire trade union campaign for equal pay to proceed.

Success was achieved when the NSW Labor Government broke the impasse in 1958 by introducing legislation to abolish wage discrimination in the public sector and in some awards governed by State Tribunals. The New South Wales *Industrial Arbitration (Female Rates) Amendment Act 1958* provided that, upon application, the Industrial Commission of New South Wales would include in awards and industrial agreements provision for equal pay between the sexes.[33] This led to 'the first breakthrough in 1959 when the New South Wales teachers award was restructured around the principle of equal pay for work of equal value and finally gained that award in 1963'.[34] However, there was to be much criticism of this Act from unionists and unions covering the manufacturing sector.

Kath, through the VTHC EP Committee, wrote to the Federal Secretary of the Australian Council of Salaried and Professional Associations (ACSPA) 'soliciting the support of "white collar" associations for the Equal Pay Campaign'. This was the first documented evidence of an approach being made for cooperation between the two largest national union organisations on equal pay—the VTHC and the ACSPA. Not only was the Secretary of the ACTU notified that ACSPA was 'willing to co-operate with it and support moves for the introduction of equal pay' but, with the approval of the ACTU, they, the ACSPA, were prepared to ask associations affiliated with ACSPA to support any rally proposed during the ACTU Congress period.[35]

The VTHC EP Committee decided to organise a special meeting to be held in Melbourne during August of 1959 in conjunction with the ACTU Congress.[36] It would seem the intention was to draw attention to the issue of equal pay and bring pressure to bear on trade union delegates attending the Congress. Documents reveal that the Equal Pay Conference took place as planned but Monk, who was President of the ACTU, acted as Chairman of the VTHC EP Conference, and this ruled out the simultaneous holding of the ACTU Congress.

In opening the VTHC EP Conference, Monk outlined the considerations of the Executive of the ACTU and its reply to the statement issued by the Minister of Labor and National Service on equal pay.[37] The Conference condemned the Federal Government for its continued disregard of the ACTU's demands for equal pay. Mr Kenny, Vice President of the NSW TLCL EP Committee, pointed out that 'recent amendments to the NSW Industrial Arbitration Act on female rates although limited in scope and falling short of the aims of the Trade Union movement, are a step in the right direction, and an important break-through in the field of legislation for equal pay for the job regardless of sex'.[38] A great deal of discussion took place on the NSW Equal Pay legislation, the need for closer contact and better co-ordination between the equal pay committees through annual meetings, and for consideration to be given to the establishment of women's bureaus. It was also suggested that another petition be organised. Miss Woodford, the Honorary Secretary of the NSW EP Committee, addressed the conference.

A circular distributed by the Combined EP Committee of NSW outlined the importance of the establishment of a women's bureau and detailed information under brief headings vitally important to women. The areas featured were Technical Training for Women, Widow as Wage-Earner, Part-Time Work,

Communal Domestic Services, Married Women at Work, Automation, Women in Australia, Social Attitudes, Psychological Aspects, Equal Opportunity, Equal Remuneration, Women in Trade Unions, Apprenticeships for Women.[39]

Reflecting on these years 1956 to 1959 in the fight for equal pay, it is interesting to note the preponderance of male trade union leaders in attendance at equal pay conferences. One questions whether most of them were there because they were genuinely interested or whether they wished to be seen as being interested.

We also need to remind ourselves that when presenting submissions before the various wage tribunals in the early years, men and women who researched the material in support of equal pay had very little empirical data on which to substantiate claims. Almost no statistics were kept on women apart from sparse details provided by the census. Industries, companies, the Public Service and the trade union movement had very little detail concerning the make-up of female staff or membership. These structures considered such information of little importance or significance and as yet computers, which in time would simplify the process, were still on the drawing boards.

By the end of the 1950s the steady influx of women entering the paid workforce, together with the stimulus generated by Kath's commitment in the trade union movement, saw a heightening interest and involvement in the equal pay struggle. But there was far more to do.

6

1960 to 1962,
the fight escalates

Kath turned sixty-five years of age in 1960, the year her ex-husband Percy Clarey died. Her energy and activities remained undiminished. Circulars were sent to all unions from the Victorian Trades Hall Council Equal Pay Committee reminding them of the Federal Unions conference and urging that all steps be taken to see that they not only had representation but that delegates from other States had a woman member. (It wasn't unusual for union delegations at these equal pay conferences to comprise only men.)

The application of pressure was always necessary and the VTHC EP Committee decided to request unions to introduce the question of equal pay at all meetings of their members where wages were discussed, particularly in regard to the campaign for an increase in the basic wage. Unions were urged to forward extra copies of bulletins, speakers notes etc. to shop stewards and shop committees for distribution. It was also agreed that the ACTU organise a deputation to the Federal Government following the Conference.[1]

At the meeting of the ACTU EP Committee on 22 February 1960, Kath recommended an equal pay campaign linked to the basic wage claim to bring the issue of equal pay to the fore.[2] On the very next day at the Federal Unions Conference, it was decided that a National Equal Pay Week be conducted in six

Australian States by the ACTU State Branches commencing on March 28. This was to be the first Equal Pay Week, an opportunity for action and publicity.[3]

Don MacSween, Secretary of the Clothing Trades Union, took the opportunity to inform the Conference that clothing trade women were receiving only 50 per cent of the male margins, a chronic situation in the clothing trades.

The Sydney EP Committee drew attention to the dearth of information on women in industry and decided to organise a survey on women and the associated problems relating to their work during Equal Pay Week.[4]

At the VTHC meeting on the Thursday night prior to Equal Pay Week, a Special Report on Equal Pay was given. The gallery was open and one had to obtain permission from a union for admission.

Among other activities during National Equal Pay Week, the

Equal Pay Rally outside Parliament House, Victoria, 1960

Photo courtesy of the Union of Australian Women, Melbourne

Business and Professional Women's Clubs of Sydney arranged a Symposium on 'Womanpower' with representatives of all women's organisations from Sydney in attendance. Some of the areas covered were Women Pioneers, Women in Industry, Women in The Public Service, University Women and Women's Voluntary Organisations.[5]

In Melbourne, a public meeting was held with speakers from various organisations. Gil Hayes, Kath Williams and Don Macsween conducted a Question and Answer Session. Albert Monk as President of the ACTU met the press on Channel 7 and several radio broadcasts were organised on 3KZ. Channel 2 screened films on equal pay during the week.[6]

Kath followed up Equal Pay Week with a circular to all unions expressing the need to examine the comprehensive round of activities which had been carried out during the week. She sought this information for future use and requested that unions inform the Equal Pay Committee of the number of

Kath Williams and Bill Brown, Furnishing Trades Union Secretary, lead the THC Equal Pay march along Swanston Street in 1960.

factory meetings held, the name of the factories, and details of the distribution of literature and other activities. A request for finance was also made to help cover the costs still outstanding. Kath was well aware of how unions functioned and was checking up to gauge the extent of participation by individual unions.

Correspondence of March 30 from the ACTU to the Melbourne Trades Hall Council indicated a difference of opinion among ACTU EP Committees and attempted to pull the Victorian THC EP Committee into line. It would seem that the ACTU State Branches Conference of EP Committees had agreed upon a method of action whereas the Victorian EP Committee had adopted a line of action conflicting with the decision of the Meeting.[7] While the decision agreed to was that approaches be made by constituents of each member of the Federal and State Parliament, requesting the member's support for the principle of equal pay, the VTHC EP Committee asked members of EP Committees and other interested organisations to approach Members of Parliament and if their answer was no or evasive, then the member was to be told he would lose support in the next election.[8]

This obvious difference of opinion displays an overall dissatisfaction on the part of the VTHC EP Committee and frustration with the slow progress towards achieving equal pay. The VTHC EP Committee wanted a bolder approach implemented. At this stage the committee had been operating for five years and Kath, with the support of the committee, indicated their preparedness to take the lead in putting pressure on the politicians. Jack Hutson, the representative of the Amalgamated Engineering Union on the EP Committee, recalls the only visible sign Kath revealed any frustration was towards the procrastination and slowness of the trade union movement and Labor Party in applying pressure or action to implement equal pay.[9]

Kath sent a letter to Stout, the Secretary of the VTHC informing him of two resolutions passed at the EP Committee requesting that the VTHC Executive consider the widening of the EP Committee to include all affiliated organisations and that the VTHC Executive empower the committee to invite two observers, one from the State Parliamentary Labor Party and one from the Federal Parliamentary Labor Party, to attend committee meetings.[10]

Kath and the committee clearly wanted more participation by all unions, 'new blood' to share the work needing to be done, bringing fresh dynamism into the proceedings. The committee may have thought that the presence of politicians at their meetings would validate the campaign for equal pay and give further strength to the cause.

Kath, on behalf of the EP Committee, wrote to the Secretary of the VTHC. She requested that the anticipated deputation to Bill McMahon (successor to Harold Holt as Federal Minister for Labour and National Service in September 1960) include representatives of all affiliated organisations and invitations be sent to outside organisations as observers. She also stressed the urgency of this matter.[11]

There can be no doubt that Kath's initiatives brought about closer co-operation between the ACTU and white collar organisations. Among those making contributions on the Deputation to McMahon were Mr Riley from ASCPA, Mr Smith of the High Council of Public Service Organisations and Miss B. Collins of the EP Committee of the Queensland Branch of the ACTU. Miss Collins emphasised the interest among women when realising they were being exploited because of their sex—the commonly used phrase until academia altered sex to gender in the late 1970s—even though their return to the employer was always equal to or higher than that of men employed alongside them.[12]

Kath, as a member of the deputation, in her lengthy submission noted that 'the family wage is no longer the concept or basis of the basic wage. The social element in the basic wage no longer stood [sic]. Deserted wives and civilian widows are limited to women's wages.' She concluded her contribution: 'The ACTU policy was for equal pay for the sexes with no discrimination of sex. That is, the full basic wage and equal margins' and 'Equal Pay for Equal Work the first step.'[13] Deputations on any issue rarely expect a positive response, nevertheless it was a good opportunity for the equal pay committee and the unions to put pressure on the government.

For some members of the VTHC EP Committee, the concept of equal pay for equal work was extremely limited. The severe segregation of the Australian workforce where women and men perform different tasks in the workplace prevents the vast majority of women from receiving any benefits from equal pay for equal work. It was for this reason that Kath and several other members of the committee thought that equal pay for equal work was a misleading concept. This dilemma was often discussed by the committee.

Before the year was over, the VTHC EP Committee was planning for the 1961 Equal Pay Week. A meeting was arranged for January and the distributed circular listed suggestions for a seminar to be organised by the ACTU in Sydney or Melbourne. An appeal was made for more assistance from rank and file unionists as well as shop stewards to ease the burden of all the work required to organise Equal Pay Week. A request was also made for the 'ACTU to prepare a leaflet advertising the Seminar, and containing ACTU Policy on Equal Pay'.[14] With the volume of work continually increasing, Kath sought assistance with the typing of material and other tasks but the impetus and organisation was driven by her.

Early in January 1961, printing trade employers were 'pressing their claims for the variation of the Graphic Arts award to enable females to be employed on all male work under the Award at substantially reduced rates'.[15] This attempt to use women as cheap labour against men was being made possible by the continued introduction of modern technology and again, the male union leadership was having difficulty in dealing with this issue. The printing trade, was extremely vulnerable; more efficient machinery was being installed which manufactured large volumes of similar products and the employers wanted to recruit women into the industry to operate these machines on lower rates of pay, depriving men of their jobs. It was obvious that an all out campaign for equal pay was necessary but despite the efforts of the VTHC EP Committee it did not occur.

The 1961 speakers' notes distributed by VTHC EP Committee made note of the ACTU Congress, commending all who helped to develop the equal pay campaign, and called for the strengthening of the movement on a national basis through its State EP Committees. The notes further testified that thirty-four countries had ratified the 1951 Equal Pay Convention, forty-three gave equal pay to civil servants, seventy-seven gave equal pay to teachers, and thirty-eight had equal pay legislation.

Kath sent a draft of a Model Bill[16] on Equal Pay to the Secretary of the VTHC requesting that it be sent on to the ACTU. This Model Bill, drawn up by a solicitor and examined by a barrister, was designed as an amendment to the Labor and Industry Acts of Victoria. In her covering letter Kath reminded the ACTU that the Labor Party had decided not to bring legislation forward on equal pay until such time as a Model Bill was drafted and had been approved by the party so that uniform legislation could be put forward. The Equal Pay for Equal Work Bill to be enacted in NSW, proved to be extremely narrow in its application and was not wanted. The VTHC EP Committee felt that their Model Bill was watertight, one that

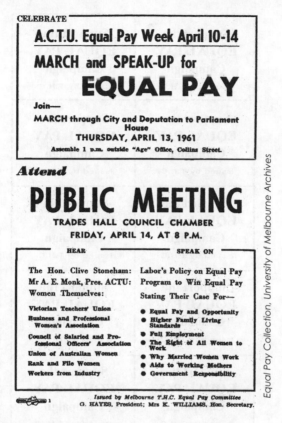

CELEBRATE

A.C.T.U. Equal Pay Week April 10-14

MARCH and SPEAK-UP for

EQUAL PAY

Join—

MARCH through City and Deputation to Parliament House
THURSDAY, APRIL 13, 1961
Assemble 1 p.m. outside "Age" Office, Collins Street.

Attend

PUBLIC MEETING

TRADES HALL COUNCIL CHAMBER
FRIDAY, APRIL 14, AT 8 P.M.

HEAR	SPEAK ON
The Hon. Clive Stoneham:	Labor's Policy on Equal Pay
Mr A. E. Monk, Pres. ACTU:	Program to Win Equal Pay
Women Themselves:	Stating Their Case For—
Victorian Teachers' Union	● Equal Pay and Opportunity
Business and Professional Women's Association	● Higher Family Living Standards
Council of Salaried and Professional Officers' Association	● Full Employment
	● The Right of All Women to Work
Union of Australian Women	● Why Married Women Work
Rank and File Women	● Aids to Working Mothers
Workers from Industry	● Government Responsibility

Issued by Melbourne T.H.C. Equal Pay Committee
G. HAYES, President; Mrs K. WILLIAMS, Hon. Secretary.

Equal Pay Collection, University of Melbourne Archives

Leaflet issued by the VTHC Equal Pay Committee, 1961

could be adapted to other States and the Commonwealth. With the Tasmanian Government preparing to bring forward equal pay legislation in this, their election year, it was felt that this draft would be useful to the ACTU.[17] It was much stronger than the Bill enacted in NSW.

Meanwhile, the ACSPA National EP Committee was well under way and letters were sent notifying the various affiliated associations of a meeting on 14 April 1961 requesting they attend.[18] The Federal Council of the Clothing and Allied Trades

Support the **EQUAL PAY** **Campaign** Issued by T.H.C.	**Support the** **EQUAL PAY** **Campaign** Issued by T.H.C.
Support the **EQUAL PAY** **Campaign** Issued by T.H.C.	**Support the** **EQUAL PAY** **Campaign** Issued by T.H.C.
Support the **EQUAL PAY** **Campaign** Issued by T.H.C.	**Support the** **EQUAL PAY** **Campaign** Issued by T.H.C.
Support the **EQUAL PAY** **Campaign** Issued by T.H.C.	**Support the** **EQUAL PAY** **Campaign** Issued by T.H.C.
Support the **EQUAL PAY** **Campaign** Issued by T.H.C.	**Support the** **EQUAL PAY** **Campaign** Issued by T.H.C.

F. Riley Collection, State Library of Victoria

Stickers distributed for placing on walls of workplaces and toilets

Union notified the ACTU of its alarm at a report that the Equal Pay Bill to be submitted to the Tasmanian Parliament by the Labour Ministry was similar to the original NSW Bill. This Bill contained the same iniquitous provision which excluded from its benefits, females in industries which were predominantly female.[19] The letter went on to urge the ACTU to complete the Model Bill for use in the different States and that representations be made immediately to the Tasmanian government with the object of preventing a repetition of the New South Wales injustices.

What was the ACTU doing to prevent a repetition of the NSW Equal Pay Bill from being enacted in Tasmania and where did the ALP stand on this issue?

Kath also wrote on behalf of the EP Committee to Mr. R. D. Williams, Secretary of the ACSPA, outlining the program of activities for the 1961 Equal Pay Week and providing information on the National Seminar. Kath also invited ACSPA to provide a speaker for the public meeting to be held in April.[20]

Women's organisations such as the League of Women Voters and the Victorian Medical Women's Society wrote to the ACTU conveying their best wishes for successful meetings during Equal Pay Week and their appreciation of the ACTU's efforts in the campaign for equal pay and for working with other groups.

Equal Pay Week was highlighted by a city demonstration followed by a march through the crowded lunchtime streets of Melbourne to Parliament House. The Committee's intention was to interview members of State Parliament and demand the introduction of equal pay for the sexes. A brief news item appeared on ABC television displaying the women and men marchers carrying their banners.[21]

Early in March 1961, the ACTU notified all ACTU Officers, State Branch Secretaries and Secretaries of Affiliated Unions that an Equal Pay Seminar was to be held in the Trades Hall, Sydney, in April. Delegates were requested to attend as well as representatives from the EP Committees. Interested organisations were also invited to participate and to take part in the discussion groups on the papers to be submitted.

It was proposed that three papers be submitted—the first by President A. E. Monk on behalf of the ACTU, detailing the Trade Union attitudes and international considerations of Equal

Clothing Trades Union Collection, University of Melbourne Archives

Women marching for equal pay in Melbourne, 1961

Pay; the second by Mrs Helen Crisp, devoted to the principal aspects of The Role of Women in the Campaign for Equal Pay, and the third by S. E. Imer, Assistant General Secretary of the Administrative and Clerical Officers' Association, on behalf of the High Council of Public Service Unions.[22]

In the absence of Mr Monk, the Senior Vice President, J. D. Kenny, a New South Wales MLC, delivered the first paper on behalf of the ACTU. In his address he said the present State Government equal pay legislation, which did not grant equal pay for all women, needed urgent amendment'. The State Government was going to be asked to amend the legislation to 'Not withstanding anything contrary in any other Act, every wage-fixing authority when fixing the salaries or wages of employees shall have regard to the principle that differentiations based on sex in scales of salary or wages shall be eliminated'.[23]

At the end of the second day of the Seminar in Sydney, the Sydney *Daily Telegraph* reported '*EQUAL PAY REQUEST TO STATE GOVERNMENT*', and 'The State Labor Council will ask the NSW State Government to grant equal pay to women'.[24]

When addressing the conference on the following day, Mr Imer said it was in 1950 that the Women's basic wage became 75 per cent of the male rate, not the adoption of any scientific formula from the study of the rates then paid but solely as a very convenient percentage. Mr Imer noted that one of the three Judges on the bench thought the existing 54 per cent of the male wage was quite enough, while the other two thought the 75 per cent formula was an easy escape from their dilemma. Their judgement gave a paper increase which good employers were already paying, and thereby reinforced the traditional view of the courts and tribunals that women's labour was inherently inferior to that of men.

Mrs Helen Crisp, who came from Canberra, began her lengthy contribution to the seminar by speaking of the granting of equal pay to women in the British Public Service in 1955 and its implementation over a six-year period. She drew attention to the fact that this granting of equal pay to the Public Service in England did not automatically extend to women employed in the private sector. She went on to say that equal pay had not been regarded as a really live issue in Canberra for some years. She described how, in 1951, the Professional Officers' Association and the CSIRO Officers' Association had applied to the Public Service Arbitrator for equal pay for all their women officers who were professionally qualified and occupying professional positions, these women (although their numbers were small) took a lively part in the proceedings, both through their professional organisations and the Canberra Association of Women Graduates. Mrs Crisp explained how the Arbitrator, though he refused their claim on the ground of the complexities in the basic wage system, made it plain that he considered the women concerned were doing work of equal value citing his words:

> There appears to be no doubt, and indeed, it is not disputed that
> the professional qualifications of female professional employees

are equal in standard to those of male professional employees, that generally employees of both sexes perform duties of a similar nature and that the female employees are not less efficient than the male employees.[25]

Mrs Crisp went on to be critical of Kath: 'Mrs Williams' battle cry that equal pay is a class question and we have to give a class answer is quite unrealistic to today's setting'.[26] She later added, 'since I have been here, at least one woman has told me that she could not possibly speak for her organisation in such a political atmosphere'.[27]

Perhaps Kath, in her contribution, may have alluded to capitalism as being responsible for the exploitation of women. Perhaps the woman Mrs Crisp referred to considered the struggle for equal pay as being non-political and understood politics in terms of party political only; this being the case, any questioning of the status quo would have been threatening. Nevertheless, when referring to Kath's contribution on how the VTHC EP Committee helped women in unions prepare five miscellaneous papers, Mrs. Crisp described this action as 'a very good move'.

She also said there were two groups of women who had to be considered in any campaign of this kind: those who benefit from it and those who can help to bring it to a successful conclusion. They may overlap but not necessarily. And her remarks still stand in today's Australia:

> Of those who will benefit, I don't think there is any doubt that on the whole, women in higher education and training (and I don't just mean academic training) feel more strongly the injustice of pay differentiated according to sex. The sense of injustice which Barbara Wootten [sic] has called the 'driving force' on the women's side in the move for equal pay ...
>
> On the other hand, many of the women and girls who naturally gravitate to jobs requiring less training (and who would no doubt

appreciate equal pay or rather, pay evaluated on the same basis as a man's pay in the same job would be) are not prepared to fight for it. Increasingly they are married women with domestic responsibilities who have insufficient time, insufficient security of tenure in their jobs, and an insufficiently long range view of their employment to allow them to take part in such a campaign. Call them a pool of cheap labour or whatever you like. But they are difficult to organise. Or they are young things filling in time between school and marriage, often doing a very good job but never looking on their work as a life long career.[28]

These last comments raise so many questions, for example, what background did these women come from? Did poverty force them to leave school at an early age? Did they have a low self-image? Did they have any expectations? Did their backgrounds encourage them to have expectations? Is it possible to look upon assembly-line work as a career? Is it possible to look upon any work where the operative has no say or control over their labour as a career? Is it realistic to expect women working in a female industry to campaign for equal pay when, due to the regulations and awards, they will never be entitled to it?

Mrs Crisp also referred to the Federal Opposition Labor politicians creating a situation in the Senate in December 1960 when they attempted to force the women senators to vote on the equal pay issue:

Obviously some drastic move was needed to draw the attention of both Parliament and the people to the existing deadlock. I sat through the Second Reading Debate and vote on the Public Service Bill in the Senate, which unfortunately, was not broadcast, because I was interested to see whether the four women on the Government side would make any kind of gesture in favour of equal pay. While I did not expect them to put their sex before their party, I did consider that they might have allowed the equal pay issue to have an airing before they stepped back into the

Party Line. For if as seems obvious, we must look for legislative rather than court action to achieve equal pay, we should be able to expect help from women in a position to give it.[29]

She went on to explain how in Federal Parliament, Labor Senator Willesee from West Australia moved: 'That the Bill be recommitted for the purpose of establishing in the Bill the principle that the rates or scales of rates of salary payable to female officers shall not be less than the rates, or scales of rates, of salary payable to male officers performing equivalent duties'. She noted how the Senator explained that he took this action because the Standing Orders of the Senate prevented Senators from moving to amend the Act. The Government Leader in the Senate (Senator Spooner) then replied that the Government was 'not prepared to agree to the recommital of the Bill', Labor Senator Dorothy Tangney, also from West Australia, began to ask a question but was ruled out of order. Without any further debate, the motion was put, and Senator Annabelle Rankin, as the Liberal Government Whip, rounded up the Government Senators and the motion was lost. The reasons the Liberal women senators gave for defeating the motion on the recomittal of equal pay legislation was, in the main, that the whole exercise was merely a Labor Party political stunt and the correct place for deciding equal pay for equal work was in the Arbitration Court.[30] Finally, Mrs Crisp stated that, had the three women Senators risked the displeasure of their party by voting the other way, the matter would have been open for further discussion. As it was, equal pay was not debated at all.[31]

Here we had a situation where the Liberal women senators could have supported a discussion on equal pay but refused to do so.

This first National ACTU-convened Equal Pay Seminar was most successful. One hundred women from all over Australia attended. Among those present were: Miss B. Collins from the

Queensland EP Committee, Mrs Flo Davis from the Liquor Trades Union, Miss Dawes from the Liquor Industry Union, R. L. Day from the Rubber Workers' Union, Mrs. I. Greenwood from the WA Combined Equal Pay Committee, Miss Hoy from the Public Service Association of NSW, Miss McLaughlin from the Australian Federation of Business and Professional Women's Clubs, Miss Miller from the Joint Coal Board Staff, Mrs. More from the Queensland EP Committee, Miss Osborne from the Teachers Federation NSW, Mrs. Simpson from the Union of Australian Women & Shop Assistants, Mrs K. Williams from the Victorian EP Committee and Miss M. Woodford from the NSW EP Committee.

In June 1961 census figures indicated a further increase in the number of women in the workforce. The number had risen by 25 per cent over that taken at the 1954 Census, an average annual increment over the period of 3.3 per cent. In the same seven year period, the male workforce grew by only 11 per cent or 1.8 per cent per annum. 'The growth of the female workforce between 1954 and 1961 was much faster than that of the male workforce in all States of Australia'. Proportionately, more women were in the workforce in Victoria (22 per cent of the female population) than in any other State.[32] 'Of the total workforce in each State, the female component was highest in Victoria (27%) and NSW (26%)'.[33]

In July 1961, the Australian Insurance Staffs' Federation contacted the Federal Secretary of ACSPA informing him of the resolutions passed at the meeting of the Victorian Equal Pay Committee of ACSPA. The resolutions indicated their desire for provision to be made for the inclusion of equal pay in the week's official itinerary of 'white-collar festival week', that a comprehensive booklet covering every aspect of the 'Equal Pay for Equal Work' Campaign be issued to all Affiliates and that it

Cleaners walk off job in RACV dispute

Fourteen women cleaners employed by the RACV walked off the job today in protest about the dismissal of a fellow woman cleaner. They say she was not given notice.

'They claim the cleaner was dismissed without notice last week for allegedly scratching the legs of chairs with a vacuum cleaner'.

'The Miscellaneous Workers' Union city organiser Mr Ted Forbes, told the meeting that the dismissed cleaner who had worked at the RACV for eight years – was entitled to 5 days notice.'

Herald, 24 October 1961

become the ACSPA Manual on Equal Pay. The Federation wanted the resolutions placed before the ACSPA Federal Executive and also requested that, should the Federal Executive of ACSPA decide to issue a national journal, the Victorian Equal Pay Committee be permitted to submit an article for inclusion in the publication.[34]

Kath was selected to be the delegate from her union to the forthcoming ACTU Congress in 1961 which 'affirmed the policy of the Trade Union Movement of equal pay for the sexes and decided as a first step toward that objective for the Trade Unions to campaign to obtain equal remuneration for men and women workers for work of equal value'.[35] The Congress urged affiliated organisations to give practical assistance to authorised programs conducted by equal pay committees.

The NSW Division of the ACSPA, in conjunction with the ACTU, produced a leaflet in preparation for Equal Pay Week of

Barmaids on strike over equal pay, Newcastle, 1962

Tribune 1962 (day and month unknown)

1962, publicising the Equal Pay Rally to be held at Wynyard Park.[36] (Kath's letter in 1959 to ACSPA on behalf of the VTHC EP Committee had brought closer co-operation between the ACTU and ACSPA through the occasional combining of their campaign activities on equal pay and Equal Pay Week.)

Liberal Governments, Federal and State, had dominated the political scene for several years and were strongly opposed to equal pay for women and the EP Committee reviewed its role in the previous State election campaign when lobbying to defeat the Liberal Government. They considered the need to be more effective in the forthcoming Federal elections in efforts to depose the Menzies Government from office and decided to ask each of the political parties standing in forthcoming elections to state unequivocally if they would introduce equal pay for their female employees in government instrumentalities if elected. In keeping with this decision the Leader of the Parliamentary Labor Party, Arthur Calwell, stated clearly that the ALP, if returned to government in December, would take necessary action to provide equal remuneration for men and women workers for work of equal value consistent with trade union policy.

Information was sought from all unions with women members on the number of women receiving equal pay, the differences in working hours between males and females, whether employers had attempted to have male award classifications altered to enable them to introduce female labour at lower rates of pay, whether there was any discrimination against women—particularly married women—and if and where any attacks had been made against equal pay. It was stressed that unions

Women competing against each other in the Equal Pay Queen Competition, 1962

Communist Party of Australia Collection, University of Melbourne Archives should begin publishing articles on these subjects in their journals.

The EP Committees had a constant effect on the overall trade union movement and were vitally important in prodding the unions into action for equal pay, even though priority was given to the protection of men's jobs.

By 1962 the VTHC EP Committee had been functioning for six years, and while Liberal Governments continued to express the view that governments could not legislate for equal pay and argued this could only be granted by the Arbitration Commission or Wage Tribunals, the ACTU and the ACSPA seemed reluctant to mount a claim. One can only assume that this was because past experience had shown that Arbitration judges were averse to opposing governments or endangering the family wage structure and constantly rejected equal pay claims. Judges who, in the main, came from the privileged class, were reluctant to create a precedent or challenge long-standing social discriminatory practices. With the lack of industrial action in support of equal pay, the EP Committees had no choice but to continue applying pressure on governments to legislate for equal pay.

Bill Brown, from the Furniture Trades Society, and Kath were selected to represent the VTHC at the meeting of the ACTU EP Branch representatives in February 1962. Kath reported on the need for a deputation to the State Government, preceded by a demonstration, radio broadcasts, TV advertisements, lunch hour meetings and workshop activities. The campaign for the establishment of a Women's Bureau was also in progress.

The Victorian EP Committee of the ACSPA decided to organise an Equal Pay Rally during the 1962 Equal Pay Week by holding a function at Kelvin Hall in Collins Place. All executive members of affiliated associations were requested to attend and advertise the gathering at their respective workplaces.[37]

Again, the march through the city streets to Parliament House was shown on ABC television news and featured men from various trade unions also participating in support of equal pay. Mr. C. Stoneham, the Labor Opposition Leader met the marchers outside Parliament House.[38] Kath appeared twice in this news item, elegantly dressed with her hat and gloves, accessories she rarely ventured without when in public.

Around this time, the Prime Minister's Department in Canberra notified Miss E. M. Ross, Secretary of the Combined EP Committee of Western Australia, in answer to her correspondence, that:

> You are, I know, well aware of the Government's position on this matter. It is felt to be inappropriate for the Government, as an employer, to depart from the existing industrial policy regarding the female basic wage, as laid down by the Conciliation and Arbitration Commission. The Government feels that a matter of such complexity and magnitude is properly one to be decided by the arbitration system, where its implications can be thoroughly canvassed, and not by the Government acting as employer.[39]

The ACTU, the ACSPA. and the High Council of Public Service Organisations, the three Australia-wide organisations covering employees, formed a deputation in 1962 to Prime Minister Menzies, who was accompanied by McMahon, Minister for Labour and National Service, and Mr. Wheeler of the Public Service Board. The deputation, among the issues aired, stressed the need for the government to ratify the ILO convention. ACTU Minutes record: 'The Prime Minister assured the members of the Deputation that they had given him much food for thought and that he intended to instruct the Minister for Labour, Mr. McMahon, to prepare a comprehensive report for Parliament'.[40]

On hearing of Menzies' response to the deputation, Gough Whitlam, Leader of the Labor Opposition, signed a statement on behalf of the Sydney EP Committee that the Menzies Government had instructed its representative at the United Nations Status of Women Commission earlier that year, on 23 March 1962, to vote against ratifying the Equal Pay Convention to implement equal pay.[41]

In Victoria, the VTHC EP Committee issued another leaflet:

MORE FIGHT NEEDED BEHIND EQUAL PAY DEMAND
The Menzies Government has rejected Trades Hall representation for Equal Pay for female workers despite the nation-wide campaign developed on the issue it is necessary then to lift the campaign to greater heights to win Equal Pay.

The leaflet went on to indicate the differences in wages paid and examples of profits made by various companies.

During this time, trouble was brewing at Commonwealth Industrial Gases Ltd. (CIG) Preston. In the previous year, CIG had made a profit of one million pounds. The company was proposing to employ women at 75 per cent of the male rate and it made it clear that if dismissals were to take place, it would be according to the needs of the company. The company proposal was that six women be employed initially, with a gradual increase to 30 per cent at a later stage. Males were to be dismissed. The difference between male and female rates was as much as five pounds per week, because women, under the applicable award, received a percentage of the male rate only and/or lower margins for skills.

Of the 480 employees, 400 were members of the Amalgamated Engineering Union. The Shop Stewards decided to have a mass meeting in the canteen and it was agreed that any settlement of the dispute would be based on the policy of the trade union movement. They agreed that women could be employed provided they were paid the same rate for the job as men. The union told the company that they supported the Shop Stewards.[42]

The trade unions knew from experience that when women replaced men during a credit squeeze, the men were never re-employed.

The company reluctantly agreed to meet the union the following week but its attitude was still the same. When union officials held a second mass meeting in the canteen, the company ordered them out. The employees followed the officials out and agreed to stop work for the afternoon in protest: this was the first difficulty experienced by unions in negotiations with this company. After the mass meeting was over, the personnel officer refused to see union officials and ordered them off the property. The union attempted to make a request to meet the directors but was prevented from doing so. The company referred the union to their legal advisers and to the Chamber of Manufacturers and refused to allow ACTU union officials to see the shop stewards. The men stopped work and sought to discuss the matter with the directors and the Trades Hall Disputes Committee.

A conference was held with the CIG employers at the Chamber of Manufacturers with the Secretary and Assistant Secretary of the THC. Also present were representatives of the Trade Union Disputes Committee, from the AEU, ASE, Clerks, FEDFA, Ironworkers, Miscellaneous, Liquor Trades and the Transport Workers' Union. The only woman in attendance was Mrs. D. Lorback from the LTU.

All negotiations with the Company were unsuccessful and the men went on strike. Other CIG-related companies joined the strike and the canteen staff, mainly women members of the LTU, joined them. Almost 1000 workers were involved. The strikers insisted they were in total agreement that women be employed by the Company as long as they received equal pay. *This CIG workers strike in 1962 was the first strike in Victoria over equal pay.*

The strike continued and, despite further negotiations, the company refused to waiver from its course. Approximately 200 strikers gathered at the Trades Hall and expressed their disgust with the distortion of events printed in the Melbourne *Herald* over the dispute. When their meeting finished, they marched to the Herald Building, entered the property and barged into the editor-in-chief's office. They let him know just how they felt about the distortions published in his paper, and the following morning an article appeared and, although unsympathetic, it did state the reason for the strike and was closer to the truth.[43] It read: '*STOP 'EQUAL PAY' STRIKES*—Court tells 5 unions. The Commonwealth Industrial Court today ordered five metal trades unions to call off a strike at four Melbourne factories of Commonwealth Industrial Gases'.[44] It noted that the five unions involved were the Amalgamated Engineering Union, the Australasian Society of Engineers, the Electrical Trades Union, the Federated Engine-drivers and Firemen's Association and the Storemen and Packers' Union, all predominantly male unions. Men's jobs in the metal trades were now seriously threatened and the unions were prepared to make a stand.

The strike was now in its twelfth day. Justice Dunphy said the unions were in breach of their awards and, together with Justice Eggleston, not only ordered the strike to stop but also prohibited the unions from being concerned in any stoppages at the factories for a period of six months The court's decision also rendered the unions liable to heavy penalties for future stoppages.

The Trades Hall Disputes Committee defied the Court Ruling in support of ACTU policy and in support of the ILO

Convention No. 100, and the strikers would not return to work. The company finally negotiated. The strike was over and the employees returned to work. The situation returned to the way it was prior to the dispute, with one exception. The CIG canteen shop steward, Mrs C. Lynch, remarked: 'During the strike, I was very pleased indeed at the wonderful co-operation that existed between the male and female workers. Up until now most women were under the impression that they had to fight a lone battle in industry. This strike had definitely proved otherwise.'[45]

For many women in industry, this type of experience is a dramatic learning process.

At the August 1962 meeting of the VTHC EP Committee, the unions represented were the Australian Railways Union, The Amalgamated Engineering Union, Boot Trades, Butchers, Clothing Trades, Electrical Trades Union, Food Preservers, Liquor Trades and Storemen & Packers. Most of these were left-wing unions. There was now a widening of representation on the Equal Pay Committee.

In October 1962 the VTHC EP Committee invited unions and interested organisations to a Buffet Tea at Parliament House.[46] They also requested permission from the Secretary of the VTHC and the ACTU Executive to entertain visiting trade union delegates to the Asian Regional Conference. In addition, the Committee wanted to know if the ACTU had written a reply to McMahon, Minister for Labour, concerning the Government's refusal to grant the requests of the ACTU deputation held in April, and requested a copy of the letter. It would seem that this final request was made to ensure that the letter was written.

7

Kath resigns from the Communist Party of Australia

The nineteen sixties proved to be a very trying and distressing period for Kath. Deep ideological differences had developed within the CPA over a period of seven years with a tremendous struggle developing among the leadership for power and control over the Party. Battles over Marxism in Australia were fought within the leadership of the Party, not at the barricades or on the factory floor.[1]

For several years the rank and file membership of the CPA was unaware of this dispute until the differences could no longer be contained. Feelings were running high and ultimately permeated throughout the membership. It is well known that 'we usually reserve our most bitter antagonism for those who are very close to our position, but not quite close enough'.[2] All this culminated in a fierce battle at the Melbourne State Conference in April 1963.[3]

Through her position on the State Committee of the CPA, Kath was embroiled in this ideological dispute from the outset; she was not a backroom ideologue; she was a 'people person' and needed to be among people. However, she maintained very strong ideological views involving her in great conflict within the Party hierarchy. Having taken a strong dislike to the Soviet Union and their ideology during her earlier visit there, Kath developed a greater trust and belief in the political and economic changes taking place in China and she adopted the Chinese political stand in the dispute.

The ultimate split over the Russia/China policy issue came at the April State Conference and, after having endured the many years of confrontation, Kath handed in her resignation from the Australian Communist Party.

WOMAN OFFICIAL LEAVES THE REDS
by the *Herald* industrial reporter, Seaton Ashton

A Victorian woman union organiser resigned from the Australian Communist Party. She is Mrs Catherine Williams, who has been an organiser with the State Branch of the Liquor and Allied Industry Employees Union for 15 years.[4]

The article went on to say that Mrs Williams, a member of the Communist Party for twenty-seven years, was believed to be the only full-time woman union official in Victoria, was Secretary of the Trades Hall Council's Equal Pay Committee and had been active as a union official among working women. She was the eleventh Victorian union official, including four union secretaries, to resign in the party split.[5]

How did Kath feel when taking this profound step? After all these years of being involved in politics, all those years in the ALP and then twenty-seven years in the CPA. What was she thinking and feeling?

Bernie Taft when writing of his experiences in the Party said, 'The split had a debilitating effect for many people, it created confusion about and disillusionment with the Party. Quite a few people became inactive, if not immediately, then after a short period.'[6] Approximately 200 members left the CPA in Victoria and they, like most party members, were severely traumatised. Members of families ceased speaking to each other, friends were no longer friends and a great deal of bitterness was experienced. Being a member of the Communist Party had given many people a sense of belonging, it was being part of a large family of like mind. The author, Jean Devanny, warmed to this sense of belonging, claiming that 'for the first time in my life I had a warm wonderful feeling of belonging'.[7] Dorothy Gibson, a lifelong Party member, recalled the importance of the party to her: 'I owe a tremendous lot to the party. It gave direction and hope in my life and a wonderful sense of comradeship not only national but world wide, working for the common purpose ... Of creating a new sort of world.'[8]

To Kath, this breaking up of her Communist Party family was devastating. Her son Ray believed his mother suffered a 'breakdown' during this period.[9]

George Edson, who remained in the CPA, recalls receiving passionate arguments from Kath when driving her home on his way to Alphington after attending THC meetings. She genuinely believed in her assessment of the political situation, and attempted to convince her former comrades of their incorrect thinking. Being totally caught up in the turmoil, she was unable to recognise the adverse effects this involvement was having on her health.

As she attempted to cope with and escape from this traumatising situation Kath began to drink. This was her way of masking the disruption in her life, but despite this upheaval her campaigning for equal pay did not falter. 'There was no indication of any change in her attitude or conduct at the Equal Pay Committee meetings'.[10] She was very successful in hiding her feelings but the drinking continued.

8

1963 to 1964,
the ACTU and equal pay

Early in 1963 the VTHC EP Committee reminded all unions to attend the meeting to prepare for Equal Pay Week and to discuss decisions made by the ACTU Executive during the previous year. The Committee sent a circular to all the unions in appreciation of the support from various unions for the campaign being organised around the forthcoming ACTU Congress and the subsequent National Conference on Equal Pay. The ACTU Executive decided that unions with female members would conduct this EP Conference. Forty-six unions had female members. Plans were already in motion to rally wide support for the introduction of equal pay legislation in Victoria.

The EP Committee sent a bulletin to unions for distribution to industries for display on their union notice-boards: *'HELP THE WOMEN, KEEP YOUR JOB'.*[1]

The bulletin stressed that women had the right and the need for work and they could not be kept out. Where unions tried to do this they failed, hence the urgent need for equal pay. The CIG dispute was used to publicise the threat of women's cheap labor. The clothing, butchers, boot and printing trades were all cited as industries where the employers were successful in having male jobs classified as female jobs and paid at female rates.

This demand for women to have the right to work was reactivated by the Federal Council of the Vehicle Builders Union (VBU) campaign against encroachment of women into the industry. The Federal Council approved of women working in the trimming section of the industry but refused their entry into other sections, blatantly revealing their attitude to women. Many other male-dominated unions, although agreeing with this stand, preferred to remain silent. They preferred to adopt this policy rather than campaign for equal pay, even though the granting of equal pay would have prevented women from being used against them.

It wasn't long before the following handout appeared:

> *VEHICLE BUILDERS UNION*
> *TAKE HEED TAKE CARE*
> *VEHICLE BUILDERS BEWARE*
> *'ME AND LIL'*

> When I first met Lil the case was clear,
> And I talked of her in my sleep.
> I called her 'precious', I called her 'dear',
> But the boss considered her 'cheap',
> For without regard to the work we did,
> And simply as cock and hen,
> He was paying me something like 15 quid,
> While Lily got only ten.
> 'Oh, Lily' I said, 'you must leave this life,
> Such discrimination is vile.
> Let me be the breadwinner, be my wife,
> And live in superior style.'
> But Lily wrinkled her film star brow,
> And said, 'If you aren't insane,
> You had better enthuse your union now
> For the Equal Pay campaign.'

149

'Oh, never bother your lovely head
With political stuff,' says I,
'The boys will think I'm a dangerous Red
If I pitch them a yarn so high'.
But I wish I'd done it, I tell you straight,
For the minute the trade got slack
The boss kept Lil on the old cheap rate
And I was given the sack.[2]

The 1963 Equal Pay Week was to be different. Apart from the usual demonstration and march through the city streets, all the unions and organisations were asked to arrange their own functions, meetings and campaigns. Through this new approach the VTHC EP Committee intended placing responsibility on the unions to involve and activate their own members.

The VTHC EP Committee was organising a social evening in the Trades Hall Ballroom, while the Meat Industry Union was holding its own buffet tea for their women members. An 'Equal Pay song (to the tune of 'Roses are Red, My Love') was written and sung by the Mackinnon Sisters to celebrate Equal Pay Week'.[3]

In Perth, Molly Lukis, President of the West Australian Council for Equal Pay and Opportunity, and committee member Irene Greenwood made broadcasts on radio during Equal Pay Week.

With the continual stream of correspondence from the VTHC EP Committee to the unions in Victoria, there was also a constant flow of leaflets, lists of suggestions for action, speaker's notes and the occasional appeal for more funds. One such circular contained information detailing the salaries of various workers which highlighted the discrimination against women. Those listed were a postman received £16.7s.9d. while a postwoman doing the same work got £12.5.0.; a male process worker was paid £15.15.0., and a female process worker doing the same work £11.15.6. A first cook (male) in a hotel with a staff of eight or more received £21.14.0. but a female first cook with comparable responsibilities £17.17.0. The circular went on to list the healthy annual profits of several firms employing women over the previous year demonstrating how lucrative it was to employ women at lower rates of pay.[4]

The Metal Trades Federation invited Kath to speak at their Stewards and Job Delegates' Conference and the Australian Labor Party assured the Committee of its full support. Kath enjoyed speaking at job meetings where she had a responsive audience and although she at times received jibes concerning the fear of women undermining the industry, she was fully capable of dealing with the issue.

The VTHC EP Committee met in 1963 and discussed the possibility of organising a campaign around the forthcoming ACTU Congress in September and the ACTU's Interstate Executive's decision to hold a National Equal Pay Conference before the end of the year. The Committee decided to conduct such a campaign and called upon all unions to give their full support and use the objectives outlined in the agenda items submitted by the LTU for Congress as a basis for the campaign. The meeting endorsed the agenda items and the LTU wanted Congress to call upon all State Branches to immediately seek legislation on equal pay in their own States by:

1. drawing up appropriate amendments to their State Labour and Industry Acts where Equal Pay Legislation did not exist;
2. in States where EP did exist, making amendments to cover all women covered by State Tribunals;
3. State Branches organising representative deputations to present these amendments to their Governments; or where governments refused to implement, seeking Private Members Bills;

4. organising a mass campaign around this objective, and the incoming ACTU Executive convening a National Equal Pay Conference within one month of this Congress.

The meeting also wanted an invitation to be sent to the ACSPA to attend the Congress and for women rank and file workers to be encouraged to attend as visitors, the aim being to fill the gallery when equal pay was being discussed. A lengthy list of suggestions was included for methods unions could undertake as part of the responsibility to make the campaign successful.[5]

The above items submitted by the LTU reveal the constant attempts Kath made to encourage action and her powerful influence within her union. It must be said that, despite arguments with various male members in the leadership of the LTU, she received their full support and backing for the equal pay campaign.

BUT THIS IS NOT ALL

As techniques improve - employers replace male labor by female. All wage levels are thus held down WOMEN have the RIGHT and NEED TO WORK-- BUT ACTION IS NECESSARY! SUCCESS DEPENDS ON YOU!

Note.

+ The Bolte Government has refused all previous approaches by the T.H.C. on this issue.

+ Your active support is essential to achieve this object.

+ Distribute this leaflet to your work mates.

+ Organise a meeting on your job.

+ Send Resolutions of support to your Government.

+ Ask your Union to organise a function to discuss the issue.

+ Write to your local M.P.(State and Federal) organise a deputation to him.

+ Organise the widest rank and file representation to the National Equal Pay Conference.

+ Support this Campaign.

+ Fill the Gallery at the A.C.T.U. Congress when Equal Pay is being discussed.

+ Begin now to book off work mates to attend Women if possible.

Send their names and addresses to your Union which will advise you of time and date. Notice may be short. ACT NOW!

DRIVE
FOR
EQUAL PAY
1963

TWO IMPORTANT CONFERENCES

A.C.T.U. CONFERENCE

NATIONAL EQUAL PAY CONFERENCE

The Australian Council of Trade Unions Composite List, Noel Butlin Archives, Australian National University

Leaflet distributed by the VTHC Equal Pay Committee

List of Unions having Female Members.

Actors & Announcers Equity	Affiliated Teachers Union
Amal. Engineering Union	Art. Fertilisers Union
A'Asian Soc. of Engineers	Boot Trade Emp. Fed.
Brushmakers Union	Aust. Fed. of Police Assns.
Aust. Glass Workers Union	Government Workers Assoc.
Leather & Allied Trades Emp.	Meat Indust. Emp. Union
Aust. Railways Union	Rope & Cordage Workers
Textile Workers Union	Theatrical Emp. Union
Tramway Emp. Assoc.	Blind Workers' Union
Clothing & Allied Trades	Dental Technicians Assoc.
Electrical Trades Union	Fed. Clerks' Union
Cold Storage Union	Fed. Confectioners' Assoc.
Furnishing Trades Society	Fed. Ironworkers' Assoc.
Liquor & allied Trades	Fed. Marine Stewards Union
Miscellaneous Workers' Union	Municipal & Shire Council Emp.
Rubber & Allied Trades Union	Fed. Storemen & Packers Union
Tobacco & Cigarette Workers NSW	Tobacco & Cigarette Workers VIC.
Food Preservers Union	Hospital Emp. Union
Man. Grocers Union	Musicians Union
N.S.W. Teachers Fed.	Photo Engravers Union
Postal Workers Union	P.I.E.U.A.
Pulp & Paper Workers Fed.	Sheet Metal Workers Union
Vehicle Builders Fed.	Wool & Basil Workersp Fed.

Equal Pay Collection, University of Melbourne Archives

Leaflet prepared by the VTHC Equal Pay Committee which accompanied the ACTU circular to ACTU officers and secretaries of unions in 1963

Gil Hayes resigned as President of the EP Committee but remained on the Committee. His reason for relinquishing the presidency is unknown. From early 1964 Bill Brown, the State Secretary of the Furniture Trades Society, was the new President.

Over the nine years of association with Kath on the EP Committee, Gil Hayes came to admire her sincerity and ab-solute commitment and, despite their political differences, they were able to work together amicably. There can be no doubt this involvement with the EP Committee enabled Hayes to broach the struggle for equal pay within his own union resulting in its involvement in several equal pay cases. How-ever, the full extent of his union's commitment, or whether he involved the women working in the boot trades industry in the campaign, could only be revealed by research into the BTU from 1955.

The Final Draft of the Equal Pay Bill was at last completed and distributed widely. The VTHC EP Committee organised a deputation to see Mr Reid, the Minister for Labour in the Victorian Liberal State Government, to present him with the Draft of the Equal Pay Bill. Mr. Gil Hayes pointed out that NSW had already introduced an Equal Pay Act while the Tasmanian Government was in the process of introducing equal pay, which indicated that Victoria was lagging behind on a State and international basis.

In the deputation to Mr Reid, Kath pointed out that the first deputation to the Victorian Government was made in 1955, and Mr Reid acknowledged the many deputations which had taken place over the years. In all these years, Kath pointed out, nothing had happened. 'We asked you to bring in your own legislation'; she went on to add that Labor members were now taking a further step, by presenting their own legislation. She continued:

> I want to say that over the years this question of equal pay has become more and more urgent. I feel that at this point—it is absolutely urgent. First of all, the development of Victorian industry and the prosperity of the people of Victoria, is the backbone of any prosperity. It is also urgent for any government which wants to hold the confidence of the people to do something about this.[6]

Mr Hayes spoke of how women were moving into industry and pointed out how easy it was for employers to replace men employees with women. All an employer needed to do was apply to the Court for reclassifications in the awards, prove that women could do the particular job as well or better than men, then the job would be seen as women's work and the Court would then move to reclassify the male jobs as female at the lower female rate of pay.

Latoof and Callil Collection, University of Melbourne Archives

The Latoof and Callil factory at Brunswick was reputed to be the largest clothing factory in Australia. By the mid-1960s, most of the employees were married migrant women.

Kath in her contribution went to great lengths to explain the industrial situation in Victoria, the overseas markets, the expansion of industry and the purchasing power of people. She pointed out the dangers inherent when employing women as cheap labor and named various industries in point, drawing attention to the CIG strike of the previous year. She spoke of the growing support for equal pay, the results of the earlier Gallup Poll, and how she and Mr. Hayes were invited to address the Bendigo TLC and the Gippsland THC. She spoke of the number of meetings held on the job and the condemnation of the Victorian Government in not passing this important legislation:

> I feel it is short-sighted for any government at this particular stage not to do something about bringing in equal pay, because it has become the will of the majority of the people and it is the responsibility of any democratic government to carry out the will of the people.[7]

She said the Bill was intended to remove all discrimination based on sex. 'I don't want to read it through. You can read it yourselves. It is quite clear. The Bill will be much better than that brought in by the New South Wales Government or any other government.'[8]

In conclusion, Kath stated:

> We are prepared to fight on. We are prepared to make an urgent question of this at the State Elections in June. We would like to have an early answer to our deputation, as to what your Government proposes to do as soon as we can. We are going to take steps to have this introduced as a private Member's Bill if your Government doesn't see fit to bring in the legislation itself. We hope we won't have to continue on this issue in the elections. We hope you will take this up and do something.[9]

Mr Stout, President of the THC, completed his contribution with: 'Most women would be very appreciative of women's rights and the obligation of people to recognise them. Thank you for seeing us. Repeating what Mrs. Williams says, "We can buckle on our armour and charge".'[10]

Kath did not differentiate in her attitude towards politicians, and wrote to Mr Calwell, the Leader of the Opposition in Federal Parliament asking him to 'lay increased emphasis on Labor's Policy for Equal Pay' when delivering his address to the electors in the forthcoming elections.

Equal Pay Week featured its usual march through the Melbourne city streets, terminating at Parliament House where a Petition supporting equal pay was handed to Mr Stoneham, Leader of the ALP Opposition. Despite a twenty-four hour rail stoppage, 150 men and women representing industrial and white collar unions, job committees, factories, workplaces and women's organisations attended the Buffet Tea.

At the Rank and File Conference in Equal Pay Week, Kath moved a resolution to be put to the forthcoming ACTU

National Conference in Canberra in April. Mrs Audrey Sinclare from the Postal Workers Union seconded the motion. Speaking to her motion, Kath showed how, in 1964, despite the international organisation's directions to which the Australian Government was a party, Federal and State Governments had still failed to introduce equal pay to one third of the workforce, women. She spoke of the allegations that introducing equal pay would have a disastrous effect on the economy, pointing out that many countries in the western world already had equal pay. Kath added that several newly emerging independent countries and socialist countries were already paying equal pay and had written equality into their constitutions in order to ensure all women, married and single, had the right to work.

Kath pointed out that in Australia national wealth continued to increase and productivity had reached ever higher levels. Government statistics had shown that the percentage of women in the workforce had increased and women were an important factor in the accumulation of the wealth of the country. Yet purchasing power had continued to decline, while prices of food, shelter, clothing, education, and transport costs had increased, forcing more married women to work to meet the growing needs of their families:

> This has led the Australian working class to realise that the Equal Pay struggle cannot be isolated from the general wages struggle of the working-class, in particular the Basic Wage.
>
> In both campaigns the trade union movement must link the two questions and lift the consciousness of both men and women, that these two questions are interconnected. Equal Pay is a class question. The employers try to separate the working class into skilled and unskilled; industrial and white collar; men and women. They are united in their efforts to rob the working class of part of their labor in the form of 'profit'.
>
> The Trade Union Movement needs to mobilise that one-third of

the working class (women), if they are to be more successful in their struggles for an increase in the basic wage.

The trade union movement needs a united struggle, men and women together to fight for Equal Pay.[11]

The Conference agreed unanimously to support a resolution in support of the Draft Equal Pay Bill and also endorsed a motion from Marjorie Broadbent:

That the wage discrimination practiced [sic] towards Aborigines needs special attention of the whole Trade Union Movement, for instance, female Aborigines in the Northern Territory, as listed in the Northern Territory Gazette are receiving 1 pound 15 shillings and 3 pence per week and males 2 pound 16 shillings and 6 pence per week.

This meeting calls upon the Trade Union Movement and the ACTU to wage an unremitting struggle for Equal Wages for all Australian workers, black or white.[12]

Kath's motion indicated her strong support for the family wage in the expectation that women would only gain wage benefits by adhering to this concept, one which the trade unions had accepted in the early 1900s, and which had, in fact, delayed the introduction of wage justice for women. It would seem that, although Kath was well aware of the class issue, she overlooked the contradiction when campaigning for a family wage when at the same time demanding equal pay for women, a wage on which widows, single mothers and single women could live in dignity. The two were incompatible. Perhaps Kath was aware of the contradiction but was forced to compromise because the dominant male trade unions supported the family wage and that was where the strength lay.

Kath believed capitalism would never introduce equal pay for work of equal value but, despite holding these views, she gave her utmost in the struggle for pay justice for women. Kath's basis for hope was socialism which, in her opinion, was the only means by which wage justice for women could be achieved; in the meantime, she considered unity in the unions was essential while campaigning for equal pay.

Among the numerous documents I researched for this book, this was the first reference Kath made to socialism or the then socialist countries at a union meeting or conference. Was this variance from previous talks due to her departure from the CPA and her participation as a committee member in the newly formed Communist Party Marxist-Leninist (CPML) or had the minute secretaries omitted earlier references to socialism in the records?

Hilda Smith recalls how, on occasions, to overcome the feeling of isolation and tension, members of the new CPML gathered at Kath's home for social evenings. 'Often we would arrive early to make salads and Kath would be busy fixing tiles on the roof'. She was a very practical woman and besides attending to various repairs around the house, she liked doing things with wood. 'When I was slicing cabbage for the cole-slaw, Kath used to tell me off for not cutting the cabbage finely enough. When now slicing cabbage for coleslaw, I am sure Kath is up there watching me to make sure I slice it finely enough!'

'Kath was always very popular and greatly admired. Fellows used to chase her but she couldn't be bothered. She often said, "having had two husbands was quite enough".' Although Kath in good humour was able to dismiss suggestions of remarrying, she was known to have a 'friend'. She was ultra-cautious about her private life, knowing how rapidly scandal spread throughout the membership of the Party. The 1964 ACTU National Equal Pay Conference took place in Canberra with representatives from many industrial unions, white collar associations and sixteen other organisations from all over Australia.

Canberra was so chosen to coincide with the sitting of Federal Parliament and to accommodate the organisation of a deputation to see the Prime Minister. Efforts to see the Prime Minister were unsuccessful. The Minister for Labour and National Service agreed to meet a deputation, and five women were selected to make presentations.

Mr Monk presided over the Conference and suggested that the Federal Government be asked to grant equal pay on the same basis as was done by the United Kingdom Government. He believed that ACTU Officers would be unsuccessful if seeking equal pay nationally in one fell swoop, but Federal and State Governments had to be prepared to apply the principles applied by the British and New South Wales governments. He added that, if equal pay for equal work could be achieved on this basis, there was no doubt that the trade union movement would claim it as a major success.[13]

Miss Mavis Woodford pointed out how Australia was falling behind other countries in the matter of equal pay: 'A little country named Chad, attached to Ethiopia, has simply written into its Constitution that there shall be no discrimination between the sexes as far as pay is concerned.'[14]

Strike at Monash

There will be no rattle of buckets, no swish of mops and brooms and no cleaning women at Monash University today ... the university's cleaning staff went out on strike early today until 9 o'clock tomorrow morning.

They are protesting against the dismissal of 36 cleaning women.

Herald, 15 October 1964

Kath came out on the attack. There can be no doubt that after nine years of campaigning for equal pay she was tired of all the pussyfooting around. She claimed what Mr Monk had put to the conference had come as a shock. Kath wanted effect to be given to the ILO Conference decision, where one rate of pay for the job be applied irrespective of whether it was performed by male or female, and not for the Government to give equal pay to its own employees over a period of six years. In Victoria, she said, a meeting some time ago had produced a Model Bill preventing members from being sidetracked in the manner that had been put to this Conference. A deputation requested that Mr. Reid, Minister for Labour and Electrical Undertakings, introduce this Bill, but his answer was 'No'. Mr Stoneham, Leader of the Labor Opposition, promised he would introduce the Bill when an opportunity arose.[15]

Kath wanted to know if she was correct in assuming that the ACTU had already made a decision along the lines Mr. Monk had outlined. Mr. Monk intervened at this stage, saying Mrs Williams had made some statements on which he should comment. He drew attention to the fact that had it not been for the ACTU, this Canberra meeting, which was a further step in the campaign for equal pay for work of equal value, would not be taking place. He went on to say that the Conference could not turn into an attack on the ACTU and the action they had taken had done more, in spite of the work Victoria had done for the cause.[16]

Over all the years of EP Committee activities, there was little if any criticism made towards the lack of action by unions or the ACTU and Mr Monk let it be known that 'we' either go along with the decision already adopted by the ACTU or 'we' could retire gracefully.

Kath was now adamant that the campaign was to be conducted for Equal Pay for the Sexes; she was aware of what would transpire if equal pay for equal work was to prevail. She was determined to maintain unity between all women in paid employment and for the struggle to be maintained to abolish the wage differential between males and females irrespective of the job performed. She was shocked when the ACTU was promoting equal pay for equal work. She knew that if this was to succeed, women in professional and semi-professional positions, in the public service and with higher skills, would obtain equal pay while the majority of women in industry, shops, offices and factories, would remain on 75 per cent of the male salary. She knew this move, as proposed by the ACTU, would take the most confident and capable women out of the campaign once having gained equal pay.

The Conference continued with Mr J. Collins moving that the ACTU be requested to make a claim for the same margins for men and women in the clothing trades industry.[17] In support of his motion, Collins expressed his deep concern at McMahon's reply to their deputation and wanted to know why an application to the Conciliation and Arbitration Commission for equal pay had not been made.[18]

President Monk said he thought the Executive should consider the principle that would be involved should the motion be carried, and gave an undertaking that the Executive would consider the matter.[19] In light of what Mr Monk said the motion was withdrawn.

It is interesting to note that, when asked why the ACTU had not brought a claim for equal pay before the Conciliation and Arbitration Commission, Mr Monk did not answer the question but deferred the matter by placing the issue into the hands of the ACTU Executive. Why was the Conference given no explanation for the prolonged reluctance by the ACTU to commence a claim for equal pay?

Mrs Noad of the NSW TLC EP Committee then moved that

Courtesy of Megan McMurchy, Margo Oliver and Jeni Thornley

Cleaners go out on strike, 1964

Conference recommend that the ACTU consider holding a series of stoppages in support of equal pay. The motion was circumvented by an amendment. The Conference went on to congratulate the Victorian Parliamentary Labor Party for bringing down a Bill on Equal Pay before the Victorian Government and pledging its full support.[20] Was this the same Bill Kath had canvassed?

Mr. Albert Monk was born in 1900 and was President of the ACTU from 1934–1943, 1949–1969 and Secretary from 1945–1949 when he was both President of the Melbourne THC and the Victorian ALP. For thirty-five years he had been a leading bureaucrat within the trade union movement and the Labor Party, and it would seem that he had become totally isolated from the people in the workforce and the union members. He took a placatory role and had a reputation for being 'weak'. While Kath had a satisfactory working relationship with him for many years, it could be said this was due to sheer tolerance on her part in trying to get the union bureaucracy to take action. Her clash with Monk at this Conference indicates her patience had run out and she was no longer prepared to remain polite.

In April 1964 the Melbourne *Herald* reported that the Bank of NSW had employed a woman teller on equal pay with male tellers at its head office in Collins Street. It claimed this was 'the first time a woman had "invaded" the traditionally-male job in Melbourne since the Second World War, when banks employed women to replace men who were overseas … [and] This is the only case of a woman bank employee getting the same pay as a male.'

It continued: 'The Secretary of the Trades Hall Council's equal pay committee, Mrs Kath Williams, praised the bank's move as "a step in the right direction. They're setting an example other banks should follow" she said. "It's really a big break-through".'[21]

This incident must have caused a stir within the banking industry. Seventeen women members and five institutional Sub-branch Secretaries met at a meeting of the Ladies Advisory Committee of the Australian Bank Officers Association. The Report from this meeting stated the terms of the Federal Awards under which female officers were employed and the rates of pay for the categories of work performed.

This list of categories indicated lower rates of pay for women, and it was claimed there was 'a long history of banks employing female officers on duties outside these categories without paying them full male rates'.[22] It was suggested that the position could no longer be allowed to go unchallenged.

The meeting heard reports from individuals from each bank substantiating the fact that female officers were being exploited in the manner reported above. The women resolved to ask their Federal Council to investigate the matter and to take it up with the banks. They foreshadowed that, should discussions with the banks prove fruitless, immediate steps be taken through Arbitration proceedings.

In August, the *Guardian* recorded that equal pay was part of the settlement after a week-long strike at Gainsborough Furniture Manufacturing Co. (a subsidiary of Electronic Industries). The company's 250 workers struck for higher wages and were able to gain an increase of 15/- as well as equal pay. Following the signing of the agreement, another furniture manufacturer, Consolidated Home Industries, agreed to give women employees equal pay.

Before the signing of the Gainsborough agreement, three mass meetings were held at the factory, at which workers refused to accept the company's first proposals, to employ women at 75 per cent of the male rate.

Mr. Bill Brown, the State Secretary of the Furniture Trades Society and president of the VTHC EP Committee, saw the whole campaign as *'a major breakthrough in the battle for the general demands of the union movement and for equal pay for women'*.[23]

In August 1964, Kath was a delegate to the 11th World Conference in Japan on Atomic and Hydrogen Bombs. The delegation was required to travel to Nagasaki and, unfortunately, the train taking them there was double-booked. Some of the passengers stood all the way on this lengthy trip while others took turns in sitting. Conditions on the train were difficult to tolerate, the heat was stifling, there was no food or water and, despite the situation and her age, Kath insisted on taking her turn in standing on this long journey; she always was a stickler for fair play.[24]

Dear Hilda,

Sorry to be so long answering your letter. I've been flat out. Starting work straight away after that strenuous trip was no joke. I'm still tired but it was worth it. A mighty Conference and the unity and level so high.

Re your request, what's behind the objections of the ACTU to take a case to Arbitration for EP, my opinion is that they are just scared stiff. They don't want Equal Pay, just the exercise. At the National Equal Pay Meeting, these were their reasons:

1. We wouldn't get it.
2. If we did get it it would result in a Single Unit Wage and bring down men's wages to the level of women's (as if it wasn't a single unit wage now) and what a stink it would cause it they tried to reduce men's wages to women's. The whole TU Movement would be up in arms and they don't like industrial struggle.
3. It would knock the struggle for Equal Pay back for 20 years (no reason given).
4. In answer to the argument that the 1949/50 Female Basic Wage Case increased women's B W from 54% to 75%—they say, It was a different background then—The War—The 90% gained by the Women's Employment Board for women in 14 industries declared essential to the War effort etc- Although they've been campaigning now for 10 years, they say, 'the times not ripe yet'.

If you can make sense out of this, it's more than I can. At the last National Equal Pay meeting, I was away in Japan. Bill Brown was away also. We had no Rep there. So they brought down a recommendation for the ACTU Congress which keeps the Status Quo. However, a number of unions including ours have items on the Agenda for a Case to Arbitration as well as continuing pressure on Governments. How far we'll get I don't know. I'm going to try to move an amendment based on our Union's Agenda Item but whether I'll get away with it or not I don't know. I'll probably have to rush the platform again.

At present, we're trying to sound out and get support from other delegations. I don't know what the Miscellaneous Union will do. Perhaps you could ask what Items are on the Agenda on Equal Pay for discussion at your Equal Pay Committee and try in a quiet way to sound out the propositions. The THC Equal Pay Committee supports a case to Arbitration.

The AEU put the proposition forward some 3 years ago and it was agreed to. Anyway, even if unions don't agree to any change in policy, surely it is only right that delegates should have the right to debate the questions as other items, and not just have an open discussion in support of the Executive's Recommendation. (It is proposed that there be 4 Speakers to the Recommendation but NO debate), otherwise why call for Agenda items?

Well Hilda, I'm writing this in an awful hurry and will have to leave it at that at the moment. Love Kath.

PS. They must be pretty scared—when they take all this trouble to prevent debate. So we must have something which if it hits the light may get more support than they would like.

This one and only letter from Kath to Hilda Smith reveals her feelings of frustration and anger at the continual procrastination of the ACTU towards initiating a case before the Arbitration Commission for equal pay for the sexes. Her reference in the letter to 'rushing the platform again' implies she had carried out this action on previous occasions when being fed up with the delaying tactics used to avoid action.

To be a delegate and participate in the discussion when policies are made during an ACTU Conference requires confidence and courage, and none more so than for women. One can only imagine the courage Kath needed when, among this vast number of confident, powerful men, she 'rushed the platform' to get her arguments across for action on equal pay or other issues pertaining to women and work conditions. Carrying out such an action when surrounded by complacency or in some cases, hostility, calls for commitment and determination, a certain type of character capable of withstanding all opposition, and this was Kath.

9

1965 to 1967: the ACTU gears up for action as Kath begins to retire

Approaching her seventieth year and knowing her working career was coming to an end, Kath knew her requesting, pleading and demanding of equal pay legislation from governments would continue to prove fruitless. Governments were reluctant to legislate equal pay, for once having passed such an Act, women would accept this as justified making it more difficult to remove, while history has shown that the Arbitration Commission can quickly reverse previous decisions. Commercial interests dictate the terms and they consider increased profits through cheap female labour to be valid and their right. Nevertheless, Kath felt it was important to persist in the exposing of discrimination against women.

Although a small number of workplaces were successful in achieving equal pay, Kath and various left-wing union leaders believed the only way possible to get wage justice for women was to initiate a claim for 'one rate of pay for the job performed' before the Arbitration Commission.

On 8 April 1965 the Melbourne *Guardian* published a success story under the heading:

13 LABOR COUNCILS IN EQUAL PAY PACT

The Municipal Employees' Union has signed an agreement with 13 Melbourne municipal councils for equal pay for their female employees.

These councils all had a majority of Labor members. The article went on to say that the agreement provided a powerful lever for use in pressing for similar steps by Liberal-dominated municipal councils. 'It has given an advance fillip to next month's Equal Pay Week activities of the union movement'.[1]

The THC sent a letter to all unions, organisations and 'leading citizens' inviting them to the Equal Pay Conference for shop stewards and to the buffet tea which was to be followed by guest speakers. The leaflet advertising Equal Pay Week 1965 noted, 'For further information about Equal Pay Week contact Mr. R. Wallace, THC Research Officer, or Mrs. Sheila Dunleavy, Butcher's Union, Organisers of the "Week", or Mrs. Kath Williams, Hon. Secretary, THC EP Committee'. It would seem that Mr Wallace and Mrs Dunleavy, who had assisted in the organisation of previous equal pay weeks, had now become the official organisers of the 1965 Equal Pay Week. This was the first indication of Kath relinquishing what had always been her responsibility; however, invitations to attend the buffet tea were sent in her name.

The Equal Pay Conference for Shop Stewards accepted the resolution that pressure be applied on the Victorian Government to give all its employees equal pay and to initiate a Premier's Conference to arrange for the ratification of the ILO Convention No. 100 and Recommendation No. 90 of 1951.

Part 3 of the Resolution was that the Government legislate for equal pay for work of equal value as in the draft Private Member's Bill, which the Opposition had submitted to State Parliament, so that all women workers under State Wages Board Determinations would receive wage justice.

Little if anything was ever mentioned in the documentation of EP Committee meetings, conferences or seminars about the need for pressure to be applied on the ACTU to begin a case for equal pay before the Arbitration Commission.

An Information Sheet on employment figures in 1965, Australia-wide, indicated there were 122 vacancies for every 100 workers, so that work was plentiful but not for women for whom there were only 53 vacancies for every 100 women workers registered. Victoria was the only State where the number of jobs available for women exceeded the number of women seeking employment. In Victoria, there were 130 jobs offering for every 100 women but there were 226 jobs offering for every 100 men. And the jobs available for men were full-time jobs. Half the registrations for employment for women were for commercial and clerical posts.

In April, the *Australian* reported that at a seminar on employment opportunities for women in Sydney, Miss Hilton, President of the International Federation of University Women, said that more married women would have to re-enter the workforce if Australia was to maintain its living standards; and that women were realising that having a good husband, intelligent children and a nice house did not give them enough fulfilment:

> It is one of the most pathetic fallacies of our day that if a woman has a successful husband, a house and family there is nothing else in the world she could possibly want ... that often a woman's lack of opportunities for employment stemmed back to her school days when little or no science was taught to girls because it was not the womanly thing for them to learn.[2]

The newspaper also recorded Miss Alison Stephen, Principal research officer for women from the Department of Labour, as saying 'that although more married women were returning to work today, the growth of our economy would depend on continued expansion of the female workforce'.[3]

Liberal Prime Minister, Sir Robert Menzies refused to move with the times.

A. C. T. U.

National Equal Pay Week

MAY 17 to 21, 1965

Organised in Victoria through
Melbourne Trades Hall Council

PROGRAMME:

Wednesday, May 19: EQUAL PAY CONFERENCE OF:

★ Shop Stewards
★ Official representatives from jobs
★ Representatives of all interested organisations

9.30 a.m. at TRADES HALL COUNCIL CHAMBER; followed by

★ Demonstration through City to Parliament House
★ Report to meeting in Treasury Gardens on Deputation to Government

Thursday, May 20: BUFFET TEA in Ballroom, Trades Hall, 6 p.m., followed by—

★ Special Night at Trades Hall Council meeting.
★ Guest Speaker on Equal Pay
★ Open Discussion

Car Cavalcade through City each day of week prior to and during Equal Pay Week.

| Unions and Unionists begin now to— | ● Organise Job Meetings.
● Elect and book off men and women members to take part in the conference and demonstration.
● Prepare slogans for the demonstration.
● Help compile a panel of speakers by providing one. |

For further information about Equal Pay Week contact Mr R. Wallace, T.H.C. Research Officer (34-5128), or Mrs. Sheila Dunleavy, Butchers' Union (34-3231), Organisers of the "Week," or Mrs. Kath Williams, Hon. Secretary, T.H.C. Equal Pay Committee (34-3015).

SPEAKERS NOTES AND OTHER LITERATURE AVAILABLE

Make Equal Pay Week 1965 the Biggest Ever

FOR THE REASONS, SEE OVERLEAF

Equal Pay Collection, University of Melbourne Archives

The *Australian* of 15 September 1965 had the following headline and comments:

MARRIED WOMEN BAN TO STAY—MENZIES

The Federal Government would retain for the present its prohibition of married women in the Commonwealth Public Service, the Prime Minister, Sir Robert Menzies, said in the House of Representatives yesterday [my emphasis].

The newspaper also reported that, when Mr Hayden drew attention to the recent statement made by Mr McMahon,

Minister for Labour and National Service, 'that more married women should be employed by industry,' Mr Menzies replied, 'the Government had looked at it from time to time but the marriage bar was a matter of policy',[4]

Early in 1965, the Shop Assistants' Union was successful in obtaining equal margins for women in certain occupations, margins being the extra allowance paid for skills over and above the basic wage.

In September the Brisbane *Courier Mail* announced that women in the South Australian Public Service were to obtain equal pay to be phased in over five years, while schoolteachers were to obtain equal pay the following year.[5]

In October Mr Jordan, Secretary of the VTHC, gave a report on the EP Committee to the THC, outlining a plan of action for the unions to undertake around the campaign for Equal Pay. Among the points he made was a request that the Labour College Film Centre be asked to film the activities, that the THC devote the next meeting of Council to a discussion on the decision of the Wages Board and that all unions be notified of decisions made.[6]

The VTHC Minutes for October recorded the move taken by the Retail Traders' Association of Victoria who returned to the Wages Board seeking to reduce the wages of female shop assistants by £3.17.0. This action was in retailiation to the Board's decision earlier in the year to grant shop assistants equal margins.[7]

Obtaining any increase in wages required great effort, support and expense and often succeeded only after strike action. Going through all the procedures necessary to gain a wage increase and being successful didn't automatically mean that it all ended there. Employers always resisted wage increases and, when granted, almost always sought a reversal of the decision.

Hilda Smith became assistant secretary of the EP Committee of the Federated Miscellaneous Workers' Union and undertook a survey of female photographic workers. Apart from interviewing women in her own workshop, she visited nine other workplaces covered by her union. She recalls sitting up all night typing over 100 copies on an old typewriter. Her questionnaire sought women's attitudes to:

If Women Get Equal Pay—

- Will they lose their jobs to men?
- Will women have to do heavier work?
- Can employers afford equal pay?
- Are women less capable than men?
- Why do you think employers refuse to give equal pay?
- Would you like a speaker to visit your place of employment to discuss Equal Pay?

Having collected approximately seventy replies, Hilda spent time at home collating the answers and typing the final document. She was pleased with the results and response from the women and was full of enthusiasm when handing the completed questionnaires to the Secretary of the union. In anticipation of a report on the survey and findings appearing in the Union Journal, when some time had elapsed and nothing had transpired, she was shocked when the Union Secretary told her he had unfortunately 'lost' all the material.

Marjorie Broadbent recalled attending the Christmas break-up party of the Miscellaneous Workers Union EP Committee held under the stairway in the basement of the Trades Hall, a very gloomy and dingy atmosphere for a party. The venue was selected by the Union.

Two circulars were sent to all affiliated unions from the THC EP Committee, one advising them of the forthcoming 1965 Equal Pay Week and the other being a programme for the Week. The need for participation and commitment to the various tasks required in organising the Week was stressed, and attention was drawn to the making of a film on equal pay which was commenced during the previous Equal Pay Week and was to be completed during Equal Pay Week.[8]

While the initial circular highlighted the gains that eleven years of campaigning had achieved (for example the NSW Labor Government's *Industrial Arbitration (Female Rates) Amendment Act* No. 42 of 1958, and the South Australian Labor Government's promise of an equal pay Act), the fact remained that the majority of Australia's growing workforce were still suffering the double exploitation of unequal pay which, in turn, held down all levels through competition between the cheap labour of women and the dearer labour of men. As well, there was substantial evidence that the resistance of employers and

---

HOSPITAL STAFFS STOP IN PAY LOG PROTEST
WALK OUT HITS SERVICES: CALL FOR NATIONAL STRIKE

More than 2000 workers at three big city hospitals and four country institutions held protest stoppages today.

The stoppages were in protest against the log of claims drawn up by Victorian hospital managements, which the Hospital Employees' Federation says seeks pay cuts.

In another move in the dispute today, Victorian members of the No. 1 branch of the federation's Federal Council decided to ask the Council for a nationwide stoppage …

This is the first time the union has threatened a national stoppage.

Herald, 3 November 1965

---

governments to equal pay was hardening, as was their resistance to any wage rise for any section of workers.

Meanwhile, the Bolte Liberal Government in Victoria continued to refuse to legislate for equal pay or even grant it to its own employees, despite repeated demands by the trade unions, the Victorian Teachers' Union and public service organisations. Employers continued to plead for more women in the workforce, and the Victorian Employers' Federation, in co-operation with the Department of Labour, Australian Industries Development Association, and the Committee for Economic Development of Australia organised a National Conference on 'Women Who Work' for May 3 and 4 1966.

Prior to the start of the conference, a picket line of clothing industry unionists, with banners demanding equal pay for women, demonstrated outside the conference building until broken up by a police order.

When reporting the first day of the conference, the *Australian* noted that a meeting of the Cabinet prevented Mr Bury, the Federal Minister for Labour and National Service, from making his speech. 'But it was delivered on his behalf by the Victorian Liberal MHR, Mr Don Chipp' who later resigned from the Party and started the Australian Democrats 'to keep the bastards honest'. Mr Chipp read the lengthy, prepared speech, part of which said:

> The Government does not oppose the principle of equal wages for men and women for work of equal worth, but if there were equal pay there would be less opportunity for pay rises to be made in the general wage area, ... [and] the question of the cost to the economy had to be considered.[9]

The nursing profession was long noted for its docility and endured its bleakest period during the fifties when gains were at an all-time low. While NSW nurses had gained an increase in the female basic wage from 54 per cent to 75 per cent of the male rate by 1950, nothing was to follow until, with 'the awakening of nurses in the 1960s to their economic disadvantages.

From 1947 they also enjoyed the same standard working hours as other workers but, by the 1960s, the nurses were becoming increasingly dissatisfied with their pay and conditions and the NSWNA was forced to act. Three thousand nurses packed the Sydney Town Hall to air their grievances and urge support for a pay increase. Following the meeting, the nurses distributed leaflets as they marched through the Sydney streets while a deputation went to Parliament House to tackle the local members.[10]

The New South Wales Nurses Association (NSWNA) began to have more success'.[11] At the NSWNA annual conference in 1966, Mr A. H. Jago, a member of the Liberal-Country Party coalition, and newly elected Minister for Health in NSW, chastised the nurses for permitting Trade Union Councils to attend meetings in regional areas. He warned the nurses how 'mass agitation aimed at arousing emotion and excitement among the participants is a dangerous weapon. There will always be people and not only communists, anxious to exploit you for political purposes, and it is hard to keep them out.'[12] On the conclusion of the Minister's address, the NSWNA president, Sally Shiels, thanked him for his 'paternal interest' in their affairs but added that the NSWNA would take whatever action was considered advisable to 'get salary justice'.

Nurses in Melbourne were also active in campaigning for increased wages and improved working conditions and took to the streets in vast numbers.

Following Equal Pay Week, Kath gave a report on the Week's activities to the April Meeting of the ACTU State Branch EP Committees. She began with the meeting of VTHC representatives and shop stewards, the cavalcade and the march to Parliament House where the assembled campaigners were addressed by Mr Stoneham, leader of the ALP in Victoria.

In November, the *Australian* stated that the ACSPA, which represented 250 000 white collar workers, had decided to ask the Federal Government to appoint a Federal Commission to examine the status of women, including the special role in the community of working wives. And that the Association was also requesting a Women's Bureau be established within the Department of Labour.[13]

It was during 1966, when some comrades felt Kath needed company and support that a woman comrade went to live with Kath at her home in Clifton Hill but, after living together for some months, the situation became untenable. Ted, a regular visitor with his bottle of whisky, showed little concern for his sister. The woman comrade left the house.

The new Australian Communist Party—the CPML—began to crumble. Meetings were irregular, and Ted Hill, President of this Party, true to his conspiratorial mindset, instructed some members not to fraternise with one another or even recognise each other in the street. Ted Hill pressured Kath into withdrawing from all activity.[14] This isolation was destroying Kath and she was desolate. Her belief in socialism was as strong as ever, but events over recent years had led to her disillusionment with the leaders, people she had been closely associated with over many years and had greatly admired. It was as if the very foundation of her life had come apart. The close-knit family had gone.

Despite this inner despair, Kath was able to appear as if in total control, as if all was well with the world, and she succeeded in hiding her pain from most of her friends and family who were unaware of the extent of her suffering. A few of Kath's friends noticed how her garden, which had given her so much joy, gradually became sadly neglected while the colourful array of hanging baskets and pot plants withered and died. But how does one approach a person who has always maintained a private distance on feelings and personal matters?

It is doubtful if those who associated with or had occasional contact with Kath knew of her tremendous effort over the years for pay justice for women. She wasn't the type of person who continually spoke of herself or what she was doing; on the contrary, when speaking to others of the campaign, she constantly stressed the need for more participation and more action and highlighted what others had done or achieved.

Kath was seventy-two years of age and had reached the stage where she was unable to perform many of the responsibilities required of her and was gradually withdrawing. While involvement had always been Kath's way of life, her position as organiser with the LTU was very demanding, had become wearing and her attendance at THC meetings had diminished.

Yet, she was fearful of relinquishing her position in the union. The union rules required three months' notice of termination of employment before retirement or resignation, but if in poor health one could finish sooner. Kath was also aware that because of her age, there would be no worker's compensation should she have an accident while on the job. She finally made the decision and wrote to her doctor son requesting a medical certificate to enable her to cease work. She told him of her ill health and her decision to give up work.[15] The certificate arrived and she was able to resign in 1967 and collect her allowance of one year's salary.

Kath's life was now to change. From the very beginning of becoming an organiser with the LTU, knowing she was contributing to the well-being of people, she had established a career path which gave her a feeling of job satisfaction. She

179

was able to look forward to each day's events being different from those of the previous day and offering new challenges. Her ability to deal with recalcitrant hotel managers and the cut and thrust of disputation was an everyday occurrence, and her association with the women union members had always been stimulating. Kath was ill-prepared for retirement and, with her health deteriorating, she became desperately lonely and isolated, feeling she was no longer needed and of no use to society. She commenced writing a book but found the lack of company, stimulation and involvement with people unbearable.[16]

Working in male-dominated structures is particularly difficult for women. Two decades earlier, in 1942, like Kath, Muriel Heagney showed loyalty to her party and reluctance to publicly disparage the labor movement of which she had for so long been a part. However, in a letter to a fellow unionist, she wrote:

> Frankly I have given up hope of achieving anything worth while immediately because here in Australia the Labour [sic] Movement and the ACTU executive officers are so terribly reactionary in their views on women workers. One commences about half a mile behind the starting post in a mile race here when women are involved in any issue, and the trade union officials and Labor [sic] ministers as a rule are more difficult to deal with than many bad employers of labour.[17]

Even though Muriel felt like this at the time, like Kath, she continued to campaign.

10

The ACTU changes policy: from urging legislation to preparing a claim for equal pay

By the end of 1966, the combined efforts of the unions and equal pay committees had produced a number of successes, more frequently within the professions and the organised workforce. Some Labor State governments began to phase in equal pay for several categories of female employees from the late 1950s, but Liberal Governments, both Commonwealth and State, would not introduce equal pay in their Public Services. These governments constantly suggested that unions should seek equal pay through the Arbitration Commission, but the ACTU would not take up this suggestion having resolved, in 1964, 'that the unions be advised that ACTU policy is to continue the campaign for the Government to legislate relating to Equal Pay and this precludes the ACTU at this stage, from taking a major case to the Commission for Equal Pay'.[1]

The many years of campaigning for equal pay, and the continual passing of responsibility from the Arbitration Commission and Wage Tribunals to governments and back over the provision of equal pay became a game played out in almost every wage tribunal. It was obvious that these institutions were not prepared to oppose governments. All members of such commissions and tribunals are beholden to governments for their livelihood, and history reveals their unwillingness to set a precedent. The entire situation was a farcical exercise where almost all of the claims relating to the implementation of equal pay were rejected.

Part of this farce was in the shifting terminology which was designed to play politics, while some of the complexities in this rejection included legislation. In New South Wales, following the passage of the *Industrial Arbitration (Female Rates) Amendment Act of New South Wales*, 1958, No. 42, the equal pay formula applied to teachers and to women in the professional division of the Public Service other than dietitians, physiotherapists, social workers and child welfare officers. For females employed in the Administrative and Clerical Division, changes in its structure had altered the application of the equal pay provisions since 1959. Initially, equal pay applied only to those in graded positions, that is, above the base range. However, an agreement was made in 1962 to include females on the base range at the fifth year of the incremental scale. Following an agreement in July 1964, there was a reconstruction of the grading scale and all females attaining twenty-one years of age were placed on clerical work of the same type as performed by males and received the full male rate of pay. Females employed in predominantly female occupations—such as typists, stenographers, accounting machinists, etc.—were at all times excluded from the equal pay provisions. In the case of these positions, the wage was the female basic wage plus the appropriate margin for that position. In the General Division adult females doing work similar to males were paid the male rate.[2]

In Victoria, female officers in the Professional Division, were paid less than males occupying corresponding positions. Prior to the introduction of the total wage in August 1967, females received 75 per cent proportion of the male base rate. Females, generally, were not employed in the Administrative Division, but in the Technical and General Division where normal female classifications of typist, assistant, etc., applied. In this division only a few positions were open to both sexes, and, in these, the female positions were placed in a lower grade on the scale than the male equivalents, on the ground that the duties were not strictly comparable. Following a decision of the Industrial Appeals Court in 1965 awarding equal margins (extra pay for extra skills) to female nurses employed under the Hospital Nurses' Board determination, the Public Service Board introduced equal margins for psychiatric nurses employed within the Service. As in the case of other nurses they received 75 per cent of the male basic wage.[3]

Big headlines in the *Australian* of 9 November 1966 featured:

> EQUAL PAY BID FOR GOVERNMENT WOMEN DOCTORS
> *The Public Service Arbitrator, Mr. E. A. Chambers, has been asked to grant equal pay to women doctors employed by the Commonwealth Government.*
>
> The Repatriation Medical Officers' Association and the Commonwealth Medical Officers' Association are seeking a new base salary level of $6420–$8308. About 600 doctors employed by the Commonwealth Government, men and women, are covered by the claim.

The article went on to show that women doctors received an annual salary of $400 less than men.

Meanwhile, after many years of having its equal pay claims dismissed, the Clothing Trades Union in 1961 decided to claim for equal margins, a move which eventually established a precedent in the industry and proved to be beneficial to women. A Full Bench of the Arbitration Commission heard the case but there was no decision until April 1967. Both parties agreed it was unjust that women performing the same work as men should be paid a lower margin and the decision granting equal margins for equal work was granted.

In concluding its decision, the Commission stated:

It seems to us to be industrially unjust that women performing the same work as men should be paid a lower margin, We endorse the principle of equal margins for equal work. We have examined the work done to see whether work done by men and women is the same and where it is and where the current male rate is a proper evaluation of the work we have awarded that rate to females.[4]

The Bench stated:

We invite the unions, the employers and the Commonwealth to give careful study to these questions (i.e. equal rates, abolition of locality differentials and economic repercussions) with the knowledge that the Commission is available to assist by conciliation or arbitration in the resolution of the problem.[5]

It would seem that this was a deliberate decision to facilitate the introduction of the Total Wage. However, only a small section of women in the Clothing Trades Industry was eligible for this increase.

This case and its decision on payment of margins were the underlying factors which brought about the change in policy of the ACTU in taking a case to Arbitration. With the Arbitration Commission affirming the concept of equal margins for equal work, the ACTU was encouraged to act more vigorously.

The announcement had come at last. Almost twenty years of talking, writing, demonstrating, coercion, and agitation by Kath, the EP Committees, the UAW, women's organisations, and, in the main, various left-wing unions, was at last coming to fruition. As part of the continuum of effort, it is important here not to overlook the efforts of Muriel Heagney and all the other women who over the many years participated in the campaign.

The most important of the ACTU Executive's recommend-

ations was that Congress authorise the Executive to prepare material in support of a claim for Equal Pay for work of Equal Value to be pursued by Conciliation and/or Arbitration as may seem suitable in the future. The Executive also recommended that Equal Pay Committees co-ordinate activities through the ACTU State Branches for developing a National Campaign to achieve this important objective.

The concept of equal pay for work of equal value was a new move.

Table 1: Three important concepts

equal pay	work of equal value	pay justice for women
for the same job	equal pay for different jobs of the same worth ? nurse = turner and fitter	a liveable wage so women can live with dignity independently

EARLY MOVE FOR EQUAL PAY LIKELY

was the headline for an article by Geoffrey Gleghorn in *The Australian Financial Review* of 7 June 1967:

Initiative for a concerted move for equal pay for work of equal value, irrespective of sex, is likely to come from a meeting of the High Council of Commonwealth Public Service Organisations in Melbourne.

The equal pay move would follow Monday's pronouncement by the Full Bench of the Arbitration Commission. In its joint statement on the national wage cases the Bench gave the green light to unions and organisations to seek gradual implementation of the equal pay principle.

The ACTU, in support of the claim for Equal Pay for Work of Equal Value, notified all the trade union and professional organisations of the decision and asked for their assistance.

The ACSPA notified its affiliated bodies that a meeting of representatives from their affiliated associations had met and decided that, in relation to the 1968 National Wage Case, discussions were to take place with the ACTU, the High Council of Commonwealth Public Service Organisations and the result of these discussions would be conveyed to them.[6] The points agreed to were:

(1) EQUAL PAY

That this meeting of ACSPA affiliated associations draws attention to the principle of equal pay for equal work established in the decision of the Arbitration Commission through the Clothing Trades Case and 1967 National Wage Case pronouncement.

ACSPA calls on all parties including the Commonwealth Government to acknowledge this principle and to take immediate practical steps towards its implementation.

Attention was also drawn to the arbitration action to initiate moves to eliminate the amount that would equal the basic wage difference between male and female workers and indicated its support in the test cases to be arranged.

Proposals were also made to take action in pursuance of pay rates which should incorporate salary amounts equal to erstwhile margins payable to male workers where female workers perform work of equal character and value.

The ACSPA and the meeting also applauded divisions and affiliated associations that were actively campaigning for equal pay and urged all other divisions and affiliated associations to actively plan and participate in equal pay campaigns. Proposals were also made to take action in pursuance of pay rates which should incorporate salary amounts equal to erstwhile margins payable to male workers where female workers perform work of equal character and value.

While the activity of the THC Committee on equal pay had declined, and Kath's involvement was less than it had been, elsewhere other women began organising around numerous women's issues. Mrs Julie Dahlitz and Mrs N. Murray-Smith were involved in organising a Public Seminar on Working Mothers and their Children, a further effort in understanding the constantly developing increase of married women into the workforce and the problems faced.

EQUALITY FOR WOMEN TALK OUT.
WILSON HALL—MELBOURNE UNIVERSITY,
FRIDAY, OCTOBER 6, 1967

The Talk Out was organised by the Technical Teachers' Association of Victoria and the Victorian Secondary Teachers' Association. Sponsoring organisations were the Australian Council of Salaried and Professional Associations, the National Council of Women, the Soroptimists Club, Victorian Women Graduates, the VTHC EP Committee, the Hospital Employees' Federation No. 2 Branch, the Women's Central Organisations Committee, the ALP, the Senior Mistresses' Association, the Technical Schools Headmistresses' Association, the Business & Professional Women's Club, Action for Better Education, and the Union of Australian Women.[7]

The program topics included philosophical, political and historical aspects of women's position, economic equality, educational equality, employment equality and a report from the Working Mothers Seminar.

In her contribution to the Talk Out, Mrs Kathleen Trend, former President of the Victorian Status of Women Association, said, 'a College should be established in Melbourne for the older women who wanted to go back to work but lacked qualifications because they married and had children early in life'.[8] Mr J. McLaren, a lecturer at the Melbourne Secondary Teacher's College, made a profound comment, saying, 'society's view gave men an air of arrogance'. He went on to say how this arrogance in men rendered them not less than human but something inhuman.[9] Mr Galbally, Labor Leader in the Victorian Legislative Council, also addressed the gathering.

In the same month, the Victorian Secondary Teachers Association distributed the following circular:

TEACHERS TRIBUNAL[10]

For 21 years, the Victorian Teachers Tribunal has consistently refused to concede the principle of equal pay for male and female teachers bound by its awards.

This policy reached its absurd peak when the Tribunal fixed differential salaries for senior positions. For example, the Assistant Director-General of Education was worth $12,000 p.a. if male but only $11,574 if female.

The circular went on to detail the various discrepancies in salary between female and male school principals, and described how the Teachers Tribunal never justified its blatant discrimination against women teachers and the only direct indications of its attitude had been in recent years when the Tribunal's Chairman (Mr L. F. C. Garlick) issued statements that his Tribunal felt that any equal pay decision for teachers should rest with the State government.

Sir Henry Bolte, for his part, found it easy to reply to Mr Garlick and his Tribunal: 'Despite what Mr Garlick may say, this matter (of equal pay) is entirely up to independent wage Tribunals and Courts'.[11]

The circular also pointed out that in other States and countries the teaching profession had been in the vanguard of the struggle to end discrimination on the basis of sex. In New South Wales, South Australia, Tasmania and New Zealand, equal pay was either in force or was on the way in. Victoria was now the social isolate in this matter.

As the major autonomous secondary teacher's organisation in the Commonwealth of Australia, the Victorian Secondary Teachers Association, advocated the immediate implementation of equal pay for equal work and the immediate ending of all discrimination on the basis of sex.[12]

The VSTA Circular shows Mr Bolte's arrogance.

With the developing interest by professional women into the dearth of women in the professions, senior positions and academia, answers were sought on whether this resulted from lack of interest, opportunity, encouragement, or stemmed from problems within the education system.

Professor Schonell, in his January 1967 Presidential address to ANZAAS, said,

> While there are many causes for early leaving girls in secondary courses, undoubtedly one strong force is the outmoded attitudes towards higher education for girls still held by educated members of the public, parents and even teachers. These outmoded attitudes lessen motivation and aspiration and deprive the girl of encouragement from people most likely to influence her. They are reinforced by the opposition in Australia to advancing women to posts of responsibility in government departments and to the primitive attitudes which have prevailed towards the continued employment of married women. These conditions must make us one of the most backward nations of the Western world in the training and adequate employment of women with higher educational qualifications.[13]

Kath again came to the fore when, in February 1968, the VTHC EP Committee sent out a circular to all affiliated unions letting them know how it continually promoted the cause of equal pay and challenged every attempt to downgrade women's wages.[14] Attention was drawn to the vigilance of the Committee in preventing 2000 women shop assistants in Victoria in 1965 from losing full equal pay which they had received since 1916.[15] Also noted was a report in the *Age*

Equal Pay for Equal Work is becoming more urgent each year for both Men and Women Workers

THERE are over one million women workers in Australia and their numbers are growing rapidly. They make up almost one third of all Australian wage and salary earners. (Commonwealth Statistics, March, 1965.)

The Commonwealth Treasury, in a report issued on 27/4/65, predicted that over the next five years the rate of increase of women workers in the total work force will be double that of men workers. The report also says that by 1976 married women are expected to provide about 13.4 per cent of the total compared with about 11 per cent in 1966, 10 per cent now, and 7 per cent in 1954. Married women will provide about 23 per cent of the increase over the 10 years.

On 15/1/65, the Victorian Employers' Federation urged its members to make more use of women workers. It pointed out that there were 1,013,618 women between 15 and 50 years of age who don't, but could, work. The Federation claimed that Australia cannot afford to have these women remain out of industry. Over the last seven years the number of married women in regular employment has increased by 88 per cent.

It is vital to every Australian worker that this growing body of women workers is not used by employers to reduce wage levels that exist now. It is also vital that women workers are not used to dampen down the demands of workers for higher wages, better conditions, and a greater share of production generally.

There must therefore be, in addition to the immediate vigilance and action of individual Unions in relation to their own awards and industries, a continuing campaign individually and collectively aimed at attaining Equal Pay for the Sexes.

Australian Council of Trade Unions' policy on Equal Pay is that affiliated Unions and State Branches approach Governments to bring down legislation providing that all wage-fixing authorities shall eliminate wage and salary differentiations based on sex. Further that the Commonwealth Government be pressed to implement ILO Convention No. 100 and Article 5 of Recommendation 90 of equal remuneration for men and women workers for work of equal value. This Convention and Recommendation was adopted in 1951, but the Australian Government has so far failed to ratify them although they have been ratified by many countries less wealthy than Australia.

EQUAL PAY FOR EQUAL WORK – WHO'S RESPONSIBILITY ?

The demand for Equal Pay for work of equal value is as vital for Men as for Women

All workers must unite and campaign in a common cause for Equal Pay for the sexes

Industrial Print, Carlton—34-2730, 34-4336   *Authorised by M. C. C. Jordan, Secretary Melbourne Trades Hall Council.*

Leaflet issued in the late 1960s

for 8 February 1968 which spoke of the recent attempt in the Arbitration Commission to set aside the first Equal Pay Award for women in Commonwealth Hostels granted by Commissioner Clarkson and the need to vigorously oppose these threats. A call was made for all unions to support the decision of the ACTU and to rally in support of equal pay for work of equal value, pointing out that this was not an issue for women only, but an issue for the whole trade union movement.[16] Kath's signature appeared on this circular together with Bill Brown's, the President: she may have resigned from her job, but she had not relinquished her position on the EP Committee.

Correspondence to the secretary of the VTHC, indicated that discussions had taken place between the President of the EP Committee, Bill Brown, George Seelaf of the Meat Industry Union and Mr Wallace, Industrial Officer of the VTHC. Concern was expressed at the declining interest in Equal Pay Week and the future of the Committee responsible for its organisation. It would seem that these three men had decided on a program for the next equal pay week, which was to include a reception organised by the VTHC Executive and conducted on a 'higher plane'. Those invited were two representatives from each affiliated union (officials), affiliated unions, women's groups, women's organisations, the ACSPA, the High Council of CPSO, the VTHC EP Committee, the State Parliamentary Labor Party and the ALP.[17] This was an obvious attempt to involve more powerful and influential people on to the committee.

When the 1968 Equal Pay Week was approaching, Bill Brown notified the Equal Pay Week Committee that Mrs K. Williams had *not* resigned as Secretary of this committee and would attend the reception with a friend.[18] It would appear that Bill Brown, as President of the VTHC EP Committee, sent this note to prevent Kath from feeling overlooked, especially when, over the years, she had constantly appealed to the various trade unions to take an active role in organising this special week. Now that others were involved and taking the initiative, it would seem that Kath was in danger of becoming another forgotten toiler in an unfeeling structure.

The ACTU Executive proceeded with the claim for equal pay for work of equal value and all necessary steps were taken to implement the claim. State Trade and Labor Councils, Secretaries of Affiliated Unions, the Secretary of ACSPA and the Secretary of the High Council, were all requested to forward details to the ACTU of legislation, determinations, awards, agreements, and administrative decisions and of any other method where the principle of equal pay had been implemented, or was in the process of being implemented, or was foreshadowed for some specific time in the future.

How ironic it was that the ACTU decided to mount a case for equal pay during the very year Kath retired from work.

The greater number of women then in the workforce, together with the campaigning for equal pay, inspired the holding of the Symposium on Work Evaluation In Relation To Equal Pay, for which documents were prepared by the Women's Bureau, Department of Labour and National Service, (1968) Melbourne, for distribution. These documents for the first time outlined research into women employees, noting the various number of women's occupations, whether these occupations were receiving equal pay and, if so, through which structure: Awards of arbitral authorities, legislative action, legislative action and awards, etc, administrative action of governments or established practice.[19]

Now that the ACTU had made the decision to go to arbitration, things really got under way. Towards the end of the year, white-collar associations were notified by the ACSPA of a meeting to consider all aspects of the welfare of working women and the need to establish a committee to plan action to improve conditions. It was suggested that this committee would co-ordinate the work of all the diverse committees now operating on issues such as equal pay but would in no way replace them. However, it was intended to be more than just another 'equal pay committee'. In the run up to the equal pay case, the committee was to call for affiliations from various unions and other interested groups while its objectives were to be industrial in nature and have endorsement through the ACSPA. This development led to the formation of the Victorian Employed Women's Organisation Council (VEWOC).

We do not know how Kath felt about the formation of VEWOC, but with her experience of trade unionism and her frequent statements on the need for unity, there can be no doubt that she was well aware of the aim of the white-collar unions to gain equal pay for their own members. She was constantly alert to the threat of splitting the alliance of employed women resulting in the more educated, skilled and confident women obtaining equal pay while the majority of working women continued to be disregarded. Did she see this new organisation as splitting the campaign, as usurping control of the equal pay campaign away from the VTHC EP Committee or was she pleased to see women from the white-collar unions becoming more involved in the campaign?

VEWOC held its first public meeting in the Lower Melbourne Town Hall on 10 April 1968, with Don MacSween as Chairman. Among the list of prestigious speakers, were Kathleen Trend, James Munro, Joyce Cameron, Diana Sonenberg, Bill Brown, Mary Hiscock and Roy Cameron. MacSween and Bill Brown were both members of the Victorian Trades Hall Council EP Committee.[20]

Kath was in attendance at this meeting and invited Marjorie

Broadbent to have a drink with her following the meeting. Kath took this opportunity to tell Marjorie that Ted Hill had ceased calling the central Committee of the CPML together.[21] There were no more meetings. Kath was further isolated and alone. With all this time on her hands, she spent more time writing her book.

In 1968, Hilda Smith who had been mentored by Kath to take her place on the EP Committee, delivered the THC Research and Information Bureau Speech during Equal Pay Week. She began:

> Mr. S. M. Gilmour of the Victorian Employers Federation, when summing up the results of the 'Women at Work' Conference recently held in Melbourne, remarked 'that the equal Pay issue was not one of major importance in the total problems associated with the status and opportunities for women in the work force'.
>
> With due respect to Mr. Gilmour and certainly acknowledging the need for equal opportunity, and more assistance to working mothers, I unequivocally state that equal pay is THE major issue for the people concerned. And not just for women but for working men too.

Hilda pointed out that despite women receiving less money then men, they were forced to pay the same rents, fares and prices for goods and services as men:

> Most women work because they just cannot manage on their husband's wages. But what of the single women, the widows, the deserted wives; living on a take home wage of around $26 a week; many of them with dependents to provide for. I hope no one tries to tell them that they go to work because they are bored with daytime television programmes.
>
> The classic answer to the demand for EP is that the economy could not stand it. This was said over 100 years ago when the demand was raised to stop children under ten working twelve hours a day.

Hilda went on to speak of the enormous profits being made and the ability of industry to pay equal pay:

> It is, and always has been a catch cry, a diversion from the real issue, which is that it is a woman's RIGHT to receive equal pay. Unequal pay is discrimination based on sex, and not anything else, and is used by employers to keep the work force divided.

Once again, a woman was expressing arguments in favour of equal pay, arguments which had been constantly repeated for more than sixty years. She used statistics to indicate how women's work was demeaned as of less value while men's work had higher value, hence higher wages. Hilda concluded her talk:

> If we had equal pay there would be none of this classifying of jobs as female ones, as an excuse to legalise cheap labour. To start with, the female basic wage must be lifted to that of the male rate, and not at the expense of margins either.
> There is no justification whatever for this inequality to continue and it is high time that men and women got angry enough to demand that this discrimination cease.

Having made a decision to present a claim for equal pay, the Executive of the ACTU chose the Meat Industry Interim Award as a test case, partly because it covered a substantial proportion of female workers and partly because it was one of the few awards with equal margins for adult females.

In the weeks prior to and during the 1969 Equal Pay Case hearing, the unions were active in distributing thousands of leaflets on the job, addressing meetings at numerous meat works and other industries and made great efforts to gain publicity for the campaign.

As Jim Hagen recounts, average weekly earnings increased in the [nineteen] fifties and sixties. So did the gross national product. Between 1947 and 1969, the real value of award rates increased by 31 per cent while real earnings during this same period rose by 78 per cent. This wages drift resulted from both over-award and overtime payment. While women were expected to work overtime in some industries, the vast majority of women did not benefit from working overtime and nor had they received over-award payments.[22]

11

The equal pay case of 1969

R. J. Hawke, an ex-Rhodes scholar qualified in both economics and law, had held the position of research officer with the ACTU since 1958. Hawke supervised the research in preparation for the equal pay case and as the advocate for the ACTU presented the case. His qualifications and experience gave him 'immense advantages in working up the kind of case the Commission wanted to hear and in examining evidence and argument put before the Court by employers.[1]

In view of the complications that would arise from a case based on equal pay for work of equal value, it would seem that the ACTU decided instead to claim for an amount of $8.20 per week to be inserted into the female award, thereby eliminating the 25 per cent differential between male and female basic wage rates. This would achieve one rate for the job, and a measure of equal pay. The claim further sought increases be paid to all females irrespective of the work they performed. The ACSPA, the HCCPSO and several other white-collar unions intervened in the case, as did the Commonwealth Government.

Several employers in the manufacturing industries were willing to pay equal pay; however, employers in predominantly female industries—clothing, retailing, banking and commerce —were strongly opposed to the concept.

The Meat Industry Union covered the expenses of the

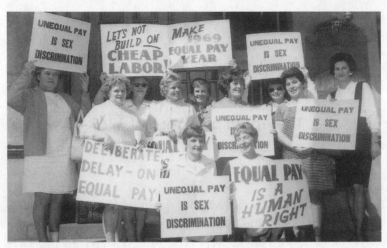

Author's Private Collection

Women from the meat works demonstrating prior to the hearing of the 1969 Equal Pay Case

women shop stewards to gather at the court and listen to the case presented. Before entering the court, the women with their placards walked up and down the pavement demonstrating their views and chanting slogans on equal pay. Several demonstrations through the city streets took place during the hearings and women from various industries and the Union of Australian Women participated.

I was able to attend the hearing and, on entering the court, immediately felt the oppressiveness of the atmosphere. People spoke in whispers as they do at funerals and eventually we ceased talking for it was impossible to relate in such an atmosphere. The door opened at the rear of the Court and in walked the judge and commissioners. All males. Everyone stood to attention until the important men were seated and the proceedings began. The seats in front of the Bench were all occupied by men, the 'fors', and 'againsts'.[2]

The evidence given by Bob Hawke was profound and

irrefutable. Numbers of women sat silent in the court and listened to the proceedings day after day. 'It was as if we were mute, while the men presented evidence for and against our worth'.[3]

EQUAL PAY DECISION 1969[4]
(From the Meat Industry Union News-Letter)

The Full Bench of the Commonwealth Conciliation & Arbitration Commission rejected the claim by the Unions and stated 'While we accept the concept of "equal pay for equal work", implying as it does the elimination of discrimination based on sex alone, we realise that the concept is difficult of precise definition and even more difficult to apply with precision.'

The extent of which [sic] we are prepared to implement the principle of equal pay for equal work is to introduce into the Award (Meat Industry Award (Ed.)) [sic] and determinations (Public Service Determination (Ed.)) before us the principles of the State Acts to the extent of the claims.

In the words of the Commission—'While we accept the concept of "equal pay for equal work" may sound fine but what women workers want is the same rate of pay for the job they are doing as a man would receive for doing the same job.'

The Commission laid down nine principles to be taken into consideration by Commissioners when deciding which women were to receive equal pay. Part of these principles include—'The female must be an adult; it must be established that certain work covered by the Award is performed by both males and females; the work performed by both males and females under such award should be of the same or like nature and of equal value, but mere similarity in name of male and female classifications may not be enough to establish that males and females do work of a like nature, consideration is to be given to whether the female employees are performing the same work or work of a like nature as male employees and doing the same range and volume of work as male employees under the same conditions.

'The above are only some of the principles, so it can be readily seen that the "cards are stacked" against women receiving equal pay.'

The Commission dodged the issue.

As a result of this decision, approximately 18 per cent of females in the workforce received equal pay, the majority being in the public service.[5] Once again, the vast majority of women were deprived of wage justice and the private sector retained its source of cheap labour.

The outcome of the case was a bitter disappointment to the trade union movement and to all women and resulted in a feeling of hopelessness, disillusionment and a dampening of action among most of the trade union officials. A feeling of dejection and what can we do now prevailed.

It was during this period that Diana Sonenberg, the Secretary of the Insurance Staff's Federation and a member of VEWOC, invited me to attend their next meeting. We were the only two to arrive and, knowing how people had become so despondent, we discussed the need for more dramatic action. I made a decision to protest against pay injustice meted out to women by chaining myself to the doors of the Commonwealth Building, holding a placard which read:

NO MORE MALE & FEMALE RATES—ONE RATE ONLY

This took place on 21 October 1969. Carrying banners of support, Betty Olle and Yvonne Smith from the UAW and Val Ogden accompanied me for moral support.[6]

Ten days following this initial chain up, Thelma Solomon, Alva Geiki and I chained ourselves across the doors of the Arbitration Court Building in protest against the institution which denied women pay justice.[7]

VEWOC held a public meeting in protest at the outcome of

Author's Private Collection

Zelda D'Aprano chained across the doors of the Commonwealth Building in protest against the unsatisfactory decision of the 1969 Equal Pay Case, October 1969

the Equal Pay Case and brought down the following Resolution, that this meeting:

- NOTES that more than one-third of the Australian workforce are women and that most receive AT LEAST $8.20 per week LESS than men;

- CRITICISES the employers submissions which were placed before the Commission;

201

- DEPRECATES the Commonwealth Government's submission which said it supported the principle of equal pay for equal work whereas the Government actually OPPOSED the unions claim:

- CONDEMNS THE Commission's decision which refused the unions claim and granted 'equal pay for equal work' on nine *strict conditions*, a decision which will only grant equal Pay to very few women, AND WHICH

- CONTINUES THE DISCRIMINATION AGAINST WOMEN WORKERS BASED SOLELY UPON SEX;

- CALLS for the elimination of ALL DISCRIMINATION AGAINST WOMEN WORKERS;

- RECOMMENDS to the Victorian Employed Womens' Organisations Council that *as a matter of urgency* it ask its affiliates and all unions & associates and union councils, where appropriate, to –

  (a) make direct approaches to employers seeking immediate payment of the $8.20 per week differential to all adult women workers, with proportionate increases for young female workers;

  (b) arrange regular publicity in union/association journals to advise female workers and the community of the precise effects of the decision and its limited effects;

  (c) hold protest meetings of male and female workers on the job and other locations as determined;

  (d) continue the campaign for the removal of this blatant wage differential.

A rate for the job is indispensable to wage justice.[8]

The Amalgamated Engineering Union was not prepared to allow any further delays in granting the women members of this union equal pay.

The *Australian* of 28 January contained the heading:

UNION CLAIMS 'UNBEATABLE'

EQUAL PAY CASE

and reported that Mr. D. McBride, the trade union advocate in the Commonwealth Arbitration Court, said women in the metal industry worked alongside men, did the same work and at the same pace. He went on to say that the metal union claims for equal pay for women working in the industry were completely beyond challenge. Union officials believed women in the metal trades satisfied the nine qualifications for granting equal pay, set down in June by the full bench of the Commonwealth Arbitration Commission. Some major factories had signed private agreements with metal unions to pay equal wages to women.

The *Herald* of 23 February 1970 ran the following article:

MORE WOMEN

GET PAY RISE

In a far-reaching decision today, Commissioner T. C. Winter started Australia's 72,000 women metal trades process workers on the road to full equal pay by January 1, 1972.

The article continued, 'Employers said the question of an appeal would be considered seriously'. It went on to say, 'Last Friday by agreement, 1300 women in the vehicle manufacturing industry were granted increases which will culminate in full equal pay by the beginning of 1972'.

All was not settled yet. A heading in the *Herald* of March 12 read:

ALL OUT!—FOR THE GIRLS

Widespread strikes and stoppages, aimed at getting women process workers equal pay, could occur in metal industries soon. A meeting of metal trade union leaders decided to present direct claims on employers for equal pay.

The metal trade Employers' Association recently appealed to the Arbitration Commission against a decision by Commissioner Winter which gave about 70,000 women in the metal industry equal pay in progressive stages.

The Full Bench reserved its decision.

The State Secretary of the Metal Trades Federation of Unions, Mr. Percy Johnson said the meeting of unions had decided not to wait for the appeal decision.

'We are making direct claims on employers for the immediate payment of the 90% of the male rate granted by the commissioner' Mr. Johnson said. 'If employers do not give satisfactory replies within seven days of receiving the claim, then their workers are likely to strike or take other industrial action,' he said.[9]

It was the threat of a strike throughout the metal trades which achieved equal pay for the women workers in that industry.

It is here that one needs to ask the question: if women in all areas of employment, government institutions, offices, shops, factories and the home were to combine and go on strike would they then obtain pay justice?

Education restrictions on females assisted in the narrowing of expectations and opportunities, and resulted in the majority of female employees being found in relatively few industries and occupations compared to male employees. Furthermore, females were usually concentrated around the lower levels of occupational hierarchies. At November 1985, women constituted 73.8 per cent of clerical workers, 63.8 per cent of employees in service, sport and recreation and 53 per cent in sales. Fifty-nine per cent of female employees were concentrated in these three major occupational groups. Women made up 47 per cent of employees in professional and technical occupational groups, and of these the majority were in teaching and nursing.[10]

12

Equal pay for work of equal value

The 1969 Case decision was for Equal Pay for Equal Work, an outcome which required women to perform and produce exactly the same tasks and quantity of work as men. This was to occur in industries where men predominated and, to avoid paying equal pay, many employers changed the tasks slightly and reclassified the numerous processes women normally carried out depriving vast numbers of women from obtaining wage justice.

The 1969 Case did not produce the benefits hoped for. Hence a different approach was required. The trade union decided to prepare a case for equal pay for work of equal value. That is, though women might perform different tasks from men, the value of women's work needed to be assessed as equal to that of men's labour.

One of the great abstract ideas in economics is expressed by the word 'value'. It does not mean market prices which vary from time to time under the influence of causal accidents or manipulation; nor is it just an historical average of actual prices. Indeed, it is not simply a price, it is something which will explain how prices come to be what they are. But what is it? Where shall I find it? Like all abstract concepts, when you try to pin it down it turns out to be just a word.[1] This problem exacerbated the difficulties in presenting the case for equal pay for work of equal value.

In order to conduct a successful case around this principle, the ACTU, unions and various women's organisations had to provide evidence before the Arbitration Commission to prove that work performed by women in many an industry or service was equal to, or more skilled than the tasks performed by men employed on higher salaries in that industry.

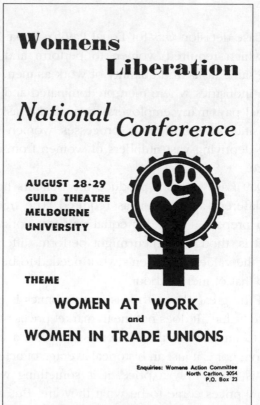

Womens Liberation

National Conference

**AUGUST 28-29
GUILD THEATRE
MELBOURNE
UNIVERSITY**

THEME

**WOMEN AT WORK
and
WOMEN IN TRADE UNIONS**

Enquiries: Womens Action Committee
North Carlton, 3054
P.O. Box 23

Women's Liberation Archives, University of Melbourne Archives

The first Women's Liberation National Conference in Melbourne 1971. The posters appeared on buildings in the city, the universities and various workplaces.

The Case was scheduled for 1972 and over twenty unions and associations were actively involved in the claim. The Women's Liberation Movement (WLM), the UAW and the National Council of Women intervened in the Case. The WLM and UAW combined their efforts and women were asked to attend the hearings to show the male-dominated establishment that women were serious in their demands.

The *WLM Newsletter* proposed action activities for July and August to focus on the equal pay case and called on women to participate in the march, attend the case throughout the hearing and to wear Women's Liberation T-Shirts. It also listed numerous activities women could undertake in support of the claim.[2]

Women gathered at the Centre to make posters in support of equal pay for work of equal value and in the following week, in conjunction with UAW women, they gathered at the city square to hear prominent speakers, distribute leaflets and display the posters. The WLM Equal Pay group, in conjunction with the UAW, issued a pamphlet in Italian, Greek and English for distribution at factories.[3] The Case was to be held during the last week of July and folders were issued to groups, the priority for distribution being poorly paid women. Groups were advised to contact the Women's Liberation Centre for further supplies of folders.[4]

The July 22 tram ride was a great success. About fifty women gathered at the City Square, and after handing out equal pay leaflets throughout the central shopping area they boarded the trams paying only a percentage of the fares. This action was repeated to highlight again the injustice of women paying full price for goods and services while obtaining only a percentage of the men's rate of pay.[5]

On the night before the Case opening, posters were pasted up all over Melbourne and a huge slogan, Equal Pay For Women, appeared on the wall of the Arbitration Commission

EQUAL PAY

PAGA UGUALE

ΙΣΗ ΑΜΟΙΒΗ

*

Issued by Women's Liberation, Union of Australian Women,
and several trade unions including the Food Preservers' Union
Clothing Trades Union, Furniture Trades Union, Butchers' Union
Textile Workers' Union, Miscellaneous Workers' Union,
Amalgamated Engineering Union.

Leaflet, 1972

F. Riley Collection, State Library of Victoria

building, but by morning the slogan was gone. Representatives of the women's movement marched with the unions on the opening day of the case, and, with her guitar in hand, Glen Tomasetti led the women gathered outside the Arbitration building in singing her famous song, 'Don't Be Too Polite Girls'. The sound of the women singing could be heard within the building and stopped the case.

This was the day Sylvie Shaw presented her submission on behalf of the WLM and her first experience in court type proceedings. She was young and extremely nervous in the intimidating atmosphere of the Arbitration Commission and was grateful for the support coming from the singing women.

Several women had assisted Sylvie in preparing her submission which she presented in two parts: one for equal pay for work of equal value, and the other for an equal minimum wage.[6] Sylvie's submission was a lengthy, well-researched document and concluded:

> The Women's Liberation Movement urges the Commission to award 'equal pay for work of equal value'. We call for rates of pay to be determined according to job content, where the sex of the worker is irrelevant. However, it is not sufficient to grant equal minimum rates for particular job classifications.
>
> Convention 100 specifically refers to the actual pre-tax payment, not just legal minima. We rely on the Commission to be consistent with Convention 100 and make an award, if legally possible, in terms which will prevent employers paying differential actual rates to males and females. Further, the Women's Liberation Movement supports the ACTU's claim to grant women the same minimum rate as men. At present the minimum wage applies only to men.
>
> Even with equal pay and removal of formal obstacles to equality of women in employment, informal discrimination will still exist. Action is required to eliminate all prejudices in society against women, as Dr. Riach, [Economics Lecturer at Monash University] succinctly explains:
>
> > It would mean bringing about a change in attitude of male employees so that they would accept females as complete equals in the work place who frequently would occupy supervisory roles over males: it would mean bringing about a change in attitude of employers so that they would assess applicants for employment *and* promotion purely on the basis of ability without regard to sex ... and ... it would mean changing the attitudes of customers so that they would accept the service without regard to the sex of the person performing it.[7]

For more than twenty years government members have been aware of discrimination in the workforce and have even expressed the desire to see the end of such discrimination, and I quote from the 1949 policy speech of Sir Robert Menzies:

> As it was my privilege to say to you in the Policy Speech of 1946, the women of Australia 'have established an unanswerable claim to economic, legal, industrial and political equality'. I hope that the time will speedily come when we can say truthfully that there is no sex discrimination in public or private office, in political or industrial opportunity.[8]

Twenty years on, we cannot say that there is no sex discrimination in public or private office, in political or industrial opportunity.

The first step to enable women to participate in the workforce on an equal basis is to grant women EQUAL PAY FOR WORK OF EQUAL VALUE [emphasis in original].

We call on the Commission to implement our proposals.[9]

Joan Curlewis presented the case for the UAW emphasising the need for women to be paid according to the rate for the job, rather than one's gender. Interviewed for the *Herald* that evening, Joan paid tribute to the UAW's 22-year fight for equal pay and to the WLM, whose approach was more suitable to the present conditions. 'They are more bolder and more defiant, less worried about being ladies'.[10]

Immediately after its election on 2 December 1972, the Whitlam Labor Federal Government appointed Mary Gaudron to act as counsel for the Commonwealth. She intervened on behalf of the Commonwealth Government in favour of women in the Case before the Arbitration Commission.

In the 1972 Case, leave to intervene was granted to the National Council of Women, the UAW and the WLM. In 1974, the National Council of Women, the Union of Australian Women and the Women's Electoral Lobby (WEL) intervened. WEL's most significant achievement for 1974 was Edna Ryan's successful submission to the Arbitration Commission for an adult minimum wage, which finally put paid to the concept of the (male) family wage. Women's groups participated strongly in the 1969, 1972 and 1974 equal pay cases, presenting well-researched information in support of women's claims. Leave to intervene in the 1969 case was granted to the Australian Federation of Business and Professional Women. The National Council of Women and the Union of Australian Women

The Commission finally arrived at their decision:

International Women's Day Rally, 1975

Courtesy of the Union of Australian Women, Melbourne

The principle of equal pay for work of equal value will be applied to all awards of the Commission. By 'equal pay for work of equal value' we mean the fixation of award rates by consideration of the work performed irrespective of the sex of the worker. The principle will apply to both adults and juniors. Because the male minimum wage takes account of family considerations, it will not apply to females.[11]

In attempting to evaluate women's labor, Australian Industrial Courts have almost always compared women's labour to that of men doing the same tasks or to men performing other tasks, the men's labour in most cases being viewed as being of more value and/or of more importance, a cultural construct of sexual discrimination. And how does one determine work of equal value? Do we base our judgements on knowledge, skills, effort, responsibility or profitability? In practice, it 'basically involves comparing the worth of a traditionally female-dominated occupation with a traditionally male-dominated occupation in a manner which is as objective as possible'.[12]

It is not surprising that in preparing a case for equal pay for work of equal value, people involved in trying to develop these presentations had great problems. 'Anyone who has worked in the development and administration of job evaluation systems is very much aware of the subjective nature of skill and responsibility requirements, as well as the difficulty of making comparative judgements as to working conditions and physical effort.'[13]

Various methods of attempted job evaluation indicate all the complexities, making it necessary at times to delete the job title from the position description to be evaluated by a committee. It certainly involved the deletion of the incumbent's name and no reference was to be made to 'he' or 'she' in the position description. Terms like 'technical officer' or 'clerical officer' were to be used. Extraordinary phrases came into the equation

Courtesy of Megan McMurchy, Margo Oliver and Jeni Thornley

3000 nurses take to the streets and march to Parliament House demanding wage increases, Sydney 1976

with references used to depict women's jobs such as 'courteous' and 'pleasant', words never used to describe men's jobs.[14]

Over the years, various cases for equal pay for work of equal value have compared the salaries and job tasks of health workers, hospital theatre sisters, ambulance drivers, health scientists in hospitals, qualified child-care staff and secretaries with those of fitters and turners.

Because of the difficulty in establishing equal value and the inherent complications, together with the enormous expense involved, unions were often deterred from undertaking claims. According to the 1972 Commission's findings, all determinations under the *Public Service Arbitration Act* were to be lodged by June 1975 but Melbourne barrister, Jocelynne Scutt, states that, 'Many of the applications were not made until after 1975'.

Between 1973 and 1981 only fifty-four such applications were made. Of these, 'only thirty-five awards were adjusted to allow equal pay for work of equal value. Work value inspections were conducted in only two of the cases.'[15]

In 1985–86 the nurses case brought matters to a head. In making his final decision on this case, on 18 February 1986, Justice Maddern finally ruled that, 'The Commission affirms the 1972 equal pay principles but rejects the idea of comparable worth'. Fourteen years after the establishment of comparable worth, in 1972, when really put to the test, the 'idea of comparable worth' was tossed out.[16]

Three authors of a government published report, *Women's Worth*, wrote (in 1987) that effective and lasting reforms in policies and practices needed to be accompanied by far-reaching changes in institutional arrangements and dominant value-systems within society; they suggested that activity promoting such reforms in organisational practice might make its own contribution to broader social change.[17]

Despite some changes in society's dominant value-system and the increasing reliance on women's paid work, albeit often part-time, now, early in the twenty-first century, the campaign for wage justice for women continues.

From 1973 when Bill Richardson became Federal Secretary of the ACSPA, many changes occurred in the functioning of EP Committees. Bill had a personal commitment to women's issues and believed there had been insufficient development of policy on women's issues by the ACSPA. Women within the organisation received tremendous support in establishing the ACSPA Committee for Women's Affairs, a committee composed in the main of non-executive members, a departure from previous practices. The objectives of the committee were to recommend policy and action for consideration at national conferences of the ACSPA and to report regularly to the Executive.[18]

Marion Miller, an Organiser with the Insurance Staffs Federation, recalls her involvement with the Women's Affairs Committee, the vital debating of issues, the research, and the freedom to form their own ideas and suggestions and that, while two male officials attended the meetings, the women were not restricted. It was necessary for this committee to formulate their ideas then report to the Executive of the ACSPA on whatever priorities or issues they considered important. They were in a position to bring women's perspectives into the debate.[19] Marion as convener of the Women's Affairs Committee played a role in the early discussions concerning the establishment of The Victorian Working Women's Centre and, as liaison to Bill Richardson, she was to become heavily involved in the decision-making process governing priorities.

One of the initial requests by the women's committee to the ACSPA Executive was for a women's resource centre, instigated in the main by Sylvie Shaw. The ACSPA responded favourably and Bill was able to obtain a grant from the International Women's Year Secretariat which made possible the establishment of The Victorian Working Women's Centre on the proviso that the Centre came under the auspices of the ACSPA who were to provide the accommodation, power, library facilities, files and general assistance. The Centre, co-ordinated by Sylvie Shaw and Mary Owens, provided a service to all working women and functioned successfully for five years, providing numerous services and a vast output of small publications in both English and other languages. The Centre finally came under the jurisdiction of the ACTU.[20]

13

Kath and male structures

During Kath's membership of the CPA—she resigned in 1967—the branch meetings and conferences placed the 'topic' of 'women and youth' at the end of the agenda. Children were rarely discussed and only appeared as part of the agenda when a woman comrade deemed it necessary; issues to do with women and youth were of minor concern when wars, the threat of war and economic matters were paramount. The problems of power and the structure of hierarchical institutions of society—whether schools, governments, government institutions, business enterprises, political parties or trade unions—were rarely discussed in depth; they were viewed only within the narrow confine of class. Patriarchy was not a widely used term.

Dorothy Hewett, poet, novelist and member of the Party when Kath was a member, wrote of her experiences in the CPA:

> Feminism and the equality of women were not causes dear to the hearts of working-class Australian men, nor were they particularly popular in the male-dominated hierarchy of the communist party. Oh, they gave it lip service occasionally—some of them even read Engels on *Women and Communism*, with his concept of the working-class woman as a 'slave of a slave'—but male supremacy was alive and well amongst the higher and lower echelons of the party.[1]

Gladys Bird, manager of the International Book Shop, recalled complaints about a party member who had the reputation of being a rabid womaniser. With a few grogs under his belt, he rough-handled a woman who rejected his advances, and when the woman complained of his behavior to the Party Leadership they told her 'You asked for it'. 'A Key paradox existed within the party: while it operated as a subculture, it none the less expected its members to conform to conventional models of behavior, conventional marriage, the nuclear family and the male breadwinner.'[2]

Equality meant sameness with men while negating the specifity of women's oppression and experience within a dominant masculinist culture. Women were expected to work with men, in unity and equity. Difference of interest was minimised, and 'sameness' was the only basis on which equality was claimed. 'Equality' within the Party as in society, maintained inequalities rather than challenged them and women's issues which were different to those of men were subordinate.

Seeing society through the models of Marxism, communist women adopted the language of class, difference and equality to create a space for themselves. The prevailing discourse constructed women as a problem requiring education and instruction in communist ideology, so that they could join their male comrades in the struggle against capitalism.

Daphne Gollan, an early communist, feminist and historian, recalled how:

> [the Party's] solution to women's problems lay in lifting women as far as their disabilities allowed, to the level of men, that it was ignorance and prejudice which caused tension between men and women, and the common struggle for emancipation would itself demonstrate the socially conditioned origins of female inferiority.[3]

This discourse of class, difference and equality had had, a long history in the Party. Not surprisingly, in 1929 at the launch of the *Woman Worker*, Edna Nelson (later Ryan) encapsulated this view when she wrote:

> The separate women's journal was not meant to entice women away from the class struggle; it was aimed to undertake the 'special task' of reaching working-class women: In answer to the fear that a separate women's bulletin might become 'feminist', it is enough to say that women taking part in the class struggle cannot be feminist. The working class movement has no time or room for feminists; they belong to and come from the leisured class.[4]

Among men of the left, there was a great fear of feminism. The claimed that it was only for middle-class women, was divisive and would split the left movement. They feared what they couldn't understand and, for the few who may have understood, they were also fearful of losing their male privileges.

As feminist Lisa Maria Hogeland recounts, 'Feminism politicises gender consciousness, inserts it into a systematic analysis of histories and structures of domination and privilege'.[5] The fear of feminism stems from the difficult and complicated questions feminists ask, about how gender consciousness can be used both for and against women, how vulnerability and difference help and hinder women's self-determination and freedom. 'Fear of feminism, then, is not fear of gender, but rather of politics. Fear of politics can be understood as fear of living in consequences, a fear of reprisals.'[6]

Many women fear the existential situation of feminism and the possible consequences. The basic feminist concept that the personal is political is profoundly threatening, it requires you to enter a world full of new meanings and implications. To stand opposed to your culture, to be critical of institutions, behaviors, discourses—when it is so clearly not in your immediate interest to do so—asks a lot.

Kath was like almost all female members of political parties of the time—she was not a feminist and neither were the vast majority of CPA or CPML women members. To have shown the slightest inkling of support for feminism in any political party would have been viewed as a serious breach of loyalty. Two of Kath's male comrades considered the matter of sufficient importance to make the point she was not a feminist, one when interviewed and the other when delivering the eulogy at her funeral.[7]

My research reveals no evidence of co-operation between Muriel Heagney and Kath Williams despite their many years of activism. There was no documentation of any approach being made to seek the support of each other. It would seem that their allegiance to their male-dominated political parties—Muriel to the ALP and Kath to the CPA and CPML—prevented them from combining their efforts in the campaign for pay justice for women.

Kath was a highly intelligent woman. She was a woman who had had two unsatisfactory marriages, had lived as a single mother while earning her own living and had a great deal of experience being involved in political parties and trade unions. For many years she had chosen to live alone, preferring solitude to living with a partner. Kath had undoubtedly made the decision that her chosen life style could not accommodate the needs or desires of a male partner and she settled for devoting her time to her son, work, and campaigning for wage justice for women and socialism. Just let us hypothesise for a moment and ask, What could Kath have expected had she seen the personal as being political and embraced feminist ideas while not dismissing her socialism? With her male comrades reflecting society's views on women, one can say with every certainty that, in the 1950s and 1960s, no trade union would have employed her had she been a feminist. Like all male institutions, the trade unions and political parties demand total loyalty to the structure. They were extremely sexist, and would have seen her not only as a threat to the Party but would have recognised she no longer believed in their 'all-knowing' or male supremacy.

Being a strong person or a stoic often comes at a price. When one has lived a life of hiding one's pain, sorrow and tears, it becomes almost impossible to allow this self- control to lapse. To be ill or suffering from disillusionment, mental pain, anguish or heartbreak is often deemed to be weakness and should under no circumstances be revealed.

Throughout her life, Kath was able to present an image of control, control over her personal, social and political existence, yet there can be no doubt she was suffering. And this suffering together with her inability to shed the well-constructed defenses built up over a lifetime left her no alternative but to escape as best she knew how. It would seem that those close to Kath who were aware of her drinking didn't recognise the symptoms of her inner despair or felt powerless to assist. This was compounded by her ability to maintain an image of being in perfect control, a subterfuge which under-mined her health.

Being a member of the Communist Party did not auto-matically put one into a society of friends, deep friendships were extremely rare and although one had a sense of belong-ing, Kath was alone. What did she think and what was she feeling about being alone? After spending three years writing, she ceased working on her book and had reached the stage where she was unable to continue. What had she written? Was it about her involvement in politics, the unions or did she also include her experiences as a woman? We will never know. Catherine Williams died on 17 April 1975. The last years of her life had been overtaken by dementia and, following her death, her documents and writings were destroyed.[8]

The *Liquor and Allied Industries Journal* made note that 'Cath Williams well known to Hotel and Restaurant workers for her work on their behalf and to thousands of other workers for her efforts to establish equal pay, has passed on. She died within several days of her eightieth birthday.' The tribute to Kath went on to pay credit to the many years of service given to the members and to the trade union movement.[9]

In a farewell article in the *Tribune*, Nell Johns of the UAW, wrote that Kath Williams was well-known in all fields of struggle for the working class but particularly loved and honoured among women. 'Kath was a friend and Comrade, sadly missed when, through ill health, she retired. Our Sympathy to her family and friends—all who knew her will remember.'[10]

In his eulogy, Frank Johnson, Executive member of the Victorian State Committee of the CPA and Kath's comrade of many years, said, 'Today it is with the deepest grief we mourn the passing of a staunch working-class woman, whose lifetime activity is part of our Australian history.' He went on to say that Cath was not a feminist and that she believed:

women's equality would be won only by men and women fighting together in overall class struggles for socialism. She was accepted nation-wide as a leading fighter for women's rights. Her activities among working women gave much strength to the demand for equal pay, and as Secretary of the Victorian Trades Hall Council Equal Pay organisation, she became a driving force in its development. Cath held no illusions as to the limitation of such demands but regarded them as a stepping stone to the more basic issues of the struggle for women's emancipation. Cath Williams was a fine Australian Patriot who upheld the true tradition of the Australian People.[11]

After all the campaigning and energy expended, Kath lived to see the introduction of equal pay for equal work in 1969 and was pleased with this result even though she believed this attainment to be the first step only. Her last message to the LTU was an expression of pleasure during the hotel strike of 1974.

14

Women, work and the fight for pay justice

Trade unions developed within industrial societies over the past 200 years for the sole purpose of protecting and increasing the living standards of employees. Australian trade unions were in existence in the 1850s,[1] and workers were taking to the streets in marches and rallies throughout the 1860s. To bring about some regulatory control over the trade unions in Queensland, the *Trade Union Act* of 1886[2] legalised trade unions.

History has shown that working people have gained far more through collective industrial action than by any other means. The need for the powerless to be able to exercise their conscience and will through collective action is of paramount importance in a democratic society.

From the beginning of the twentieth century countries such as Denmark, Italy, Greece and France recruited women into unions.[3] Australian unions did not do this and, in the main, they discouraged women from seeking employment in what were deemed to be male industries and refused membership to women. Most men in Australia of that era were conditioned to believe it was their manly duty to provide for wife and children and deemed it humiliating if their wives sought paid employment. They also failed to comprehend that the economic system requires men to be held financially responsible for their families thus binding them to their employer and turning them into wage slaves.

From the time of the establishment of the Australian Labor Party in the 1890s which became, in 1908, the Labor Party,[4] most working-class women in the early period of the 1900s to post World War 2, came from families supporting the Labor Party and had husbands who were members of unions. Unions were seen as 'men's business' and not part of women's domain. All unions, by and large, went along with this attitude and women who did enter industry were often forced to establish their own unions.

Much later, during the 1950s and 1960s when jobs were plentiful and the threat of losing one's livelihood was minimal, most women saw paid work as a temporary phase in their lives, and were reluctant to demand equal pay. Women's insecurity in the workplace stems largely from their feeling of having insufficient skills, worthless skills, and a low self-image created by a home environment where all female services are unpaid and, in the main, taken for granted. Carrying this deep sense of inner worthlessness into industry and commerce puts women into a position where they feel it is not their place to make any demands.

It is not difficult to understand why most women's unions are ultra-conservative, and why this situation is accepted. Working-class women live in a society where salary or wages determine the economic status and importance of the individual. Entering the paid workforce with little or no knowledge of trade unions or the dynamic of paid work, and having no self-worth or expectations apart from earning money, renders working-class women insecure and reluctant to take industrial action.

Another potent cause of women's conservatism stems from the fact that the majority of women work in small businesses with few staff. Men too, when employed in small establishments, are known to be less involved in union activity and more vulnerable to intimidation.

Research reveals the lack of union activity in most female industries including shop assistants, clerks, and, until the 1960s, nurses. Female members of these unions preferred males in the leadership, expecting them to know more of union matters and be in a position to be more effective. During the 1950s and 1960s these unions made token gestures towards the activities of the equal pay committees, equal pay conferences and semiars. On the rare occasions when unions did employ women as officials, the women were carefully scrutinised to ensure they didn't rock the boat.

In contrast to the female-dominated unions, the history of female organisers in the LTU reveals the impact they had on women in their industry and the willingness of women to belong to the union. This was a union that did not make 'sweetheart' deals with companies or management, deals where union dues were deducted from pay packets by the employer and given to the union in return for a compliant workforce. This practice still applies to employees in large supermarkets where agreements are made between the union and management to employ large numbers of casual staff to work all hours without overtime pay rates.

Employees are left with only one choice when all methods to safeguard hard-won conditions, gain wage justice or improve conditions fail: the withdrawal of their labour, strike action. Unions responsible for women's industries rarely if ever organise strike action. During the 1950s and 1960s, when jobs were readily available, the leadership of the Clerks' Union, Shop Assistants' Union and hospital unions were right-wing controlled and averse to any form of membership participation in union affairs. Their main role in gaining wage justice was to obtain the flow-on which resulted from strike action by militant unions to gain increases to the basic wage and cost-of-living adjustments. These non-militant unions relied on others to do the fighting for them.

Throughout their history, the trade unions have, sporadically, responded to almost all issues with the prevailing attitude of men. While in the 1930s several were prepared to take some action in support of women, in the main, such action was deeply constrained by men belonging to the patriarchal force opposed to women's economic emancipation. This dilemma in the unions remained until the number of women entering the workforce dramatically increased after World War 2 and the Women's Liberation Movement, with its more militant agenda, began to take the unions on in the early 1970s. The 'Pill' too was another vital factor, ridding women of constant pregnancies and freeing them to venture into the world.

From the very beginning of the Women's Action Committee in Victoria and the establishment of the WLM in all States at the beginning of the 1970s, a visible change began to take place among women in society which affected women in the workforce and the unions. Between 1969 and 1975 female union membership, particularly in service industries, rose dramatically: by 63 per cent, compared to 26 per cent for males. While some of the increase in women's membership could be put down to compulsory unionism and dues being taken from their salary, the women's movement was organising alternative trade union conferences and inspiring women to action.[5]

However, the presence of large numbers of women is by itself no indication of influence. Both Labor Governments and male union members have been extraordinarily tardy in thinking about women. Although there were exceptional individual unionists who supported the women's movement for many years, there were too few among the leadership to make a difference.[6] Bill Richardson from the ACSPA, however, is one such exception.

Key union executive positions, such as full-time Secretary or Assistant Secretary, have almost always been occupied by men. Sociologist Gisela Kaplan notes that the Royal Commission on Human Relationships in 1979 found that women held only 2 to 3 per cent of presidential and secretarial positions in union branches. She cites a 1980 study which 'found that women were underrepresented at each level of decision making, from shop stewards and office representatives to organisers, research officers and members of executive committees. If they held positions, they were appointed rather than elected.'[7]

It must be said that the responsibility for the lack of representation of women in the unions cannot totally be placed on the trade unions. Women are ill-equipped to understand the necessary responsibilities when entering the paid workforce. Our entire education system does not prepare or impart the means by which the young can obtain a better understanding of workplace dynamics, the unions, wage structures or how working conditions such as sick pay, holiday pay, long-service leave, maternity leave or better remuneration etc., are gained. How much is known of the numerous strikes it took for these conditions to be obtained and the sacrifice people made to improve the living conditions of all Australians?

Our culture, our literature, our television and our makers of film, in particular, do not depict life in the paid workforce—they largely ignore the industrial scene, its alienation and its ramifications. They refuse to capture what for most people takes place during work hours—the sunlight hours, which should be our best quality time—and choose to concentrate most of their efforts on 'love' and violence. Or, when depicting people at work, they reduce it to comedy with the characters doing very little work and spending their time talking and laughing—the very opposite of reality. This artificial obliteration of people from production, and the falsification of reality, encourages young people to have unreal expectations for their lives in the workforce and outside it.

Women have had scant recognition of their contribution to society. This is especially true of urban women. The first museum dedicated to the work of country women—the Pioneer Women's Hut, which was established by the immense and passionate effort of Wendy Hucker at Tumbarumba, New South Wales, in 1988—and The Australian Worker's Heritage Centre at Barcaldine, Queensland, when completed, will emphasise the work of rural women, but little recognition is given to the contribution of urban women in the paid workforce. Compared to men whose employment efforts remain tangible, be they buildings, houses, cars, trains, electricity, etc., the results of women's paid labour in the services, clothing, food, clerical, sales, and cleaning industries are wellnigh intangible, unseen or disappear within twenty-four hours. Recent exhibitions have been held in Perth on the contribution to society by Indigenous women employed in service, and in Adelaide on migrant women in industry and service; however, permanent historic museums are required, dedicated to the history of women in paid employment and their contribution to society.

Over the past thirty years women have been encouraged to undertake careers: however, this pursuit has not always produced the desired results. The banking industry has appointed many women in senior ranks and employed large numbers of part-time women at the lower echelons while putting unfair pressure on the staff to work harder. Many of the senior positions women hold in banks carry extra responsibilities yet have a lower status and salary than that obtained by the men they replaced. Despite the record profits obtained in the industry, continued dismissals and pressure placed on staff is creating an increase in stress levels. Bank staff in rural areas are told they must accept the extra workload or the banks will close. The women's movement needs to analyse this situation very seriously to determine whether these women are receiving equal opportunity or are being used as cheap labour to replace the men. It would seem that the banking industry is rapidly becoming another female industry attracting lower salaries.

With the emergence of enterprise bargaining in the 1980s, women continued to be disadvantaged. On this controversial issue, the 1985 congress of the ACTU declared that 'industry and enterprise bargaining disadvantages less organised and less industrially powerful groups', and that productivity bargaining 'disproportionately affects women workers who are clustered in service industries, the public sector and low value added manufacturing areas'.[8]

The Industrial Relations Commission echoed this view in 1991, noting that 'Enterprise Bargaining, especially bargaining for over-award payments, places those sections of the workforce where women predominate at a relative disadvantage'.[9]

The (Industrial Relations Commission) limits on enterprise bargaining do not protect women workers.

As Karen Fredericks states: 'At best, the strongest, most unionised, most strategically placed sections of the workforce to strike productivity deals, gaining or increasing over-award payments in return for productivity measures are in industries manufacturing for export'.[10] Time has shown that service industries where women predominate—teachers, nurses and clerks do not contribute to the bottom line, in the struggle to be 'internationally competitive' resulting in industry and governments drastically reducing their numbers.[11]

In two articles in the *Sydney Morning Herald*, David Dale reported that approximately 228 400 women were dismissed from their jobs in the three years to June 1997.[12] Some of these would have been among the 77 400 sacked from the Commonwealth Public Service by the Howard Government.[13]

The steady workplace retrenchments combined with the increase of younger people entering the workforce helped to bring about a decline in trade union membership. Between 1982 and 1990 union membership fell by 8 per cent for men and women alike, producing levels of 45 per cent membership for men and 35 per cent for women.[14]

According to Meredith Burgman, the ABS in March 1992 showed that its Workplace Bargaining survey revealed how 23 per cent of full-time employees had workplace negotiated increases, compared with 9 per cent of part-timers [and that] over 40 per cent of women work part-time compared with under ten [sic] per cent of men; [also that] women and especially part-timers, were under-represented in workplaces where the main source of increases were awards.[15]

In 1997 the ABS noted a significant drop in the number of women in full-time jobs: 23 000 in June of the previous year while the number of women in part-time jobs increased by 20 000. These 'part-time or casual women workers if on the dole, are entitled to earn [no more than] up to $30 per week before their unemployment payment is affected'.[16]

Part-time work is the choice for some women with families but the negative aspects of part-time work lie in the conditions that usually accompany it. Leave loading, holiday pay, health benefits and superannuation contributions, promotional opportunities and job-related training are generally denied part-time workers, particularly when most part-time work is casual.

Women entering the workforce since the 1970s expected to obtain pay justice but, for women in 1999, the earnings gap between men and women is firmly entrenched. The ABS figures for 1998 reveal that women in full-time employment received 20 per cent less in wages than men. While men earned an average wage of $714.50, women's average wage was $468.30. The contradictions which force women to live in a man's world reveals their comparative poverty: 'Whereas nearly half of all women have a gross weekly income of less than $200, only 27 per cent of men do'.[17]

The decline in women's wages and the erosion of equal pay is obvious. The headline in the *Sydney Morning Herald* of 25 February 1999 read as follows: *A million more jobless revealed.* The article claimed that figures indicate 1.7 million people in Australia want work but can't find it. The official figures are fudged by preventing part-timers, casuals, married women or persons living with an employed partner to register for the dole.

Women vary in their expectations and while women's participation in management overall (public and private sectors) had risen by 2.8 per cent in the eight years between 1986–94, during the same period the number of women in the workforce had doubled.[18] For working-class women, opportunities in middle management and corporate glass ceilings don't mean a thing: what they want is a job. Indigenous women too have their own priorities and traditions of activism with the recognition of land rights taking prime place.

Under the present monetary system, if one is not self-employed or in business, it becomes necessary to sell one's skills to an employer in order to survive. In the past, with the industrial laws intact and the unions negotiating for wages and conditions, one was as valuable to an employer as the price unions, with support from their members, could extract. Skills, whether from the hands or head, remain the only commodity a worker can sell in order to survive. With the current enforcement of enterprise contracts by firms and companies, the situation has developed where all employees are competing with each other while unaware of each other's earnings thus destroying any feeling of togetherness as encouraged by the unions.

The former Federal Minister for Industrial Relations, Mr Reith, said in 1999 that unions are unnecessary and workers can negotiate directly with their employers. No worker believes that he or she and their boss are on an equal footing. Have you ever heard of a case where a worker sacked a boss?

Moreover, the Federal Government, having destroyed much of the previous industrial legislation, continues in its desire to further curtail wages and conditions, including the abolition of the minimum wage, and is rapidly aiming for the prevention of union organisation in the workplace.

The *Sydney Morning Herald* of 7 September 1998 reported research on ten of the world's leading economies which found that Australians were among the lowest paid, despite long working hours. The hourly labour cost of an Australian manufacturing worker was 1.6 per cent below that of an American, taking into account wages and on-costs, such as sick leave and overtime payments. 'It is clear relative pay levels have declined over time. One hundred years ago Australia had the highest standard of living in the world.'[19]

Vast numbers of Australian women are finding they require more than a home and children for fulfilment and most women, according to interviews by the Australian Institute of Family Studies, choose to stay at work even if they don't need to economically.[20] But for those who need to work to survive, how do they cope on part-time or casual work or the dole?

Australia is known for having the highest incidence of occupational gender segregation in OECD countries in that the majority of Australian women are channeled into low-paying occupations such as hairdressing, librarianship, processing, retail and clerical work. Sixty-four per cent of female employees are concentrated in three major groups: clerical, sales and service industries.[21] This current pattern of occupational segregation in Australia has not always existed. Occupations which now employ few women (for example, mining and printing) were major areas of women's employment in the nineteenth century and, until the 1920s, women in Australia worked as chauffeurs, garage attendants and mechanics.[22]

The New South Wales Government's Pay Equity Inquiry, which it undertook between December 1997 and July 1998 as part of its priority to address inequitable pay and working conditions for women, studied private sector child-care workers, seafood processors, public sector librarians, clerical workers in the private sector, hairdressers, beauty therapists and first-year-enrolled public hospital nurses.

The scope and depth of the inquiry went far beyond anything ever done in Australia. It heard extensive evidence from people working in female-dominated industries and from experts in industrial relations, economics, law, job evaluation, labour markets, equal employment opportunity and sex discrimination.

Mary Rose Liverani, after attending the inquiry, said Gail Gregory, the NSW Labor Council advocate, thought everything could be set right through changes to the wage-fixing principles but, after twenty days of evidence, she realised the Inquiry was going to be the biggest matter since the equal pay case thirty years ago.[23] Gregory noted that while the women's groups knew very little about industrial relations, they had an impressive grasp of the theory underlying the arguments presented.[24] The National Pay Equity Coalition (NPEC) women's group said the inquiry proved to be a learning experience for all involved.

Mary went on to say that the evidence presented by the

NPEC at the Inquiry, argued that commonsense fails to wrestle with:

> the potentially discriminatory assumptions underlying 'skilled' work; does not ascertain whether exclusionary practices exist that limit women's access to certain areas of work or to assess the extent to which the domestic division of labour conditions both men and women's access to the workforce; ...
>
> [that] concepts of skill have historically been constructed to privilege men and to devalue what women do. The nursing profession, for instance, has achieved pay equity by emphasising the technology component of its members' skills and by downplaying the personal skills that are at the very core of nursing.[25]

Justice Glyn in her findings stated that the 1969 and 1972 EP decisions on women's employment had not brought them equal pay for equal work and that the implementation of pay equity policies should improve equity outcomes. Among her final recommendations, she expressed the need for the Industrial Relations Committee to be given greater powers to examine enterprise agreements to prevent inequities in work value and that the Commission must be in the forefront of action to develop strategies to prevent and pre-empt pay inequities.[26]

A *Sydney Morning Herald* report in December 1998[27] stated that the Inquiry singled out the child care industry where women employees predominate (90 to 95 per cent) and experience discrimination because of their gender. Child carers were paid rates below those of unskilled occupations such as shop assistants and car park attendants. Hairdressers, librarians, childcare workers, and clothing outworkers were also found to be underpaid. The article noted that Justice Leonie Glynn found that 'in industries such as hairdressing and nursing, the fact that they are dominated by women is the determining factor in the setting of wage levels'.[28] Between 1987 and 1995 the average hourly rate for full-time women and men employees slightly declined while the pay rates of female part-time workers declined substantially.

While some journalists and business leaders now refer to a 'kinder capitalism',[29] Justice Glyn drew attention in the inquiry's conclusions to the adversarial attitude shown by the Employers' Federation and the Chamber of Manufacturers (Industrial) to the inquiry.[30] These two organisations were the only two among over fifty who were granted leave to appear which failed to agree that undervaluation existed in some or all of the occupations/industries examined by the inquiry.

The 1997–1998 Pay Equity inquiry confirmed what many women and the trade unions have known for many years. But what can be done to redress the problem?

From the early 1970s when the women's movement began its feisty campaign, the trade unions, although reluctant, were forced to acknowledge the untapped strength of women and accept some women into leading roles. It was then that changes began to emerge. However, despite the commitment of the ACTU to women, by 1987 only one of its thirty-one member executive was female. Jennie George first became an executive member then went on to become the President of the ACTU. More recently, Sharan Burrow succeeded Jennie George, indicating that the trade union movement had accepted that women in the trade union movement were there to stay. The recent announcement to have 50 per cent women on the ACTU Executive has created global union history.

Fighting for wage justice for women has proved to be as tough and vicious as most campaigns fought for better pay or conditions. In recent years unions have lodged claims for equal pay (or equal remuneration for work of equal value) only to have various tactics employed by companies to avoid payment.

One of the most difficult cases went to a formal hearing, the Commission making two inconclusive decisions against the Sydney Company HPM. The company fought this tooth and nail even to the extent of sacking the twelve male general hands with whom three hundred female process workers were being compared. It was only after the women and men took combined industrial action that the case was settled. It resulted in the women receiving a higher initial wage increase than the men, and further increases that would, over the course of the agreement, result in their getting the same rate of pay as the male general hands. In the meantime, most of the general hands who had been sacked, were re-appointed to the store-person classification. The struggle continues.[31]

In October 1999 the ACTU pursued a case against the *Age* newspaper arguing that women employed in the phone room taking classified advertisements should have salaries equivalent to male press hands. The company strenuously resisted this case.

Given these situations, it remains to be seen whether any of Justice Glyn's recommendations arising out of the inquiry held in NSW in 1997–1998 come to fruition.

A 1999 article in the *Sydney Morning Herald* cites John Buchanan, of the University of Sydney's Australian Centre for Industrial Relations Research and Training, who points out that less than 15 per cent of the workforce is professional, with the strength and skills to be part of the 'selfish' workforce. It quotes him as saying that really powerful people get their voice heard while the classic full-time wage-earner model is rapidly disappearing.[32] As Janet McCalman wrote:

> It is all a question of power. Individuals with little or no money are less powerful than individuals with lots of money. A free

society depends not so much on eternal vigilance as on a continuing open contest for power. No government or élite that remains in power without challenge, no matter how idealistic their ideology, can be trusted.[33]

Trade unions are essential to the contest of democracy. An open society is kept open by conflict, contest and debate; it may not be particularly 'relaxed and comfortable' but it must be free and creative. The price of liberty really is eternal struggle.[34]

In its efforts to make capitalism work, the arbitration system institutionalised class conflict, while, in recent years and to a degree, it established the political economy of a 'fair go' with attempts to be redistributive, especially for those occupations that had little or no industrial muscle. Women in the main were the recipients of this protection despite the inadequacy of the outcome. With the advent of the Coalition Federal Government and the Reith era, most of the Industrial Relations Commission's policy of a 'fair go' was whittled away. To add extra restrictions on the ability for workers to organise, Peter Reith, former Minister for Employment, Workplace Relations and Small Business, promoted further legislation in Parliament to destroy the effectiveness of unions. However, as at January 2001, Tony Abbott, a hard task master, is now Minister for Employment, Workplace Relations and Small Business. Should the Federal Coalition Government be returned to office in the election due late in 2001, there will be little benefit to workers, particularly for those in production and services.

The deregulation of the labour market, which began in the Keating era and continues, has resulted in the continued dismissal of thousands of Australian workers and, while it has produced cost benefits for employers and gains for the members of a few powerful unions, for the powerless it has meant longer working hours, lower wages and a preponderance of part-time work. 'The rise of individualism has been matched with a collapse of concern in community. Seventy per cent of new jobs in the market are casual or contract.'[35]

The turning back of the clock concerning the lack of recognition of women and their contribution to society, plus the dominance of male perspectives, became patently obvious from reports on the recent ILO meeting in Geneva. Commenting on the meeting, the *Sydney Morning Herald* of 4 October 1999 noted that the Australian delegation, consisting of twelve male representatives, including one each from the Labor Party and Democrats, all with expenses paid by the Federal Coalition Government, were at the meeting to debate and observe proposed revisions of the Maternity Protection and Child Labour conventions; the delegation included Mr Reith who reportedly said, 'You don't have to be pregnant to present a policy position'.[36]

Ms Lisa Heap, Federal Women's Officer for the Australian Education Union and nominated by the ACTU, was not formally recognised by the all-male delegation but eventually gained entrance into the conference when the International Confederation of Free Trade Unions gave her accreditation. Ms Heap was deeply concerned when the Australian Government argued that employers should be able to conduct a pregnancy test on women seeking a job. The Australian Government had also argued at this meeting against an international standard for paid maternity leave.

Although most Australians accept the word 'reform' to mean improvement, since the advent of the Federal Coalition Government in 1998 people have come to learn that when the Prime Minister, a government Minister, or particularly Mr Reith talks of reforms or puts forward a policy, the working people will suffer. This has proved especially so for women. What have the women members of the Liberal Party, National Party,

Labor Party and Democrat Party done about the official stand taken at this ILO Conference within their parties?

Present conservative governments take an anti-woman stand through industrial legislation, and the increased costs of child care: this illustrates their determination to force women out of the paid workforce and back into the kitchen. This back door expulsion of women from paid employment is of great concern to women who desperately need to earn an income. The representatives of these very same women were excluded when, according to the *Sydney Morning Herald*, Senator Newman 'transformed her much vaunted annual roundtable with grass-roots women into a group dominated by business women, at which migrant and Aboriginal groups were also locked out ... and slashed the groups invited from 60 to 21'.[37] The women present at the annual roundtable were selected for their expected acceptance of Liberal and Coalition Party policies.

The Federal *Sex Discrimination Act* originally introduced into Parliament by Labor Senator Susan Ryan in 1981, later passed in 1984 and supplemented in 1986 by the *Affirmative Action (Equal Employment Opportunity for Women) Act*, made possible the implementation of affirmative action programs which enabled women to move into the professions and middle management.[38] Although many restrictions to wider employment choices were removed, many employers, the media, community attitudes, organisational stereotyping and other factors continue to promote a culture and atmosphere discouraging women interested in entering male-dominated areas of work.

The refusal of our Federal Government to sign the United Nations' Convention protocol on the Elimination of all forms of Discrimination Against Women,[39] should not come as a surprise to the women of Australia. With the absence of statistics on the number of job dismissals, married women seeking employment, the minimising or closure of government departments specifically concerned with women as well as huge numbers of Australian women on part-time work, what else could we expect? It would seem that the reason for the government's refusal to sign the protocol may stem from its desire to reintroduce previous discriminatory practices or introduce new practices against women in employment and society.

Trade Unions and future policy

It is interesting to look back on the late 1960s and early 1970s, when the women's movement was initiating active protests over equal pay, and note the reaction of the trade unions leaders, especially those from strong militant unions toward women active around women's issues. Each of the four union secretaries approached refused to give any support to the women.[40] What they couldn't control, they wouldn't support.

Jack Hutson, a member of the AEU, in his 1971 book, *Six Wage Concepts*, wrote, 'Three women in Melbourne at least showed appropriate reaction to the Equal Pay Decision by chaining themselves in protest to the door of the Arbitration Commission, but as for the rest there was silence'.[41] Jack's further analysis of the trade union movement's attitude towards women and women's situation in the paid workforce was far beyond the comprehension or acceptance of most of his brothers in the trade union movement.

The women's struggle for wage justice in Australia extends over more than one hundred years, a period which saw little union action for equal pay until the 1950s when there was a greater number of women in the workforce. From this date on, the intense action by Kath Williams and the equal pay committees brought forth a belated involvement of the trade unions into the campaign for equal pay. And, although from the late 1960s the ACTU, the ACSPA and other unions undoubtedly played a major role in campaigning for equal pay, this has still not been attained. The reasons for this are a combination of factors: the male chauvinist culture prevalent in almost all of the structures, including trade unions, plus the fear women have of protesting on their own behalf. Unions are only as strong as the strength of their membership, and women need to give this strength to their unions in order to gain leadership and support when needed. Trade unions are essential for safe-guarding the interests of working people and although many women since the early 1970s have become involved in their unions when joining or returning to the paid workforce, there is still a need for women to accept the responsibility that comes with this choice and participate in their unions.

Recent research by Jenny Doran of the ACTU reveals that women union members earn an average $543.00 a week compared to women who aren't union members and who average $436.00. Unionised women earn 24.5 per cent more than their non-union counterparts. Most of this differential is explained by the different treatment of union part-timers and non-union part-timers.[42] With women in part-time work constituting 73 per cent of part-time workers and 43 per cent of all women workers,[43] it becomes essential to see how beneficial belonging to a union can be.

Working-class women with ideals, insight and a 'fire in their belly' and who understand the plight of women as well as being one of their rank, women who can give leadership and who are accepted by their sisters for being one of their kind are needed as organisers. These women with leadership potential need to be nurtured, not controlled. They need to be given the skills necessary to conduct consciousness-raising, conflict resolution, deal with management and whatever else is required when faced with the many problems women experience in the paid workforce but, most of all, their ideals, passion and dynamism must be nourished.

There can be no doubt that in our competitive society, with its continual sackings, increased technology, reduction in government services and its reliance on the importation of skilled experts to avoid the cost of training our young, fewer and fewer jobs are becoming available. During the past twenty years Australia's population has increased dramatically, yet the retail sector has seen an increase of just one hundred jobs. Sixty two per cent of all jobs created since 1985 have no sick leave or annual leave entitlements. Part-time work is growing at 20 per cent per year. More than one-third of workers say they are fearful of losing their jobs.[44] Unemployment is here to stay and, in coping with this situation, we need to remove the exorbitant emphasis on paid work and mutualise the status of paid and unpaid work thus helping to put an end to the current clustering in occupations.

The trade union movement, while decreasing in membership and strength, continues to protect and guard its organisation by demanding total control. This attitude has aided the alienation of the unions from women and of women from unions. In the current economic situation, the union movement needs to develop a vision of where it is going and expand on its methods of attaining these goals. In order to obtain support from the people when conducting campaigns, new methods of organisation are required to accommodate women's needs by relinquishing total control over the decision-making process when combining activities with women's organisations and women at home. Women are in desperate need of appropriate action to increase their quality of life.

With the reluctance of those in power to accept women's

labour in the home as being worthy of appropriate remuneration, the time has come when the women's movement and the trade union movement needs to reappraise the situation. The era of each trade union jealously guarding its own little empire needs to go in place of the common good of women. All women work, and the time has arrived for women in the workforce and women in the home to combine their efforts for a united campaign around the need for pay justice for all women—through meetings, conferences, rallies, marches demonstrations and strike action if necessary.

At the UN half-decade conference for women, in Copenhagen in 1980, Marilyn Waring said, 'Women's exclusive association with the domestic and reproductive sector is at the crux of women's subordination and its perpetuation', and 'Women continue to satisfy, and continue to see reproduction unpaid, undervalued, unacknowledged'.[45]

Home economist Margaret Reid claimed that, if an activity is of such a character that it might be delegated to a paid worker, then that activity shall be deemed productive. Any activity culminating in a service or product which one can buy or hire someone else to do is an 'economic activity' even if pay is not involved.[46] How then, in economic terms, do we place a value on work performed in the home?

The natural life-promoting forces of nature, the earth, sun, rain and trees, all have a vital role to play in our survival and quality of life but are not valued by our patriarchal, capitalist-driven, global economy unless harnessed for money-making purposes. Women too come into this category. The importance of the provision of life and its sustaining tasks and services, and the mothering of the next generation of workers are, in economic terms, supplied for nothing more in return than board and lodging. This being the case, the capitalist system places no monetary value on women's total contribution in the home. While it can be said that those in power will, in the long-term, be making financial profit from the offspring of today's women, they reject Margaret Reid's theories and consider any work performed in the home by women as not being worthy of adequate, direct financial return.

This unequal distribution of power is implicitly based on the unequal distribution of paid and unpaid work, and the resulting power differential is the main obstacle to the equality of women in all parts of the world; and despite all the fast food on offer, or the leisure breaks obtainable as service commodities, a living person is also needed to introduce the qualities of a housewife, for her subordination is the 'compensation for man's dependence within the wage labour relationship.'[47]

The lengthy process of redistributing paid and unpaid work must be speeded up and, towards this end, the obligation of managing the home, rearing children and caring for the elderly should be shared in a spirit of partnership. But how can this be achieved when the organisation of the workplace is still geared to the masculine experience of autonomy, mobility and freedom from domestic responsibility?[48]

In concluding her book, *Three Masquerades*, Marilyn Waring states:

> I situate women in their own reality. We are universally, half of humankind. We are guaranteed equal rights to participate in political and civil life. Nowhere do we experience this equality in reality.
>
> I situate women in their own reality. Everywhere we work longer hours than men. We may not be paid, but no comparator is necessary. We may not be in servitude, we may even enjoy the time taken in all the production and services we furnish, but our reality is that this is work.
>
> To refuse our participation with men on equal terms in political representation, and to refuse to recognise our economic

production and reproduction as work, is a fundamental and universal breach of human rights.

Our Lives are testimony.[49]

There can be no doubt that, with the strengthening of the global economy, fewer people will be required in the paid workforce while the accumulation of wealth will be concentrated in fewer hands. This is occurring while the overwhelming majority of people are threatened with insecurity and poverty. A participatory democracy cannot survive when the global economy and self-interest is destroying our cohesiveness.[50]

Several groups of people in attempting to survive or free themselves from wage fixation in various countries have taken matters into their own hands and created alternative and /or sustainable life styles.[51]

Analysis of our economic system and culture and the history of the lengthy campaign for pay justice for women in Australia indicates beyond doubt that this goal is unachievable unless radical economic and cultural changes occur.

Eva Cox, in her desire for change, wrote, 'What we are seeking is a paradigm shift, to change both the fields of debate and the rules of the game'.[52] We could argue that our definition of equality should be a fair distribution on the basis of need, rather than one which distributes through the vagaries of the marketplace. We need to live in a society where human action enables us to develop our capacities to make collective decisions for the common good. Making decisions that involve rising above self-interest and standing in the shoes of others makes groups more civil and more likely to take different standpoints into account.

Citizenship, in liberal democratic theories, implies a level of fair treatment before the law, with a presumed sense of responsibilities and an expectation of liberties. Social democratic models add levels of material fairness and of controls aimed at greater fairness in the distribution of resources. In both cases, the benefits are both individual and communal. In societies where only those with the money can afford market essentials and pleasant goods and services, those who do not have the wherewithal are often without the essentials and barely eke out an existence. When the allocation of resources is structurally determined by gender, race, class or other ascribed characteristics injustice becomes systemic.[53]

Despite attempts by some people to create alternative life styles, the fixation of most people on wage labour, indicates their inability to conceive of any other non-hierarchical work situations. One consequence is that the hierarchy of capital and wage labour is being consolidated and intensified at the present historical moment.[54]

In a world where technology is constantly becoming more efficient and labour more alienated, there needs to be a drastic cut in work hours for all, with the workplace becoming more democratic. The rules of industry and commerce were created by men and for men who are autonomous, mobile and free from the responsibility for rearing the young. These rules are not immutable and having been made by men can be changed by men and women. For women in the workforce or at home, in order to obtain wage justice plus quality of life, it has become necessary to do away with hierarchies in the workplace. A different management structure is required where the workers have greater control, more involvement in the management process and leadership roles are shared. 'Democracy in the workplace is about what happens to the money as well as how you do your job'.[55] Such an arrangement would enable the changing around of the culture to place the priority of people first and the dollar second. It would assist in creating work satisfaction and enable greater flexibility of work hours making it possible for men to assume equal responsibility with women for the caring of children, the sick and the elderly.[56]

A system should be devised where people receive an appropriate salary from taxation when rearing children, or caring for the sick or elderly. This would be a valid method of giving just recognition and remuneration for the carrying out of these important tasks.

At this point, it becomes necessary to suggest that the society detailed in the previous two paragraphs could possibly provide the basis for an economy and lifestyle where the overwhelming majority of women could obtain proper recognition and pay justice. But can these changes be implemented? And who is going to do the work necessary to achieve this?

The last thirty years of the twentieth century saw the consciousness of women raised immeasurably, so I put it to you all now in 2001: How do you envisage a world where all women will receive just recognition and remuneration for their contribution to society?

Appendix 1

Noteworthy decisions on pay[1]

1907 Justice Higgins, Family Wage, Harvester Decision 2 CAR 1

1912 Justice Higgins, Mildura Fruit Pickers Case 6 CAR 61
First formal acceptance of equal pay for equal work for women

1913 Rural Worker's Union Case

1917 Justice Powers, Theatrical Case Judgement 11 CAR
First Case in which the Arbitration Court agreed to consider a minimum wage for women in an industry

1919 Clothing Trades Case 13 CAR
Justice Higgins said that married and/or single women were subject to the physical limitations of their sex and suffered incidents from industrial work detrimental to the female reproductive system; and set women's wage in the clothing trade at 54% of men's rate.

1920 By 1920, in New South Wales, State awards were for a family of four, while Federal awards covered a family of five.

1920 Justice Brown, Cardboard Box Makers Case 3 S.A.I.R. 11 1919–1920

1923 December. Clothing Trades Union. Justice Webb would not depart from previous awards. Women's wages set at 55% of the male wage.

1926 Federated Liquor and Allied Trades Case. Because men were the preferred workers, women lost their claim for equal pay.

1926 NSW *Industrial Arbitration Act.* The Commission maintained women's rate at 54% of the male rate while the living wage declared for adult male workers was reduced to the needs of a family of three. This in a period of inadequate contraception and large families.

1928 Justice Drake-Brockman would not depart from previous awards and rejected the Clothing Trades Union's request for equal pay.

1929 Fruitpickers Case 28 CAR 597. Equal pay was overturned by reclassifying fruitpicking as women's work. (W. M. Newton Case)

1934 The Commonwealth Arbitration Court based the basic wage firmly on the economic capacity of industry to pay thus discontinuing the Harvester principles of 1907. CAR 144

1936 NSW Industrial Commission decided adult female employees of the State to receive 54% of adult male's living wage.

1937 The ACTU conducted its first Case for equal pay.

1937 *Industrial Arbitration (Amendment) Act* affirmed women's rate of pay in all industries was 54% of the male rate. This remained until World War 2 when the Women's Employment Board decided women should receive no less than 60% and no more than 100% of the male rate. For women in vital industries, the rate was 75%.

1940 Full bench of the Industrial Commission heard a case put forward by the New South Wales branch of the Federated Clerks' Union for equal pay.

1942 Federated Clerks Union Case, Queensland, 52 CAR

1943 The Arbitration Court, in determining its basic wage case, concluded that 'work suitable for women in which they were not in competition with men for employment, should remain worth less than men's work'. Wage tribunals and wages boards in New South Wales, Queensland, South Australia and Western Australia adopted the same determination.

1944 National Security (Female Minimum Rates) Regulations Case, 54 CAR

1944 Chairman of the Women's Employment Board, Mr Justice Foster, was appointed to the Commonwealth Arbitration Court.

1944 The Commonwealth Arbitration Court decided that, in the twelve 'vital' industries where wages were compared, the work done by women didn't require any display of skill, responsibility or exposure to any unusual physical conditions and so the wages paid remained at 54% of the male basic wage. Because of the great dissatisfaction stemming from this ruling, the government, under the National Security Regulations, gazetted a 75% minimum rate for women in all vital industries.

1947 National Wage Case. Boot Trades

1947 *Conciliation and Arbitration (Amendment) Act*
The culmination of agitation by women's groups, the amendment enabled the same wage to be paid to persons of either sex performing the same work. It was now possible for a claim for equal pay to be brought before the Arbitration Commission for determination.

1949 June, Commissioner Morrison reduced the salary of barmaids to 75% of the male wage in every State except Victoria.

1949–1950 Basic Wage Inquiry. (698) The ACTU argued for equal pay irrespective of sex. The claim was rejected but

Justices Foster and Dunphy increased women's wages from 54% to 75% of the rate payable to male workers.

1951 Justice Foster, Equal Pay Case Decision

1951 March of 1951, Commissioner Galvin in New South Wales reduced rates for women in the metal trades from 90% to 75% of the male rate.

1951 Industrial Court of Queensland. Queensland Branch of the Clerks Union re Clerks Union and Switchboard Attendants Award.

1958 The first statutory direction on equal pay was inserted in the *Industrial Arbitration (Female Rates) Amendment Act, New South Wales*. Similar legislation was enacted in South Australia in 1967, Western Australia and Queensland in 1968, and for public servants in Tasmania in 1966.

1959 The NSW Teachers' Federation fought and won an equal pay decision.

1969 Equal Pay Case conducted by the ACTU. Resulted in equal pay for equal work.

1972 National Wage Case. Union argument based on equal pay for work of equal value. Resulted in women employed under Federal Awards receiving equal pay. Women employed under State awards needed to prove their case.

1974 Minimum Wage Case 147 CAR. Equal pay for minimum rates. All Federal Awards were freed of sex discrimination.

1986 Nurses Case. 300 CAR

1   Sources: ACTU, personal communication, December 1999; Bradon Ellem. 1989. *In Women's Hands: A History of Clothing Trades Unionism in Australia*. NSW: New South Wales University Press; Alina Holgate and Karen Milgrom for the Women's Legal Resources Group 1985. *She Works Hard For The Money … Equal*

Pay for Women. Victoria; Edna Ryan and Anne Conlon. 1975. *Gentle Invaders : Australian Women at Work 1788–1974,* Thomas Nelson (Australia) Limited; Jocelynn Scutt. 1992. Inequality before the Law; Department of Industrial Relations, New South Wales.

Appendix 2

The Victorian Working Women's Centre

The Working Women's Centre was established in Melbourne (1976) to meet the vital needs of women in the workforce, needs sadly neglected by the trade union movement of the time. The Centre came under the auspices of the ACSPA while Sylvie Shaw and Mary Owens, co-ordinators of the Centre, endeavoured to provide support and information where necessary and within a year had drawn up the Working Women's Centre Charter.

WORKING WOMEN'S CENTRE CHARTER[1]

We believe that stronger unionisation of women workers will increase the effectiveness of the national trade union movement and will ensure that women workers and the community both recognise the importance of trade union organisation for women.

We wish to ensure that women workers have:

* Equal access to trade union training.
* Special union training courses which will concentrate on overcoming the diffidence to which women have been conditioned.
* Inclusion of women's problems in the general education programme of trade unions.
* Equal access to higher office in trade unions.

We seek to encourage women to participate more in trade unions and to encourage unions to take positive action to make this possible.

During the five to six years of its existence, much research and effort went into producing a series of discussion papers covering a wide range of topics.

DISCUSSION PAPERS[2]
1. Should unions be concerned about 'Women's' Issues?
2. Should unions be concerned about childcare?
3. Should unions be concerned about migrant women workers?
4. Do women really get equal pay?
5. Maternity, paternity and family leave?
6. Do women have equal opportunities in employment?
7. Should unions support a mother's wage?
8. Alternative working hours
9. Training and retraining
10. Occupational health
11. Unemployment
12. Women and shift work
13. Work experience
14. Occupational health—part 2: Occupational health hazards for pregnant women
15. Equal Opportunity Bill
16. Migrant workers and their health
17. Outworkers and homeworkers
18. Women and retirement—part 1: Superannuation
19. Child care—an important industrial issue?
20. New patterns of industrial democracy for women
21. Occupational health—part 4: Psychotropic drug abuse
22. Women work and technological change
23. Trade Union training for women
24. Is there a need for health services for women at the workplace?
25. Married women working

26. Unemployment part 2: Disadvantaged youth (emphasis female)
27. Women in skilled trades
28. Current developments in part-time work
29. Women's perception of work
30. Attitudes to payments by results
31. Occupational health—part 5: Stress job dissatisfaction and mental health
32. Anti discrimination legislation
33. 'Life must go on—I forgot just why': Special problems for older women
34. Occupational health—part 6: The disabled woman worker —part 1
35. Occupational health—part 6: The disabled woman worker —part 2
36. Women and stress in industry
37. Child care debate
38. Parental and family leave
39. Women's employment
40. Women's wages
42. Hidden employment
43. Alternatives to employment

The depth of analysis in these papers and the commitment and notable influence of the women's movement indicates the early incorporation of demands beyond the usual narrow union confines of wages and conditions. The activities of the Centre together with the firm support from Bill Richardson, Federal Secretary of the ACSPA, and the demands constantly applied by the women's movement, created a climate where the ACTU was ultimately forced to take far more cognisance of women in the workforce and in trade unions.

1   Anna Pha, The Working Women's Centre: Its First Five Years, a paper towards an MA, University of Melbourne, 1982.
2   Ibid.

Interviews

Interview tapes lent by Lynda Clarey

John Arrowsmith, 7 May 1990
Fred Benbow (Junior), August 1990
Harry Bocquet, 21 September 1990
Marjorie Broadbent, 20 July 1990
Agnes and Wattie Doig, 15 September 1990
Vic and Vida Little, 18 August 1990
George Mitchell, 18 August 1990
Eric Pipgrass, 10 December 1990 (Kath's cousin)
Flo Russell, 23 April 1990, 14 January 1991, 26 November 1997
Hilda Smith, 27 August 1990

Interviews conducted by author

Marjorie Broadbent, 13 May 1998
Lynda Clarey, November 1997 (Kath's granddaughter)
Ray Clarey, November 1997 (Kath's son)
George Edson, April 1998, May 2000
Kath Holt, November 1997
Jack Hutson, November 1998
Vic and Vida Little, 18 August 1998
Mary Rose Liverani, 15 January 1999
Marion Miller, 29 October 2000

Max Ogden, July 1998
Vera Perry, January 1998
Flo Russell, 26 November 1997, 9 December 1997
Hilda Smith, June 1998
Bernie Taft, 1998
Lois Williams, November 1997 (Percy Clarey's cousin)

Notes

1
Cath the housewife

1 Education History Research Unit, Education Department Record No. 17518.
2 *Recorder*, Australian Society for the Study of Labour History, June 1975, p. 16.
3 Interview, Lois Williams, cousin of Percy Clarey, November 1997.
4 Education History Research Unit, Education Department Record No. 17518.
5 Ibid.
6 Ibid.
7 *Australian Dictionary of Biography, Vol. 13, 1940–1980*, p. 432.
8 The late Agnes Doig in interview with Kath's granddaughter, Lynda Clarey, in 1990. Lynda Clarey kindly allowed me to use this material.
9 *Public Services Act No 1024*, 1889, Section 14.
10 Education History Research Unit, Education Department Record No. 17518.
11 Eric Pipgrass in interview with Lynda Clarey, 10 December 1990.
12 Kathleen Fitzpatrick, A Cloistered Life. In Patricia Grimshaw and Alice Strahan. (Eds), *The Half Open Door*, Sydney: Hale & Iremonger, p. 120. Kathleen Fitzpatrick's definition of a middle-class family was one in which the family income, though it be small, was reasonably secure and did not arise from manual labour.

13 *Recorder*, Australian Society for the Study of Labour History, June 1975, p. 16.

14 Eric Pipgrass in interview with Lynda Clarey, 10 December 1990.

15 Marjorie Broadbent in interview with Lynda Clarey, 20 July 1990.

16 *Recorder*, June 1975, p. 16.

17 Agnes Doig in interview with Lynda Clarey, 15 September 1990.

18 ASIO. National Archives of Australia. Australian Security Intelligence Organisation.

19 *Recorder*, June 1975, p. 16.

20 Ibid.

21 Ibid.

22 Interview, Ray Clarey, November 1997.

23 Marjorie Broadbent in interview with Lynda Clarey, 20 July 1990.

24 Ibid.

25 *Australian Dictionary of Biography, Vol. 13, 1940–1980*, p. 43.

26 George Mitchell in interview with Lynda Clarey, 18 August 1990.

27 Flo Russell in interview with Lynda Clarey, 23 April 1990, 14 January 1991, 26 November 1997.

28 George Mitchell in interview with Lynda Clarey, 18 August 1990.

29 Ibid.

30 Ibid.

31 Fred Benbow (junior) in interview with Lynda Clarey, August 1990.

32 Ibid.

33 Education History Research Unit Record No. 17518.

34 Wattie Doig's letter, 10 October 1984.

35 Ibid.

36 Jim Hagan, *The History of the ACTU*, p. 128.

37 *Australian Dictionary of Biography, Vol. 13, 1940–1980*, p. 431.

38 Alleyn Best, *The History of The Liquor Trades Union in Victoria*, p. 157.

2
An early history of women and unionism

1 Megan Murphy, Margot Oliver and Jeni Thornley, *For Love or Money*, p. 39.
2 Pam Young, *Proud to Be a Rebel*, p. 49.
3 Ibid.
4 Ibid., pp. 126, 131.
5 Desley Deacon, *Managing Gender*, p. 18.
6 Pam Young, *Proud to Be a Rebel*, p. 180.
7 Ibid., p. 182.
8 Suzy Baldwin, *Unsung Heroes and Heroines of Australia*, p. 88.
9 Alleyn Best, *The History of The Liquor Trades Union in Victoria*, p. 105.
10 Desley Deacon, *Managing Gender*, p. 189.
11 Heather Radi, *200 Australian Women*, p. 187.
12 Ibid.
13 E. H. A. Smith, The Solidarity of Women—What Women have accomplished in the Confectionery Industry. *The Women's Clarion*, 1, 7 November 1921, pp. 2–3.
14 Megan McMurchy, Margot Oliver and Jeni Thornley, *For Love or Money*, p. 40.
15 Bradon Ellem, *In Women's Hands*, p. 211.
16 Kay Daniels, Mary Murnane and Anne Picot, *Women in Australia*, p. 139.
17 Bradon Ellem, *In Women's Hands*, p. 170.
18 Ibid., p. 241.
19 Joyce Stevens, *A History of International Women's Day in Words and Images*, p. 10.
20 Alleyn Best, *The History of The Liquor Trades Union*, p. 212.
21 Ibid., p. 157.
22 Ibid.
23 Ibid., p. 158.
24 Ibid.
25 Jim Hagan, *The History of the ACTU*, p. 112.
26 Ibid., p. 113.

27 Alleyn Best, *The History of The Liquor Trades Union in Victoria*, p. 164.

28 Ibid., p. 167.

29 Bradon Ellem, *In Women's Hands*, p. 221.

30 Heather Radi, *200 Australian Women*, pp. 176–7.

31 Alleyn Best, *The History of The Liquor Trades Union in Victoria*, p. 168.

32 Ibid., p. 174.

33 Stella Lees and June Senyard, *The 1950s—How Australia became a Modern Society, and Everyone got a House and Car*, p. 87.

34 Caddie, 1991, *The Autobiography of a Sydney Barmaid*. Sydney: Pan Macmillan, p. 6.

34 Ibid., p. 83.

36 Alleyn Best, *The History of The Liquor Trades Union in Victoria*, p. 174.

37 Ibid., p. 212.

38 Ibid., p. 182.

39 Ibid.

40 Ibid.

41 University of Melbourne Archives, MTHC Minutes, 3 June 1948.

42 Noel Butlin Archives, Tom and Mary Wright Collection, Mrs R. Whitfield, Equal Rate For The Job. *The Housewives Guide*, November 1948, Z 267 Box 18.

43 Ibid.

3
Women's postwar moves

1 Ann Howard, *Where Do We Go From Here?*, p. 28.

2 *Queensland Teachers Journal*, February 21 1949, p. 12

3 Department of Labour and National Service, 1958, *Equal Pay: Some Aspects of Australian and Overseas Practice*, Canberra, p. 55.

4 Ibid.

5 Ibid.

6 Stella Lees and June Senyard, *The 1950s: How Australia became a Modern Society*, p. 65.

7   Nicholas Drake, *The Fifties in Vogue*, p. 13

8   Mary Sponberg, Review of Germaine Greer's *Untamed Shrew*, *Women's Liberation Newsletter*, December 1997, held in Mitchell Library.

9   Molly Haskell, *From Reverence to Rape*, p. 235.

10 Ibid.

11 Ibid.

12 Stella Lees and June Senyard, *The 1950s*, p. 78.

13 Ted Myers, Corporate Education Resources Pty. Ltd., Discussion Notes on Time's Up, prepared with assistance from the Women's Bureau of the Department of Employment and Industrial Relations, A Women's Film Unit Production for Film Australia.

14 Jim Hagan, *The History of the ACTU*, p. 140.

15 My summary from N21/1201, Noel Butlin Archives.

16 Adapted from the House of Representatives Standing Committee on Legal and Constitutional Affairs. 1992 *Half Way to Equal*. Report of the Inquiry into Equal Opportunity and Equal Status for Women in Australia. Canberra: Australian Publishing Service.

17 Department of Labour and National Service, *Equal Pay* 1958, p. 51.

18 Alleyn Best. *The History of The Liquor Trades Union in Victoria*, p. 208.

19 Bernie Taft, *Crossing the Party Line*, p. 68.

20 *Guardian*, May 1951.

21 University of Melbourne Archives, THC Minutes, 31/7/52.

22 Jim Hagan, *The History of the ACTU*, p. 112.

23 University of Melbourne Archives, Eleanor Masters Collection.

24 Ibid.

25 Ibid.

26 Ibid.

27 Ibid.

28 Gisela Kaplan, *The Meagre Harvest*, pp. 11–12.

29 *Guardian*, 21 August 1952.

30 Noel Butlin Archives, ACSPA. Victoria Contributes to Equal Pay Movement. N10/852, pp. 30–31.

31 Ibid.

32 Interview with Vic and Vida Little, 18 August 1990.

33 Ibid.

34 John Arrowsmith in interview with Lynda Clarey, 7 May 1990.

35 Ibid.

36 Noel Butlin Archives, ACSPA. Victoria Contributes to Equal Pay Movement. N10/852

37 Alleyn Best, *History of the Liquor Trades Union in Victoria,* p. 212.

38 University of Melbourne Archives, VTHC EP Committee, Box 1.

39 University of Melbourne Archives, Resume of ACTU Activities on Equal Pay, Box 3.

40 University of Melbourne Archives, VTHC Equal Pay Committee, Box 3. 20/5/55.

41 Noel Butlin Archives, N16/676 May 20.

42 Bradon Ellem, *Hell for Leather: Industrial Relations and Politics in the Boot Trades, 1945–55,* typescript, 41 pp. Copyright now held by Belinda Probert and Ray Juriendini (see Acknowledgements). Page references refer to typescript.

43 Bradon Ellem, 'Hell for Leather', p. 54.

44 Ibid., p. 10.

45 Ibid., pp. 11–12.

46 Ibid., p. 11.

47 Ibid., p. 26.

48 Zelda D'Aprano, *Zelda.*

49 Ibid., p. 92.

50 Robert Murray. *The Split.* Melbourne: Cheshire 1970

51 Zelda D'Aprano. *Zelda,* p. 125.

52 Ibid., p. 119.

53 Ibid., p. 128.

4
Decisions on equal pay, 1891 to 1955

1 Pam Young, *Proud to Be a Rebel,* p. 66.

2 Ibid., p. 68.

3 Desley Deacon. *Managing Gender,* p. 170.

4 Megan McMurchy *et al., For Love or Money.*

5 Ibid., p. 41.

6 Pam Young, *Proud to Be a Rebel*, p. 165.
7 Edna Ryan and Anne Conlan, *Gentle Invaders*, p. 110.
8 Ibid., p. 111.
9 Jocelynne Scutt, Inequality Before the Law.
10 Megan McMurchy *et al.*, *For Love or Money*, p. 41.
11 Marilyn Lake, *getting equal*, p. 97.
12 Jocelynne Scutt, Inequality Before the Law.
13 Megan McMurchy *et al.*, *For Love or Money*, p. 91.
14 Marilyn Lake, *getting equal*, p. 178.
15 Edna Ryan and Anne Conlan, *Gentle Invaders*, pp. 122–3.
16 Marilyn Lake, *getting equal*, pp. 172, 181.
17 Jim Hagan, *The History of the ACTU*, p. 14.
18 Megan McMurchy *et al.*, *For Love or Money*, p. 86.
19 Jean Arnot, Address to Annual Conference, 1937, May 25, *Red Tape* (Public Service Journal) p. 123. State Library of New South Wales Archives.
20 Heather Radi: *Jessie Street Documents and Essays*, Broadway, NSW, Women's Redress Press.
21 Jim Hagan, *The History of the ACTU*, p. 112.
22 *Sydney Morning Herald*, Pelita Clark, 24 September 1998.
23 Ibid.
24 State Library of New South Wales Archives, Jean Arnot in *Red Tape*, September, 1946, p. 1015.
25 Noel Butlin Archives, s784.
26 Jim Hagan, *The History of the ACTU,* p. 152.
27 Jocelynne Scutt, Inequality Before the Law, p. 276.
28 Daisy Marchisotti, Equal Pay Case. 1951. In Elizabeth Windschuttle, W*omen, Class and History*, pp. 423–7.
29 Ibid.
30 Ibid.
31 Ibid.
32 Ibid.
33 Jocelynne Scutt, Inequality Before the Law p. 277.
34 Noel Butlin Archives, N16/676, VTHC. 1955.
35 Interview with Vera Perry, January 1997.
36 Noel Butlin Archives, N16/676, MTHC 1955.

37 Noel Butlin Archives, M24 ACTU Federal Union Conference on Equal Pay, 21 March 1956.
38 Alleyn Best, *The History of The Liquor Trades Union,* p. 212.
39 Noel Butlin Archives, M24 ACTU Federal Union Conference on Equal Pay, 21 March 1956.
40 *Herald,* 30 June 1956.
41 Bradon Ellem, *In Women's Hands,* p. 258.
42 Barbara Curthoys and Audrey McDonald, *More Than a Hat and Glove Brigade,* p. 51.
43 Ibid., p. 54.
44 Kath Williams, 1957, *Equality Will Be Won.* printed by Coronation Press, Melbourne.
45 Ibid., p. 4.
46 Ibid., p. 30.
47 Ibid., p. 31.
48 Ibid., p. 32.
49 Ibid.

5
The Fight for Equal Pay, 1956 to 1959

1 M24 ACTU, 21 March 1956.
2 Mitchell Library Archives, Labor Council of New South Wales. Box 23 (144)
3 Barbara Curthoys and Audrey McDonald, *More Than a Hat and Glove Brigade,* p. 50.
4 Viv Flannery, Viv Flannery. In Roberta Bonnin, '*Dazzling Prospects',* p. 22.
5 University of Melbourne Archives, VTHC Box 3.
6 Noel Butlin Archives, N16/676 ACTU.
7 *Guardian,* 28 March 1957.
8 *Herald,* 25 March 1957.
9 Ibid.
10 Ibid.
11 *Guardian,* 4 April 1957.
12 Harry Bocquet in interview with Lynda Clarey, 21 September 1990.

13 Noel Butlin Archives, N21/267 ACTU.
14 Ibid.
15 *Sun,* 14 January 1958.
16 Ibid.
17 *Guardian,* 10 February 1958.
18 Noel Butlin Archives, N16/676 ACTU.
19 Ibid.
20 Ibid.
21 *Sun,* 16 May 1958.
22 Noel Butlin Archives, N21/267 ACTU.
23 Mitchell Library Archives, Labor Council of New South Wales Collection, Box 23 (144).
24 Noel Butlin Archives, N16/676 ACTU.
25 University of Melbourne Archives, Box 23 EP Committee.
26 University of Melbourne Archives, Box 3 EP Committee.
27 Ibid.
28 Noel Butlin Archives, 69/285 ACTU
29 Justice Gleeson, in the Martin Kreiwaldt Memorial Address 1994, *Sydney Morning Herald,* 4 April 1994.
30 Marjorie Broadbent in interview with Lynda Clarey, 20 July 1990.
31 Hilda Smith in interview with Lynda Clarey, 27 August 1990.
32 Interview with Ray Clarey, November 1997.
33 Noel Butlin Archives, N10/230 ACSPA, 9 June 1959.
34 University of Melbourne Archives. VTHC Equal Pay Committee Box 3 1959. Resume of ACTU Activities on Equal Pay.
35 Noel Butlin Archives, N10/230 ACSPA.
36 Noel Butlin Archives, 69/291 ACTU.
37 Ibid.
38 Noel Butlin Archives, 69/291 ACTU.
39 Ibid.

6
1960 to 1962, the fight escalates

1 Noel Butlin Archives, N21/1209 ACTU, 16 February 1969.
2 Noel Butlin Archives, N 21/1209 ACTU, 22 February 1960.

3 Ibid.

4 Mitchell Library Archives, Labor Council of New South Wales. Boxes 24 & 25 (144).

5 Noel Butlin Archives, 69/295 ACTU.

6 Noel Butlin Archives, N21/1209 ACTU. The whereabouts of films mentioned are unknown.

7 Noel Butlin Archives, N 21/1209 ACTU 30/3/1960.

8 Ibid.

9 Jack Hutson's written answers to questionnaire, 5 October 1998.

10 Noel Butlin Archives, N21/1209.

11 Noel Butlin Archives, N21/1209 9 August.

12 University of Melbourne Archives, Box 3 September 1960.

13 Ibid.

14 University of Melbourne Archives, Box 3 VTHC Equal Pay Committee 12 December 1960.

15 Noel Butlin Archives, 69/295 ACTU. From the *Printing Trades Journal*, January 1961, pp. 2–3.

16 University of Melbourne Archives, Box 3, VTHC Equal Pay Committee, copy of initial draft Bill.

17 Noel Butlin Archives, N21/1209 ACTU, 22 March 1961.

18 Noel Butlin Archives, N10/232 ACSPA.

19 Noel Butlin Archives, N21/1201 ACTU.

20 Noel Butlin Archives, N10/232 ACSPA.

21 ABC Television Archives.

22 Noel Butlin Archives, 69/295 ACTU.

23 Ibid.

24 Noel Butlin Archives, 69/295 ACTU. *Daily Telegraph* April 18, 1961.

25 Ibid.

26 Noel Butlin Archives, 69/284 ACTU, p. 3

27 Ibid., p. 7.

28 Ibid., p. 3.

29 Noel Butlin Archives, 69/295 p. 8.

30 Ibid., p. 9.

31 Ibid., p. 8.

32 Department of Labour and National Service, *Equal Pay: Some*

Aspects of Australian and Overseas Practice, Canberra, 1963, p. 69.
33 Ibid.
34 Noel Butlin Archives, N10/232 ACSPA.
35 Noel Butlin Archives, N21/1209 ACTU.
36 Mitchell Library Archives, Labor Council of New South Wales, Boxes 24 & 25 (144).
37 Noel Butlin Archives, N23/44 ACSPA.
38 ABC Television Archives.
39 Noel Butlin Archives, N21/1201 ACTU.
40 Noel Butlin Archives, N23/44 ACTU.
41 Noel Butlin Archives, N21/1201 ACTU.
42 University of Melbourne Archives, VTHC Disputes Committee Minutes, 27 July 1962–29 August 1962.
43 Interview with Max Ogden, 25 November 1997.
44 *Herald,* 7 August 1962.
45 Alleyn Best, *History of the Liquor Trades Union in Victoria,* p. 202.
46 Noel Butlin Archives, N21/1207 ACTU.

7
Kath resigns from the Communist Party

1 Cited in Diane Bell and Renate Klein, *Radically Speaking,* p. 168.
2 Hugh Mackay, *Sydney Morning Herald,* 14 February 1998.
3 Bernie Taft, *Crossing the Party Line,* p. 130.
4 *Herald* 1963 (precise date unknown).
5 Ibid.
6 Bernie Taft, *Crossing the Party Line,* p. 131.
7 Joy Damousi, *Women Come Rally,* p. 132.
8 Ibid., p. 133.
9 Interview with Ray Clarey, 25 November. 1997.
10 Interview with Jack Hutson, 5 October 1998.

8
1963 to 1964, the ACTU and Equal Pay

1 University of Melbourne Archives, Box 3, VTHC EP Committee, February 1963.

2 Unknown Poet. Lent by Hilda Smith.
3 University of Melbourne Archives, Box 3, VTHC EP Committee 1963.
4 Noel Butlin Archives, N69/302 VTHC EP Committee circular, 1963.
5 University of Melbourne Archives, Box 23, EP Committee, July 1963.
6 Noel Butlin Archives, N21/1211 ACTU 1964, p. 6.
7 Ibid., p. 7.
8 Ibid.
9 Ibid., pp. 7–8.
10 Ibid., p. 8.
11 Noel Butlin Archives, N21/1201 ACTU March 1964.
12 Ibid.
13 Noel Butlin Archives, N69/304 ACTU April 1964, p. 2.
14 Ibid., p. 3.
15 Ibid.
15 Ibid.
17 Ibid., p. 7.
18 Ibid.
19 Ibid.
20 Noel Butlin Archives, N69/304 ACTU.
21 *Herald,* 21 April 1964.
22 Noel Butlin Archives, N16/676 Bank Association.
23 *Guardian,* 6 August 1964.
24 Marjorie Broadbent in interview with Lynda Clarey, 20 July 1990.

9
1965 to 1967: The ACTU gears up for action as Kath begins to retire

1 *Guardian,* 8 April 1965.
2 *Australian,* 14 August 1965.
3 Ibid.
4 *Australian,* 15 September 1965.
5 *Courier Mail,* 4 September 1965.

6 University of Melbourne Archives, VTHC Minutes, 21 October 1965.

7 Ibid. University of Melbourne Archives, Box 1 VTHC EP Committee, April 1966. This particular document states the Retail Association had equal pay from 1913 while in Chapter 10 endnote 15 another document referred to quotes 1916 as the date. The shop assistants referred to may have been from one section of the industry only. Unable to obtain confirmation from Retail Association.

8 University of Melbourne Archives, 1965 and 1966. All attempts to locate this film were unsuccessful. A search was made through ABC Television; the ACTU; Cine Media, Victoria; Clothing Trades Union; *Labor History Bulletins*; Liquor and Miscellaneous Union; The National Film and Sound Archives, Canberra; the VTHC, and an advertisement was placed in *Green Left Weekly*.

9 *Australian*, 4 May 1966.

10 Mary Dickenson, *An Unsentimental Union*, p. 130.

11 Ibid.

12 NSW Nurses Association Journal *The Lamp*, August 1966, pp. 8–9.

13 *Australian*, 19 October 1966.

14 Interview with Ray Clarey, 25 November 1997.

15 Lynda Clarey papers, private collection.

16 Interview with Ray Clarey, 25 November 1997.

17 Jennie Bremner, In the Cause of Equality. In Margaret Bevege *et al.*, *Worth Her Salt*, p. 292.

10
The ACTU changes policy

1 Jim Hagan, *The History of the ACTU*, p. 400.

2 Department of Labour and National Service, *Equal Pay: Some Aspects of Australian and Overseas Practice*, Canberra 1968, p. 75.

3 Ibid.

4 Jim Hagan, *The History of the ACTU*, p. 401.

5 Ibid.

6 Noel Butlin Archives, E 192/9/6 ACSPA.

7 *Sun*, 7 October 1967.
8 Ibid.
9 Ibid.
10 Victorian Secondary Teachers Association, October 1967.
11 Ibid.
12 Ibid.
13 Leaflet distributed at Talk Out.
14 Noel Butlin Archives, N21/1212 ACTU.
15 University of Melbourne Archives, Box 1 VTHC EP Committee. April 1966. This document states the Retail Association had equal pay from 1916 while the document drawn on in chapter 9 quotes 1913 as the date. The shop assistants referred to may have been from one section of the industry only. Unable to obtain confirmation from the Retail Association.
16 Ibid.
17 University of Melbourne Archives, Box 1, THC EP Committee.
18 Ibid.
19 Symposium: Work Evaluation In Relation to Equal Pay, 8 May 1968.
20 Noel Butlin Archives, N21/1212 ACTU.
21 Interview with Marjorie Broadbent, 13 May 1998.
22 Jim Hagan, *The History of the ACTU,* p. 213.

11
The Equal Pay Case of 1969

1 Jim Hagan, *The History of the ACTU,* p. 220.
2 Zelda D'Aprano, *Zelda,* p. 166.
3 Ibid.
4 From the *Meat Industry Union News-Letter,* June 1969.
5 Jocelynne Scutt, Inequality Before the Law, p. 278.
6 Zelda D'Aprano, *Zelda,* p. 316.
7 Zelda D'Aprano, *Zelda,* p. 174.
8 Document from Hilda Smith.
9 *Herald,* 12 March, 1970.
10 Mitchell Library Achives, Australia Women's Bureau, 1986.

12
Equal pay for work of equal value

1 Joan Robinson, *An Essay on Marxian Economics,* 2nd ed., New York: St Martins Press, 1966.

2 *Women's Liberation Newsletter,* August 1972, Women's Liberation Archives.

3 *Women's Liberation Newsletter,* July 1972, p. 3.

4 Ibid.

5 *Women's Liberation Newsletter,* August 1972, p. 4.

6 Zelda D'Aprano, *Zelda,* pp. 318–19.

7 P. Riarch, Equal Pay and Equal Opportunity. *Journal of Industrial Relations.* Vol. 11, No. 2, July 1969. Cited in Sylvie Shaw's submission to the Arbitration Commission on Equal Pay for Work of Equal Value, 1972.

8 Joint Opposition Policy, 1949, November 10. Cited in Sylvie Shaw's submission to the Arbitration Commission on Equal Pay for Work of Equal Value, 1972.

9 From Sylvie Shaw's submission to the Arbitration Commission on Equal Pay for Work of Equal Value, 1972.

10 Suzane Fabian and Morag Loh, *Left-Wing Ladies,* p. 110.

11 Commonwealth Arbitration Commission, Legal Report, *National Wage and Equal Pay Case 1972,* 1047 CAR 172, p. 179.

12 Alina Holgate and Karen Milgrom, *She Works Hard for the Money,* report for the Women's Legal Resources Group, Melbourne, 1985, p. 35.

13 Clare Burton *et al., Women's Worth,* p. 4, citing Livernash, the editor of a book published by an employer's group in the United States.

14 Clare Burton *et al., Women's Worth,* p. 125.

15 Statement concerning a case by Jocelynne Scutt, Inequality before the Law, p. 279.

16 Australian Industrial Commission. Document No: PO55CR Mis O67/86 MD Print G2250 p. 8.

17 Clare Burton *et al., Women's Worth,* p. 138.

18 Anna Pha, The Women's Working Centre. Paper submitted for an MA, University of Melbourne, 1982.
19 Interview with Marion Miller, 29 October 2000.
20 Anna Pha, Working Women's Centre.

13
Kath and Male Structures

1 Dorothy Hewett, *Wild Card: An Autobiography*, 1923–1958, McPhee-Gribble, 1990, p. 175.
2 Joy Damousi, *Women Come Rally*, p. 138.
3 Daphne Gollan. Memoirs of Cleopatra Sweatfigure. In E. Windschuttle (Ed.) *Women, Class and History*.
4 Ibid., p. 144. *Worker's Weekly*, 18 January 1929, p. 3.
5 Lisa Maria Hogeland, Fear of Feminism, *Ms Magazine*, November/December, 1994.
6 Ibid.
7 Interview with Harry Bocquet, 21 September 1990. Frank Johnson at Kath's funeral, 21 April 1975.
8 Interview with Ray Clarey, November 1997.
9 *The Liquor and Allied Industries Union Journal*, April–May 1975.
10 *Tribune*, 29 April 1975. Lynda Clarey's papers.
11 At Kath's funeral, 21 April 1975.

14
Women, work and the fight for pay justice

1 Jim Hagan, *The History of the ACTU*, p. 4.
2 Pam Young, *Proud to Be a Rebel*, p. 162.
3 Gisela Kaplan, *The Meagre Harvest*, p. 12.
4 Jim Hagan, *The History of the ACTU*, pp. 8–10.
5 Gisela Kaplan, *The Meagre Harvest*, p. 74.
6 Ibid., pp. 74–5.
7 Ibid.
8 Karen Fredericks, Enterprise Bargaining no Bargain. *Refractory Girl*, Issue 46, p. 44.

9   Australian Industrial Relations Commission's April 1991 Wage Case, Print J7400, p. 56.
10 Karen Fredericks, Enterprise Bargaining no Bargain. *Refractory Girl*, Issue 46, p. 43.
11 Ibid.
12 *Sydney Morning Herald*, David Dale, 9 September 1998.
13 *Sydney Morning Herald*, 30 April 1998.
14 ABS, 1992. *Social Indicators*, Catalogue 4101. Canberra: Australian Bureau of Statistics.
15 Meredith Burgmann, The Chips Are Down, *Refractory Girl*, Issue 47/48, p. 67.
16 Information from Centrelink, Port Macquarie, 25 October 1999.
17 *Sydney Morning Herald*, Marilyn Lake, Shorter week for true equality, October 1999.
18 Gisela Kaplan, *The Meagre Harvest*, p. 174.
19 *Sydney Morning Herald*, 7 September 1998, interviewing Greg Bamber and Russell Lansbury, editors of *International and Comparative Industrial Relations: A Study of Industrialised Market Economics*, St. Leonards: Allen & Unwin, 1993 (2nd edition).
20 *Weekend Australian*, Tracy Sutherland, 12–13 July, 1997.
21 Ted Myers, Corporate Education Resources Pty Ltd., Discussion Notes on Times Up, a co-production with the Women's Bureau of the Department of Employment and Industrial Relations. A Women's Film Unit Production for Film Australia. Film Australia, p. 2.
22 Philippa Hall. Skills & Training: Opportunities and Obstacles for Women. In M. Davis and Valerie Pratt (Eds). *Making the Link: Affirmative Action and Industrial Relations*. Sydney: Affirmative Action Agency & Labour-Management Studies Foundation, Graduate School of Management, Macquarie University. 1994, p. 14.
23 Interview with Mary Rose Liverani. 15 January 1999.
24 Ibid.
25 Ibid.
26 Department of Industrial Relations, NSW, 1998, *Pay Equity Inquiry*. Summary of Findings and Recommendations.

27 *Sydney Morning Herald*, Malcolm Brown, Still underpaid after all these years, 26 December 1998.

28 Ibid.

29 *Sydney Morning Herald*, Helen Trinca, A Kinder Capitalism, 17 July 1999.

30 Department of Industrial Relations, New South Wales, *Pay Equity Inquiry*, Summary of Findings and Recommendations.

31 Jenny Doran, ACTU, personal correspondence, 12 October 1999.

32 *Weekend Australian*, Shelley Gare, Unmanageable and out in force, 28–29 August 1999, p. 22.

33 *Age*, Janet McCalman, We need unions like it or not, 11 November 1998.

34 Ibid.

35 *Weekend Australian*, Shelley Gare, Unmanagable and out in force, (quoting John Buchanan of the University of Sydney's Australian Centre for Industrial Research and Training), 28–29 August 1999.

36 *Sydney Morning Herald*, Jackie Dent, Motherhood—too important to leave to women, 4 October 1999.

37 *Sydney Morning Herald*, Lisa Hudson, Grassroots women lose voice, 22 October 1999, p. 3.

38 Susan Ryan, *Catching the Waves: Life In and Out of Politics*, Sydney: Harper Collins, 1999, pp. 241–4.

39 *Sydney Morning Herald*, United Nations, 9 September 2000, p. 20.

40 Zelda D'Aprano, *Zelda*.

41 Jack Hutson, *Six Wage Concepts*, p. 170.

42 Jenny Doran, 1999, *Equal Pay: A Union Priority*, ACTU, March.

43 Ibid.

44 Susan Carcary, The Second Wave, *Capital Women*, Issue No. 61, September 1999, p. 1.

45 Marilyn Waring, *Women, Politics and Power*, p. 232.

46 Marilyn Waring, *Counting For Nothing*, p. 21.

47 Veronika Bennholdt-Thomsen and Maria Mies, *The Subsistence Perspective: Beyond The Globalised Economy*, North Melbourne: Spinifex Press, 1999, p. 172.

48 Ibid.

49 Marilyn Waring, *Three Masquerades*, p. 163.
50 John Ralston Saul, *The Unconscious Civilisation.*
51 Veronika Bennholdt-Thomsen and Maria Mies, *The Subsistence Perspective*, 1999, p. 22.
52 Eva Cox, 1984, Social Justice for whom?. In Dorothy H. Broom, *Unfinished Business*, p. 189.
53 Ibid., p. 192
54 Veronika Bennholdt-Thomsen and Maria Mies, *The Subsistence Perspective.*
55 Miranda Corzy, 1999, Utopia at Work: Equality between Women and Men, and Flexibility for All, *Refractory Girl*, Issue 53, Spring, p. 24.
56 Susan Biggs and Kerry Fallon Horgan, 'Time on, Time Out!'.

Bibliography

Archival material

ABC Television Archives

Mitchell Library Archives, State Library of New South Wales
'For Love or Money' Collection
Labor Council of New South Wales Collection
    Boxes 23, 24, 25 (144)

Noel Butlin Archives, Australian National Archives
Association of Draughting, Supervisory and Technical
    Employees, Federal Office
    E 192/9/6
Australian Bank Employees' Union
    N16/676
Australian Council of Salaried & Professional Associations
    N10/852
    N10/230
    N10/232
    N23/44

Australian Council of Trade Unions

Composite List	Documents
N21/1201	M24
N21/1207	S784
N21/1209	69/285
N21/1211	6/291
N21/1212	69/295
N21/1213	69/284
	69/302
	69/304
	E192/9/6
	Z767

Tom and Mary Wright Collection, Deposit List Z267, Box 18

State Library of Victoria
La Trobe Collection
F. Riley Collection
Union of Australian Women, Melbourne

University of Melbourne Archives
Clothing Trades Union Collection
Communist Party of Australia Collection
Eleanor Masters Collection
Federated Liquor Trades Union Collection
Latoof and Calill
Melbourne Trades Hall Equal Pay Collection
 Box 1 & 3 VTHC EP Committee
Myer Collection
VTHC Disputes Committee Minutes 27/7/1962–29/8/1962
VTHC Minutes 3/6/1948, 31/7/1952, 28/10/1965
Western Australian Museum
 Collection of History Department
Women's Liberation Archives

Books and articles

Australian Dictionary of Biography, Vol. 13 1940–1980. Melbourne: Melbourne University Press.

Aveling, Marian and Joy Damousi (Eds). 1991. *Stepping Out of History: Documents of Women At Work in Australia*. North Sydney: Allen & Unwin.

Baldwin, Suzy (Ed.). 1988. *Unsung Heroes and Heroines of Australia*. Elwood, Victoria: Greenhouse Publications.

Bell, Diane and Renate Klein (Eds). 1996. *Radically Speaking: Feminism Reclaimed*. North Melbourne: Spinifex Press.

Bennholdt-Thomsen, Veronika and Maria Mies. 1999. *The Subsistence Perspective: Beyond The Globalised Economy*. London and New York: Zed Books; Melbourne: Spinifex Press.

Best, Alleyn. 1990. *The History of the Liquor Trades Union in Victoria*, Victorian Branch, Published by the Union. North Melbourne: Victorian Branch, Federated Liquor and Allied Industries Employees' Union of Australia.

Bevege, Margaret, Margaret James, Carmel Shute (Eds). 1982. *Worth Her Salt—Women at Work in Australia*. Sydney: Hale & Iremonger.

Biggs, Susan and Kerry Fallon. 1999. *'Time On, Time Out!' Flexible Work Solutions to Keep Your Life in Balance*. St. Leonards: Allen & Unwin.

Blake. L. J. (Gen. ed.). 1973. *'Vision and Realisation': A Centenary History of State Education in Victoria*, Vols. 1–3. Melbourne: Education Department of Victoria.

Bonnin, Roberta (Ed.). 1988. *'Dazzling Prospects': Women in the Queensland Teachers' Union since 1945*. Queensland: Queensland Teachers' Union.

Broom, Dorothy H. (Ed.). 1984. *'Unfinished Business': Social Justice for Women in Australia*. Sydney: George Allen & Unwin.

Brownfoot, Janice, and Dianne Scott. 1977. *The Unequal Half: Women in Australia Since 1788*, New Studies in Australian Society Series. Sydney: Reed Education.

Burton, Clare, Raven Hag and Gay Thompson. 1987. *Women's Worth: Pay Equity and Job Evaluation in Australia.* Canberra: Australian Government Publishing Service.

Caine, Barbara (Ed.). 1998. *Australian Feminism: A Companion.* Melbourne: Oxford University Press.

Curthoys, Barbara and Audrey McDonald. 1996. *More Than a Hat And Glove Brigade: The Story of the Union of Australian Women.* Sydney: UAW Book Press.

Cusack, Dymphna. 1953 Introduction. *Caddie.* London: Constable.

Commonwealth of Australia. 1992. *Half Way to Equal: Report of the Inquiry into Equal Opportunity and Equal Status for Women in Australia.* House of Representatives Standing Committee on Legal and Constitutional Affairs. Canberra: Australian Government Publishing Service, April, p. 286.

Damousi, Joy. 1994. *Women Come Rally: Socialism, Communism and Gender in Australia, 1890–1955.* South Melbourne: Oxford University Press.

Daniels, Kay, Mary Murnane and Ann Picot. 1977. *Women In Australia: An Annotated Guide to Records.* Vol. 2. Canberra: Australian Government Publishing Service.

D'Aprano, Zelda. 1995. *Zelda.* North Melbourne: Spinifex Press.

Deacon, Desley. 1989. *Managing Gender: The State, the New Middle Class and Women Workers 1830–1930.* Melbourne: Oxford University Press.

Dickenson, Mary. 1993. *An Unsentimental Union: The NSW Nurses Association 1931–1992.* Sydney: Hale & Iremonger.

Docherty, James. 1981. *The Emily Mac: The Story of The Emily McPherson College 1906–1979.* Melbourne: Ormond Book and Educational Supplies.

Drake, Nicholas. 1987. *The Fifties in Vogue*. London: Heinemann.

Duke, Jas, Peter Lyssiotis and Vivienne Méhes. 1986. Authors and publishers of *Industrial Woman*. Melbourne: The Small Publishers' Collective.

Ellem, Bradon. 1989. *In Women's Hands? A History of Clothing Trades Unionism in Australia*. The Modern History Series. Kensington, NSW: University of New South Wales Press.

Eveline, Joan and Lorraine Hayden (Eds). 1999. *Carrying The Banner: Women Leadership and Activism in Australia*. Nedlands: University of Western Australia Press.

Fabian, Suzane and Morag Loh. 2000. *Left-Wing Ladies: The Union of Australian Women in Victoria, 1950–1998*. Melbourne: Hyland House.

Figes, Eve. 1970. *Patriarchal Attitudes: Women in Society*. London: Faber & Faber.

Fitzpatrick, Kathleen. 1983. A Cloistered Life, in Patricia Grimshaw and Alice Strahan (Eds), *The Half-Open Door*. Sydney: Hale & Iremonger.

Frances, Raelene and Bruce Scates. 1993. *Women at Work in Australia: From The Gold Rushes to World War II*. Melbourne: Cambridge University Press.

Grimshaw, Patricia, and Alice Strahan (Eds). 1983. *The Half-Open Door*. Sydney: Hale & Iremonger.

Hagan, Jim. 1981. *The History of the ACTU*. Melbourne: Longman Cheshire.

Harper, Jan and Lyn Richards. 1979. *Mothers and Working Mothers*. Ringwood: Penguin.

Haskell, Molly. 1974. *From Reverence to Rape*. Baltimore: Penguin.

Hewett, Dorothy. 1990. *Wild Card: An Autobiography 1923–1958*. Ringwood: McPhee Gribble and Penguin Books.

Howard, Ann. 1994. *Where Do We Go From Here?* Sydney: Tarka Publishing.

Hutson, Jack, 1971. *Six Wage Concepts*. Sydney: Amalgamated Engineering Union.

Kaplan, Gisela. 1996. *The Meagre Harvest: The Australian Women's Movement 1950s–1990s*. Sydney: Allen & Unwin.

Kingston, B. 1975. *My Wife, My Daughter and Poor Mary Ann: Women and Work in Australia*. Melbourne: Nelson.

Kirkby, Diane. 1997. *Barmaids: A History of Women's Work in Pubs*. Cambridge: Cambridge University Press.

Lake, Marilyn, 1999. *getting equal: The History of Australian Feminism*. Sydney: Allen & Unwin.

Lees, Stella and June Senyard. 1987. *The 1950s: How Australia became a Modern Society, and Everyone got a House and Car*. Melbourne: Hyland House.

Lonsdale, Michele. 1997. *Liberating Women: The Changing Lives of Australian Women since the 1950s*. New York: Cambridge University Press.

MacIntyre, Stuart and Richard Mitchell. 1989. *Foundations of Arbitration: The Origins and Effects of State Compulsory Arbitration, 1890–1914*. Melbourne: Oxford University Press.

McMurchy, Megan, Margo Oliver and Jeni Thornley. 1983. *For Love or Money: A Pictorial History of Women and Work in Australia*. Ringwood: Penguin Books.

Murray, Robert. 1970. *The Split: Australian Labor in the Fifties*. Melbourne: Longman Cheshire.

Radi, Heather (Ed.) 1988. *200 Australian Women: A Redress Anthology*. Broadway, Sydney: Women's Redress Press.

Reeves, Andrew. 1990. *Another Day Another Dollar: Working Lives in Australian History*. Carlton North: McCulloch Publishing.

Rydon, Joan and R. N. Spann. *1996 NSW Politics: An Electoral and Political Chronicle, 1901–1917.* Sydney: NSW Parliamentary Library & Department of Government.

Ryan, Edna and Anne Conlon. 1975. *Gentle Invaders: Australian Women at Work 1788–1974.* Melbourne: Nelson.

Ryan, Susan. 1999. *Catching the Waves: Life In and Out of Politics.* HarperCollins. Australia.

Saul, John Ralston. 1997. *The Unconscious Civilisation.* Ringwood: Penguin.

Saunders, Kay and Raymond Evans (Eds). 1992. *Gender Relations in Australia: Domination and Negotiation.* Sydney: Harcourt, Brace, Jovanovich.

Scutt, Jocelynne. 1992. Inequality before the Law—Gender, Arbitration and Wages. In Kay Saunders and Raymond Evans (Eds). *Gender Relations in Australia: Domination and Negotiation.* Sydney: Harcourt, Brace, Jovanovich, pp. 266–86.

Shields, John (Ed.). 1992. *All Our Labours: Oral Histories of Working Life in Twentieth Century Sydney.* Kensington, NSW: New South Wales University Press.

Skelton, Kath. 1990. *Miss Gymkhana, R. G. Menzies and Me: Small Town in the Fifties.* Ringwood: McPhee Gribble and Penguin.

Stevens, Joyce. 1985. *A History of International Women's Day in Words and Images.* Sydney: IWD Press.

Sweetman, E., C. Long, and J. Smyth. 1922. *A History of State Education in Victoria.* Published for The Education Department of Victoria by Critchley Parker, Melbourne.

Taft, Bernie. 1994. *Crossing the Party Line.* Newham, Victoria: Scribe Publications.

Waring, Marilyn. 1985. *Women, Politics and Power.* Wellington: Unwin paperbacks. Port Nicholson Press.

Waring, Marilyn. 1996. *Counting for Nothing: What Men Value and What Women are Worth*. New Zealand: Bridget Williams Books Ltd.

Waring, Marilyn. 1996. *Three Masquerades: Essays on Equality, Work and Hu(man) Rights*. St Leonards: Allen & Unwin.

Windschuttle, Elizabeth (Ed). 1980. *Women, Class and History: Feminist Perspectives in Australia 1788–1978*. Australia: Fontana/Collins.

Young, Pam. 1991. *Proud to be a Rebel: The Life and Times of Emma Miller*. St. Lucia: University of Queensland Press.

Index

INDEX

Clarey, Bruce 6, 10
Clarey, Percy James 2–5, 16, 105,
106, 120
marriage to KW 6
break up 10–13
custody arrangements
10–11, 12
political career 9, 10, 13, 18–19
trade union career 4–5, 13, 19
views on employment of
women 39–40
Clarey, Raymond 7, 115
custody of 10–11, 11–12
in Portland 14, 15, 16
in Wonthaggi 19
Clerks' Union 225–6
Clothing and Allied Trades Union
127–8
Clothing Trades Case (1919) 77
Clothing Trades Union 26, 27, 77,
183–4
Collaretti, Gus 67, 70–3
College of Domestic Economy 2
Collins, Berenice 84–5
Collins, J. 162
Collins, Miss B. (Qld EP
Committee) 124, 134
Commonwealth Court of
Conciliation and Arbitration,
and equal pay 55–6
Commonwealth Industrial Gases
Ltd. 141–4
Commonwealth Service
Association 57
Communist Party of Australia 9,
18, 37
attempt to proscribe 58
declared illegal 14
KW and
joins 13
in Portland 14, 16
resigns 145–7
State Committee

elected to 20
and equal pay 58–9
membership 116
in Wonthaggi 17–18, 19
patriarchal structures 216–19
Communist Party Marxist–Leninist
159, 178, 194
Cooper, Leontine 74
Coull, Jim 19, 39, 64–5
Council of Action for Equal Pay
78, 79, 82
Cox, Eva 245–6
Crisp, Helen 130, 131–4
Cross, Doogie 14
CSIRO Officers' Association 131
Curlewis, Joan 210

Dahlitz, Julie 187
Daly, Jean 63
D'Aprano, Zelda 105, 200, 201
Davis, Flo 30, 30, 90–1, 100, 135
Dawes, Miss _ (Liquor Industry
Union) 135
Day, R.L. 135
Dempsey, Irene 55
Denham, _ (Premier of Qld) 26
Devanny, Jean 147
Diwell, Daisy 30
Doig, Agnes 5, 9, 17, 19
Doig, Wattie 17, 19
domestic work see work in the
home
Don, Ruth 101
Dunkley, Louisa 32, 75
Dunleavy, Sheila 170
Dwyer, Kate 24

Edson, George 147
Edwards, Elizabeth 74
Electrical Trades Union, and equal
pay 48
Emily McPherson College see
College of Domestic Economy

288

Zelda
Zelda D'Aprano
An essential contribution to the history of the women's movement.

Her accounts of poverty and gender inequity and her own political, sexual and intellectual maturation are presented with blinding honesty and an indefatigable sense of humour. In a genuine expression of sisterhood experiences, ideas and practical accounts are expressed through an intimate disclosure of both her body and mind. Drawing on her own experience, D'Aprano brings to life the difficult issues that face all women.

Asheley Jones Pandora

ISBN: 1875559-30-2

Kick the Tin
Doris Kartinyeri
When Doris Kartinyeri was a month old, her mother died, and Doris was removed from the hospital and placed in Colebrook Home. A moving testimony from one of the Stolen Generation.
ISBN: 1875559-95-7

Women's Circus: Leaping off the Edge
Adrienne Liebmann, Jen Jordan, Deb Lewis, Louise Radcliffe-Brown, Patricia Sykes and Jean Taylor (Eds.)

This is a big, rowdy, colorful, three-ring circus of a book, packed with death-defying feats and acts that will thrill and amaze—not the least of which is their breathtaking commitment to feminist process.

Carolyn Gage

ISBN: 1-875559-55-8

If you would like to know more about Spinifex Press
write for a free catalogue or visit our website

SPINIFEX PRESS
PO Box 212 North Melbourne
Victoria 3051 Australia
<http://www.spinifexpress.com.au>